Roman Religion
A Sourcebook

THE FOCUS CLASSICAL SOURCES

Roman Sports and Spectacles • *Anne Mahoney 2001*
Roman Religion • *Valerie Warrior 2002*

Roman Religion
A Sourcebook

Valerie M. Warrior

Focus Publishing
R. Pullins Company
Newburyport MA

ISBN 1-58510-030-7

10 9 8 7 6 5 4 3 2 1

Cover: Altar of Scipio Orfitus. Rome, Musei Capitolini. Photo by Sansaini, neg. no. 57.373. Courtesy of the German Archeological Institute.

CONTENTS

PROLOGUE

LIVY 43.13.2. As I write of antiquity, not only does my own mind become in some way or other old-fashioned, but also a certain religious feeling *(religio)* keeps me from regarding those matters which the wisest men of former times decided required action on the part of the state as something unworthy to be reported in my History.

> With these words the historian Livy (Titus Livius, c. 59 BCE — 17 CE), writing in the age of the emperor Augustus, confronts the question of whether to report religious matters that his contemporaries might find unimportant and inappropriate. Livy is convinced that he should respect the wisdom of former times and include what he has found in his sources.
>
> This book presents the religion of ancient Rome through to the fourth century BCE *via the ancient sources,* the major emphasis being on the republic and early empire. Some background in Roman history is assumed, but readers are encouraged to consult the *Oxford Classical Dictionary,* ed. Simon Hornblower and Antony Spawforth, 3rd edition (1996) which has articles by some of the foremost scholars of Roman religion and history. Nonetheless, modern interpretations are secondary, an aid to learning. My hope is that the notes throughout this book make the ancient texts speak more clearly for themselves. The reader should feel free to dip into later sections for a first reading, using the cross references, glossary and index.
>
> Study of the ancient sources is not as simple as it might seem at first sight. 'Consider the source' is a rule that must be borne in mind throughout this selection of readings. Most of the extant literary testimony, particularly on early Roman religion, is written *looking back.* First, therefore, we must ask, who is the author, in what genre was he writing, and when did he live; that is, how far is he removed in time from the events he is describing. Only then will one be in a position to assess the value of a source.
>
> Testimony that is more or less contemporaneous with the event that is described is offered by inscriptions commemorating laws and various kinds

of dedication. Epitaphs from tombs throughout the Roman empire often yield valuable information about the lives of more ordinary people who would not otherwise find their way into the history books. By considering the source and sharing the struggle of the various writers to look back and reconstruct the past, we can hope to learn from double contrasts in time and perspective.

The reader, however, must bear in mind that any modern reconstruction of Roman religion is necessarily incomplete. The extant evidence is like a jig-saw puzzle with many of the pieces missing. Nor should we attempt to superimpose upon this incomplete picture our preconceptions about the components of a religion. An ethical element, for example, is mostly absent from traditional Roman religion. As Cicero notes, when the Romans wanted to be informed about what was morally right, what was morally wrong and what was neither one nor the other, they turned to philosophers for such answers, not to diviners whose task it was to interpret the will of the gods.[1] For the Romans *religio* was not a matter of 'faith' or 'belief' in a creed or doctrine, but, rather *cultus deorum*, worship of the gods.[2]

The focus is on selected Roman descriptions of Roman action and opinion in areas that they or we would call 'religion,' proceeding thematically and more or less chronologically. The ancient sources are to be viewed with utmost respect as the primary means by which an accurate understanding of the past can be gained. However strange or different ancient views may seem, we ought to read and reflect upon the ancient testimony. By contrasting Roman action and opinion with our own, we may come to better understand ourselves and the culture in which we live. The reader is thus urged to adopt the perspective implied by the above quotation from Livy.

ACKNOWLEDGEMENTS

Keith Whitaker reviewed an early draft and Christopher McDonough provided suggestions at a later stage. Their work stimulated my thought and resulting revisions. Technical assistance by Cynthia Zawalich, Melissa Massello, Melissa Wood, and Ron Pullins brought the book to and through production. Throughout, my husband Thomas Stone posed questions and gave encouragement.

VALERIE M. WARRIOR
CAMBRIDGE, MASSACHUSETTS
SEPTEMBER 2002

---

[1] Cicero, *On divination* 2.10-11.
[2] Cicero, *On the nature of the gods* 2.8.

INTRODUCTION

1.1 CICERO, *ON THE NATURE OF THE GODS* **2.8.** We Romans are far superior in *religio*, by which I mean, the worship *(cultus)* of the gods.

1.2 FESTUS **284 L.** The rituals of the state *(publica sacra)* are celebrated at the expense of the state for the people.... Private rituals *(privata)* are those celebrated for individuals, households *(familiae)*, and the family *(gentes)*.

> The above excerpts from ancient sources show a sense of the superiority of Roman religion and the distinction between state and private rituals (*sacra*), state religion being an enlarged version of private religion. Three quotations from plays of Plautus (fl. c. 205–184 BCE) presumably reflect widespread religious outlooks.

1.3 PLAUTUS, *TWO BACCHISES* **144.** How something turns out is in the hands of the gods.

1.4 PLAUTUS, *MERCHANT* **225,** *ROPE* **593.** The gods make sport of men in strange ways.

1.5 PLAUTUS, *LITTLE CARTHAGINIAN* **1187-8.** Jupiter ... through whom we live the span of our lives, in whose control are all men's hopes of life, grant that this day may be free from harm.

> The Roman world was filled with deities. The divine takes a multitude of forms, and can be experienced within the human mind and heart as awe inspired by nature itself. Some spirits (*numina*) are spoken about as distinct from human beings, but many others are presented as gods small and great, having gender and many other human characteristics, both physical and emotional.
>
> A preliminary selection of readings yields a picture of diverse divine presence throughout the life of individual, family, and state. There were numerous lesser divinities of the environment, non-anthropomorphized 'spirits' of streams, woods, plowing, even mildew or blight, a disease that affects crops (*Robigo*).
>
> Seneca the Younger, writing in the early Empire, reflects on the religious awe that is inspired by nature.

1.6 SENECA THE YOUNGER, LETTERS 41.3. If you have ever come upon a grove that is thick with ancient trees which rise far above their usual height and block the view of the sky with their cover of intertwining branches, then the loftiness of the forest and the seclusion of the spot and your wonder at the unbroken shade in the midst of open space will create in you a feeling of the divine *(numen)*. Or, if a cave made by the deep erosion of rocks supports a mountain with its arch, a place not made by hands but hollowed out by natural causes into spaciousness, then your mind will be aroused by a feeling of religious awe *(religio)*. We venerate the sources of mighty rivers, we build an altar where a great stream suddenly bursts forth from a hidden source, we worship hot springs, and we deem lakes sacred because of their darkness or immeasurable depth.

> Each Roman family had its own Lar (plural, Lares), a deity that protected the household. This protection, however, was contingent upon the head of the family (*pater familias*) maintaining the god's worship. In his comedy *Pot of Gold*, Plautus has a Lar speak the prologue. The Lar tells how he caused the death of the owner of the house because the latter had neglected his worship, but he is going to help the daughter of the present owner because she is attentive to his cult.

1.7 PLAUTUS, POT OF GOLD 1–27. So that no one may wonder who I am, I'll briefly introduce myself. I am the Lar of the family of this home that you saw me come from. For many years now I have been in possession of this house. I looked after it for the father and grandfather of the present occupant. As a suppliant,[1] the grandfather secretly entrusted to me a pot of gold. He buried it in the center of the hearth, supplicating me to guard it for him....

After the death of the man who entrusted the gold to me, I began to observe whether his son would pay me greater honor than his father. But his devotion to me soon diminished, and I had a smaller and smaller share of honor. So I did the same by him, and he died. He left a son who now occupies this house, a man of the same sort as his father and grandfather. He has one daughter. She is constantly praying to me every day, with gifts of incense or wine or something. She gives me garlands. Because of her devotion, I have caused her father Euclio to discover the treasure here so that he might more easily find her a husband, if he is willing.

> There were also the greater, anthropomorphized gods of Roman state religion: Jupiter, Juno, Mars, Venus, Apollo, Diana, Ceres, Bacchus, Minerva, Mercury, and Vulcan. By the middle republic these gods had been assimilated with the Olympian gods of Greek mythology: Jupiter with Zeus, Juno with Hera, Mars with Ares, Venus with Aphrodite, Diana with Artemis, Ceres with Demeter, Minerva with Athena, Mercury with Hermes, and Vulcan with Hephaestus. Apollo and Bacchus/Dionysus were known by their Greek names, although the latter deity was also identified with the Roman Liber. Assimilation,

---

[1] *suppliant*: one who makes a prayer of entreaty to a god, by formally addressing a particular deity at an altar or shrine. Such prayers were usually accompanied by offerings to the deity.

Panel from the altar of Scipio Orfitus, 295 CE, depicting the pouring of meal (*immolatio*), flour mixed with salt, over the sacrificial victim by the main sacrificant who is veiled. A young male attendant (*camillus*) holds the steer. Rome, Museo Capitolini. Photo by Sansaini, neg. no. 57.373. Courtesy of the German Archeaological Institute.

however, does not imply a strict equivalence or correspondence with the Greek counterpart. For example, the cult of Apollo was brought to Rome at a time of plague and he was worshipped as Apollo Medicus. Mars was originally an Italic agricultural deity, who later assumed the warlike characteristics of the Greek Ares as the Romans engaged as much in war as in agriculture.

These gods frequently assumed cult epithets that were essentially Roman or Italic. For example, Jupiter the Best and Greatest (Optimus Maximus) is an essentially Roman deity, having his temple on the Capitoline hill in Rome, and his cult bears little resemblance to the Zeus of Greek literature and mythology. Jupiter was also worshipped as Jupiter the Stayer in Battle (Stator) or as the Thunderer (Tonans) in separate and distinct temples.

All these gods, both greater and lesser, public and private, demanded the veneration and worship (*cultus*) of mortals. The noun *cultus* is a cognate of the verb *colere*, which has a variety of meanings: to till and so cultivate the soil, tend, care for, cherish, honor and esteem, and is thus used figuratively of men's cultivation or worship of the gods and also of the gods' protection of men, as well as giving us the word 'cult.'

The aim of *cultus* was to gain the favor of the gods (*pax deorum*) and avert their anger. This principle is often described by modern scholars as the *do ut des* concept (I give so that you may give). Valerius Maximus, writing in the early first century CE, comments on the Romans of earlier times:

1.8 VALERIUS MAXIMUS, *MEMORABLE WORDS AND DEEDS* **2.5.6.** They venerated the other gods in order to make them beneficent, but they paid cult to Fever with temples to make her less harmful.[2]

Although this may seem somewhat pragmatic, what should be emphasised is the hope rather than the presumption of reciprocity.[3] The relationship between man and gods was like a contract that had to be constantly maintained by regular prayer and sacrifice. Otherwise, the gods' favor could not be assured, as is apparent from the Lar's speech in Plautus' *Pot of Gold*.

The main features of Roman worship, especially the prominence of animal sacrifice, are summarized by the poet Lucretius, in an albeit negative picture of Roman piety:

1.9 LUCRETIUS, *ON THE NATURE OF THINGS* **5.1197–1201.** It is no piety *(pietas)* to appear often with covered head,[4] turning to a stone, approaching every altar, nor to fall prostrate on the ground, with palms outstretched before the shrines of the gods, showering the altars with the blood of beasts and piling vow upon vow.

Worship, as the above passage shows, was a ritual that required both prayer and sacrifice, the latter being an offering to the gods of an object that was of value to the donor. Sacrifice could be as simple as an offering of the fruits of the earth, flowers, wine (bloodless sacrifice), or of an animal (blood-sacrifice). Incense, a particularly expensive item, was also offered.

The poet Horace (65-8 BCE) promises to sacrifice a kid to the spring of Bandusia, a fountain near his birthplace, at the festival of the Fontinalia, a festival at which flowers were thrown into fountains and wells dressed with flowers.[5] In sharp contrast to the regular practice, Horace vividly describes the blood sacrifice that he will make.

1.10 HORACE, *ODES* **3.13.1-8.** O spring of Bandusia, more shining than glass, worthy of sweet wine and flowers, tomorrow you will be honored with the gift of a young kid. His brow, just swelling with budding horns, marks him out for love and battles. But in vain. For this offspring of the lively flock will stain your cool waters with its own red blood.

---

[2] That is, they vowed and dedicated temples to Fever in order to avert this malady. Compare the apotropaic purpose behind the cult of *Robigo* in 6.10 and 6.11.

[3] Dowden (1992) 3: the *do ut des* concept 'focuses too much on the hope of a future gift and too little on the relationship and bond which my gift establishes here and now.'

[4] It was an essential part of Roman ritual to have the head covered when making a sacrifice; see illustrations on pp. 3, 24, 36.

[5] *Fontinalia*: a festival in honor of *Fons*, the god of fountains, celebrated on 13 October.

In his treatise *On the nature of the gods*, Cicero (106-43 BCE) discerns two major divisions in the religion of the Roman state: sacred rites and auspices, the latter being signs that were considered to have been sent by the gods as an indication of their favor or disfavor toward an action that was already in progress or under consideration.[6] These two divisions were under the supervision of two different priesthoods, the pontiffs and the augurs.[7] Prophecies, portents and prodigies constitute a third category.[8] All three categories were vital for the well-being of the state.

1.11 CICERO, ON THE NATURE OF THE GODS **1.122.** The *pontifices* are in charge of the sacred rites (*sacra*), and the augurs in charge of the auspices (*auspicia*).

1.12 CICERO, *ON THE NATURE OF THE GODS* **3.5** The whole religious practice (*religio*) of the Roman people is divided into ritual (*sacra*) and auspices (*auspicia*). A third category is added, consisting of whatever prophetic warnings the interpreters of the Sibylline books or the *haruspices* have derived from portents and prodigies.[9] I have always thought that none of these areas of religion was to be despised, since I am convinced that Romulus by his auspices and Numa by his establishment of ritual laid the foundations of our state which assuredly could never have been as great as it is had we not maintained the fullest measure of divine favor.[10]

In a treatise on divination (the art of interpreting signs believed to have been sent by the gods), Cicero summarizes the tradition concerning the interpretation of auspices.

[6] *auspices* (*auspicia,* singular *auspicium*): literally the observation of birds, but more widely applied to a variety of signs deemed to indicate the will of the gods. Auspices were both public and private, although private auspices fell into disuse, except for weddings (Cicero, *On divination* 1.28).

[7] *pontifices* (singular, *pontifex*): official priests of the state who were appointed for life. *augurs*: official diviners and priests of the state, also appointed for life. On the various duties of the pontiffs and augurs, see chapter 5.

[8] *portents and prodigies*: unusual or unnatural occurrences that were believed to have been sent by the gods as an indication of a future event. The term prodigy (*prodigium*), as opposed to a portent or omen, should strictly refer to a sign that has been accepted by the state authorities as indicating that the *pax deorum* has been broken or is about to be ruptured. On the six stages of dealing with a prodigy, see chapter 7.

[9] *Sibylline books*: a collection of oracles (divine utterances or prophecies) that was kept in the temple of Jupiter on the Capitoline Hill and was said to have been bought from the Sibyl of Cumae by the fifth king of Rome, Tarquin the Elder; see 2.9. These books were consulted by the *quindecimviri sacris faciundis*, the board of priests for the performance of sacred rites. *haruspices* (singular, *haruspex*): priests, diviners who specialized in extispicy (inspecting the entrails of sacrificial victims), who originally came from Etruria (see illustration, p. 57). The term *haruspex* is also used more generally of soothsayers and diviners. They, unlike the *pontifices* and augurs, were not state officials until the reign of Claudius (41-54 CE).

[10] *Romulus*: legendary founder and first king of Rome.
Numa: legendary king who succeeded Romulus.

1.13 CICERO, *ON DIVINATION* **1.3.** Nor is there only one kind of divination that has been employed in public and private. For, without mentioning other nations, how many kinds have our people embraced? Tradition has it that first of all Romulus, the father of this city, not only founded the city in obedience to the auspices, but he himself was an excellent augur. Then the rest of the kings employed augurs; and, again, after the expulsion of the kings, no public business was ever transacted at home or abroad without first taking the auspices.

Moreover, since our ancestors thought that the lore (*disciplina*) of the *haruspices* had great efficacy in seeking advice and interpreting and expiating unusual occurrences (*monstra*), they gradually introduced that art in its entirety from Etruria, so that it should not appear that they had neglected any kind of divination.

> Cicero discerns two kinds of divination, the artificial (external) and the natural (internal), and comments on the importance of divination in the life of the state.

1.14 CICERO, *ON DIVINATION* **1.12.** There are two kinds of divination: one is based on skill *(ars)*, the other on nature *(natura)*. For what nation or state can fail to be influenced by the pronouncements of interpreters of entrails, prodigies and lightnings, those of augurs or astrologers,[11] or of lots — all of which are almost entirely dependent on skill *(ars)* — or, to mention the two kinds that are classed as 'natural,' the forewarning of dreams or of prophecy?

> Cicero admits but also defends the fallibility of divination.

1.15 CICERO, *ON DIVINATION* **1.24-25.** So it is with the responses of soothsayers (*haruspices*), and indeed with every kind of divination that is the result of opinion. For this kind of divination depends on inference and beyond inference it cannot go. Sometimes perhaps this kind of divination is deceptive, but nevertheless in most cases it guides us towards the truth. For it is derived from boundless eternity and within that period it has become an art through the repeated observation and recording of almost countless instances in which the same outcome has been preceded by the same signs.

> There were five types of auspical signs: from the sky (thunder and lightning), birds (their number, flight, cries, and feeding), sacred chickens and their feeding, unusual behavior of quadrupeds (e.g., speaking), and unusual, threatening occurrences (*dira*). These signs were either encountered by chance, i.e., unsolicited *(oblativa)*,or they were actively sought, i.e., solicited (*impetrativa*). Auspices were valid for one day only, that is, they pertained only to time, not to substance.[12]
>
> Auspices were taken before elections, a census, assemblies, the passing of laws, military operations and even before crossing the sacred boundary (*pomerium*) of Rome. In the following passage, Cicero describes how, during the Hannibalic

---

[11]   Astrology was never accepted as a part of state religion, see 12.23-12.32.

[12]   The technical difference between auspices and auguries (*auguria*) should be noted: the latter are auspices that pertain to both substance and time and could only be conducted by augurs.

war, the consul Flaminius disregarded both solicited and unsolicited signs with the result that he and his army were slaughtered in the ensuing battle.

1.16 CICERO, *ON DIVINATION* **1.77.** Didn't the consul C. Flaminius neglect the signs of future happenings and so bring great disaster on the state in the Second Punic War? After purifying his army he moved his army to Arretium and, as he was leading his legions against Hannibal, his horse suddenly threw him without any reason in front of the statue of Jupiter the Stayer in battle. But he did not regard this as a matter for religious concern (*religio*), though it was apparent to the experts that this was a sign for him not to engage in battle. Again, when auspices had been taken by means of the *tripudium*,[13] the keeper of the chickens advised postponing the battle. Flaminius then asked: 'What would you think should be done if the chickens should never eat?' 'You should remain inactive,' was the reply. Whereupon Flaminius declared, 'Fine auspices, indeed, if they advise action when the chickens are hungry and no action when they are full!' So he ordered the standards to be pulled up and the army to follow him. Then, since the standard bearer of the first company could not loosen his standard, several soldiers came up to help, but to no avail. When this was announced to Flaminius, he ignored it, as was his custom. And so, within three hours, his army was cut to pieces and he himself slain.

Cicero implies the uniqueness of Roman state religion.

1.17 CICERO, *IN DEFENCE OF FLACCUS* **69.** Each state has its own religion (*religio*), we have ours.

That religion was an integral part of Roman political life is apparent from an incidental remark by the historian Livy that a magistrate would not address an assembly without first making a prayer.

1.18 LIVY **39.15.** The consuls mounted the Rostra and called an informal meeting of the people.[14] When the consul had pronounced the regular formula of prayer which magistrates are accustomed to make before they address the people, he began thus: 'Never before has this formal prayer to the gods been not only so suitable but also so necessary, a prayer that reminds us that these are the gods whom our ancestors resolved to worship, venerate and pray to....'

Six features of Roman religion

Six 'features' of Roman religion will serve as organizing categories, both for the religion of the family and that of the state. Nowhere are these six presented as such by ancient testimony. These categories, therefore, should be viewed with caution, as aids to the process of beginning a study of ancient Roman religion. Both the following and the earlier excerpts from the ancient testimony should help the reader understand the mind-set of the ancient Romans, while also comparing the Roman outlook with viewpoints that one finds today.

---

[13] *tripudium*: the ritual feeding of sacred chickens before a battle. The birds' refusal to eat was thought to indicate the gods' opposition to the proposed course of action.

[14] *Rostra*: the speakers' platform in the Roman Forum.

Lectisternium: drawing of a relief from Eleusis in Greece. The inscription gives the name of the dedicator.

(1) The gods exist but their benevolence cannot be taken for granted. The relationship between gods and men requires constant upkeep by means of regular prayer and sacrifice in order to ensure their benevolence or favor *(pax deorum* or *deum)* and avoid their anger *(ira)*, as is apparent in the above speech by the Lar in Plautus' *Pot of Gold.*

In Plautus' comedy *Merchant,* a woman places a laurel branch on an altar and prays for the well-being of her son.

1.19 PLAUTUS, *MERCHANT* 678-9. Apollo, I pray that in your benevolence (*propitius*) you bestow favor (*pax*), good health (*salus*) and good sense (*sanitas*) on our household (*familia*), and in your benevolence may you also spare my son.

(2) *do ut des,* **I give in order that you may give**. This contractual principle is illustrated by the state's religious response to a plague that broke out in 399 BCE in the middle of Rome's war against the neighboring city of Veii. On the advice of the Sibylline books, the Senate ordered a banquet in honor of the gods (*lectisternium*) to be celebrated by the state and by individual families.[15]

1.20 LIVY 5.13.5-7. Plague was rife, affecting all living creatures. Since no cause nor end to this incurable disease was found, the Senate decided to consult the Sibylline books. Over a period of eight days the *duumvirs* celebrated the first *lectisternium* ever held in Rome in order to win the favor of Apollo, Latona, Diana, Hercules, Mercury and Neptune, spreading couches for them that were as richly furnished as was possible at that time.[16] The ritual was also celebrated in private houses. Throughout the city doors were left open and food of all kinds was set out for general consumption. Everyone alike, we are told, both known and unknown, was invited in and hospitably entertained.

A few years later, also because of plague, the Romans again resorted to a *lectisternium.* This is one the few occasions that Livy explicitly mentions *pax deorum*; elsewhere it is assumed.

1.21 LIVY 7.2.2. Both in that and in the following year (365 and 364 BCE) there was a plague. Nothing memorable was done in the latter year, except for the

---

15   *lectisternium*: literally a draping of couches, a banquet in honor of the gods at which the statues of the gods were placed on draped couches outside the temples.

16   *duumvirs*: two officials, priests who were in charge of the performance of sacred rites (*sacris faciundis*) and who thus acted as interpreters of the Sibylline books. At first there were two, then ten, fifteen, and finally sixteen. See Glossary under *quindecimviri. Latona*: the mother of Apollo and Diana.

performance of a *lectisternium* in order to beg for the *pax deorum*.

> A votive tablet poignantly records a woman's gratitude to the goddess Minerva the Mindful, or the one who listens, for answering her prayer.

1.22 *CIL* 11.1305, *ILS* 3135. In payment of her vow Tullia Superiana <dedicates this plaque> willingly and deservedly to Minerva the Mindful for having restored her hair.

> The poet Ovid (43 BCE – 17 CE) is somewhat flippant, if not also cynical, about such gift-giving.

1.23 Ovid, *Art of Love* 3.653-4. Gifts, believe me, win over both men and gods. Jupiter himself is placated by the offering of gifts.

> **(3) The gods communicate their will to man by sending messages — auspices, portents, prodigies, dreams and prophecies — that were usually interpreted by various specialists in divination.** Three groups of experts practised divination: augurs, quindecimvirs (the board of priests for the performance of sacred rites), and *haruspices*. The first two were state officials appointed for life. The *haruspices* were not state officials, but were summoned as needed. Augurs and *haruspices* would be consulted on signs from birds and from the sky, but the former were more concerned with auspices that expressed the divine will concerning a specific act or a disregard of auspices, whereas the *haruspices* dealt with signs that indicated future happenings, i.e., portents, prodigies and omens.
>
> The biographer Suetonius (c. 70 CE – c. 130 CE) tells the famous story of Publius Claudius Pulcher who, in the First Punic War, disregarded unfavorable auspices before a naval battle and threw the sacred chickens into the sea.[17]

1.24 Suetonius, *Life of Tiberius* 2. Claudius Pulcher began a naval battle off Sicily, although the sacred chickens would not eat when he took the auspices. In defiance of religiosity (*religio*), he flung them into the sea, ordering them to drink since they would not eat. He lost the battle.

> Cicero tells the story of how the Carthaginian general Hannibal heeded the warning of the goddess Juno who appeared to him in a dream.

1.25 Cicero, *On Divination* 1.48. Coelius writes that Hannibal wished to carry off a golden column that was in the shrine of Juno at Lacinium.[18] However, he did not know whether it was solid or gilded, and so he bored into it. Finding it was solid, he decided to remove it. But when he was asleep, Juno appeared to him and warned him not to do it, threatening that if he did she would cause the loss of his good eye. That clever man did not neglect the warning. From the gold filings, moreover, he had the image of a calf made which he placed on the top of the column.

> Cicero reports a clash between the *haruspices* and an augur. Cicero's

---

[17] That these chickens would not eat before the battle was thought to indicate the gods' disapproval of the proposed engagement.

[18] *Coelius*: an early Roman historian whose work only survives in quotations such as this. *Lacinium*: a promontory in southern Italy.

conclusion is that both kinds of divination were proved correct.

1.26 CICERO, *ON THE NATURE OF THE GODS* **2.10-11.** In the consulship of P. Scipio and C. Figulus (162 BCE), both Roman augural lore and that of the Etruscan *haruspices* were confirmed by the eventual outcome. Gracchus, then consul for the second time, was conducting the election of his successors. The first returning officer suddenly dropped dead as he was reporting the results. Gracchus nonetheless proceeded with the election. Perceiving, however, that the matter had caused the people to feel some religious concern *(religio)*, he referred the matter to the Senate.

The Senate decided that it must be referred to 'the customary officials.' *Haruspices* were brought in and pronounced that the returning officer for the elections had been out of order.[19] Thereupon, so I heard from my father, Gracchus burst into a rage: 'Is that so, indeed? Was I not in order? I took the auspices and put the names to the vote both as consul and as augur. You Etruscan barbarians, who do think you are, claiming the right to judge the auspices of the Roman people and be interpreters of the conduct of our elections?' And so he ordered them to depart.

Afterwards, however, he sent a letter from his province to the college of augurs, saying that while reading some books he had realised that there had been a flaw *(vitium)*. After setting up his augural observation post in the gardens of Scipio, he had crossed the *pomerium* to hold a meeting of the Senate but, when returning, had forgotten to take the auspices. Therefore the election of the consuls was flawed.

The Senate decided that the consuls must resign. This they did. What greater example than this do we seek? A very wise Roman, perhaps one of the most outstanding, preferred to confess an error that could have been concealed rather than let a religious problem *(religio)* affect the state. The consuls preferred to lay down their office immediately rather than hold on to it for a moment in the face of a religious problem *(religio)*. The authority of the augurs is great; is not also the skill of the *haruspices* divinely inspired?

(4) Ritual and its correct performance are critically important. As the above example from Cicero shows, any imperfection or flaw *(vitium)* in either the prayer or the sacrifice could offend the gods and thus incur their anger.

Before making a sacrifice a character in Plautus anxiously enquires:

1.27 PLAUTUS, *LITTLE CARTHAGINIAN* 253 - 4. Are all the things here that are needed to secure the *pax deum*?

A flaw or error *(vitium)* in either a prayer or sacrificial victim would necessitate the whole ceremony being repeated. Three major categories of public actions could be affected by a flaw: elections, the legislative assemblies, and other functions of the magistrates, including festivals and military operations.

In the following excerpts, at the inauguration of the consuls of 176 BCE one of

[19] The *haruspices* interpreted the presiding officer's death as a *prodigium*. Gracchus, however, relied on his position as augur, choosing not to regard the consul's death as a bad auspice. Thus he dismissed the objections of the *haruspices*.

the sacrificial victims was found to be flawed and the Latin festival, celebrated before the consuls went off on campaign, had to be repeated because of an omission in the prayer.

1.28 LIVY 41.14.7. The consuls, Gnaeus Cornelius and Quintus Petilius, on the day they entered office, each sacrificed an ox to Jupiter, as is customary, but no head on the liver was found in the victim sacrificed by Petilius. When this was announced to the Senate, he was ordered to keep sacrificing an ox until a favorable omen was secured....

1.29 LIVY 41.16.1-2. The Latin festival was held on 4 May, and a religious problem arose because, at the sacrifice of one victim, the magistrate of Lanuvium omitted from his prayer the words 'for the Roman people, the Quirites.'[20] When this was reported to the Senate and referred by that body to the college of pontiffs, the pontiffs decided that the Latin festival should be repeated, since it had not been correctly performed, and that the people of Lanuvium, on whom the repetition was incumbent, should furnish the victims.

(5) The gods' concern is more with material success than ethical behavior. They grant success, prosperity, health, and have little if any concern with the behavior of humans toward other humans.

1.30 CICERO, ON THE NATURE OF THE GODS 3.87. We give thanks to the gods when we achieve political office or some benefit to our family estate, or if we happen upon some good or avoid some misfortune, and we do not think that our own reputation has been enhanced. Did anyone ever give thanks to the gods because he was a good man? No, he did so because he is rich, honored and secure. Jupiter is called 'Best and Greatest' not because he makes men just, moderate and wise, but because he makes them healthy, secure, wealthy and prosperous.

This attitude is apparent in the following words of three characters in Plautus.

1.31 PLAUTUS, CURCULIO 527-532. Since I've managed that business well, I must go to the temple here and give thanks.... I've got the money, and the fact is that the gods put money in the hands of a man to whom they are well disposed. So now I'll attend to the business of sacrificing to them. It's my intention to look out for myself.

1.32 PLAUTUS, CURCULIO 557. When the gods are favorable to a man, he is a man they are not angry with, I guess.

1.33 PLAUTUS, PERSIAN 205-6. The gods will bless me. Why me? Well, by heaven, that's their will. But if they were to treat me as I deserve, by heaven, they would hate me and do me ill.

(6) Religion and politics are interconnected. The administration of politics and religion was often in the hands of the same men. Thus religion was under state control and protected the state. Most state priesthoods were lifetime appointments but not a full-time occupation. Thus a man could be a pontifex or an augur and also take part in political life, a point that is illustrated

---

[20] *Lanuvium*: a city outside Rome where the main part of the festival was enacted. *Quirites*: an ancient title of the Romans.

by the career of Julius Caesar, who became a pontifex in his early twenties and later had a distinguished political and military career, in addition to being elected chief pontifex (*pontifex maximus*). Many priests, as ex-magistrates, were members of the Senate, a body that was frequently consulted on religious issues. Thus it is often difficult, if not impossible, to distinguish 'religious' from 'political' issues.

Cicero avers that this interconnection of functions that are regarded as distinct in many cultures was intentional.

1.34 CICERO, *ON HIS HOUSE* 1.1. Among the many divinely inspired institutions established by our ancestors, nothing is more outstanding than their desire to have the same individuals in control over worship of the gods and the vital interests of the state. Their objective was to ensure that the most eminent and illustrious citizens maintain religion by their good government of the state, and maintain the state by their wise interpretation of religion.

Polybius, a Greek historian living in Rome in the mid-second century BCE, reflects on the utility of religion to the Roman state as a means of social control, opining that the state was held together by fear, awe, and respect for the supernatural (*deisidaimonia*).

1.35 POLYBIUS 6.56.6-12. In my opinion, the area in which the Roman constitution is most conspicuously superior is their concept of the gods. It seems to me that the very thing that is a matter of reproach among other peoples is what holds the Roman state together: I mean *deisidaimonia*.

Religious matters are dramatized and introduced into their public and private life to such an extent that nothing could exceed them in importance. Many people may find this amazing. My own opinion is that they have adopted these practices for the sake of the common people. For if you could form a state entirely from wise men, this approach perhaps would not have been necessary. But since every mass of people is fickle, and full of lawless desires, irrational passion, and violent anger, it is essential that they be controlled by invisible terrors and suchlike pageantry.

Cicero articulates the patriotic belief that Rome owed her success and greatness to acknowledging the gods.

1.36 CICERO, *ON THE REPLY OF THE HARUSPICES* 19. We owe the creation, increase and retention of our empire to the will of the gods.... We have excelled every race and nation in piety *(pietas)*, devotion to religion *(religio)*, and in that singular wisdom which recognizes that everything is ruled and controlled by the will of the gods.

A generation later, after a long period of civil war that culminated in the battle of Actium, Horace attributes Rome's recent problems both at home and abroad to the Romans' neglect of the gods.

1.37 HORACE, *ODES* 3.6.1-20. You will be paying for your ancestors' omissions (*delicta*), O Roman, though you do not deserve to do so, until you have restored the temples and crumbling shrines of the gods and the statues that are filthy with black smoke.

You rule an empire because you acknowledge that you are subordinate to the gods. From them comes every beginning. To them the outcome must be attributed. Because they have been neglected, the gods have visited many evils on sorrowing Italy.

Twice now the Parthians have crushed our attacks that were undertaken without good auspices....[21] The Dacians and Aethiopians almost destroyed Rome when it was beset with civil strife....[22]

Our age is teeming with vice and has polluted first the marriage bed, then our race and our homes. A stream of disaster rising from this source has flooded our country and our people.

> The historian Livy relates how Quintus Fabius Maximus, the newly appointed dictator,[23] addressed the Senate after news of the consul's death in the military disaster at Trasimene during the war against Hannibal (218-201 BCE).[24] Several expiations, or remedial actions, are prescribed to deal with the anger of the gods, thus corroborating Polybius' statement about *deisidaimonia*.

1.38 LIVY 22.9.7-10. Beginning with religious matters, Fabius convinced the Senate that the consul Flaminius had been in error more through his neglect of the rituals and auspices than through his recklessness and ignorance. So he said that they ought to enquire of the gods themselves how the gods' anger *(ira)* could be appeased. Thus he prevailed on them to do what is rarely done except when dreadful prodigies have been announced: the board of ten *(decemvirs)* was ordered to consult the Sibylline books.[25]

When these priests had inspected the fatal books, they reported to the Senate that the vow which had been made to Mars on account of this war had not been duly performed, and must be performed anew and on a larger scale. Great games must be vowed to Jupiter, and temples to Venus Erycina and Mind. Finally a *supplicatio* and *lectisternium* must be celebrated and a Sacred Spring vowed, if they should prove victorious and the state remain the same as it had been before the outbreak of hostilities.[26]

---

[21] The Parthians had inflicted crushing and ignominious defeats on Marcus Licinius Crassus at Carrhae in 53 BCE, and on the forces of Marcus Antonius in 36 BCE.

[22] *Dacians and Aethiopians*: an allusion to the battle of Actium in which Octavian, soon to style himelf Augustus, defeated the forces of Antony and Cleopatra. Dacian bowmen served under Antony at Actium and Egyptians, here called *Aethiopians*, manned the fleet.

[23] *dictator*: an extraordinary magistrate appointed for a maximum period of six months, whose power (*imperium*) overrode that of the two consuls. Such appointments were made in times of extreme crisis, usually to deal with a military emergency. This use of the office was discontinued after the Hannibalic War.

[24] *Trasimene*: a battle in 217 BCE in which Hannibal inflicted huge losses on the Roman army.

[25] *decemvirs*: see Glossary under *quindecimviri*.

[26] *supplicatio* : a period of collective prayers and offerings to the gods by the whole state. *lectisternium*: see Glossary. *Sacred Spring*: all the animals born in a certain spring were consecrated and sacrificed to the gods; see 4.15.

STORIES OF EARLY ROMAN RELIGION
AND THE IMPORTANCE OF DIVINATION[1]

The traditional date of the foundation of Rome by the eponymous Romulus is 753 BCE. But the stories we have concerning the period of the kings (c. 753-510 BCE) were written several centuries after the events they purport to describe. The literary sources are consistent in retrojecting Rome's religious institutions back to her mythical past. Variants in the legends, however, are apparent, especially in the versions of Livy and Ovid who were writing during the time of Augustus (27 BCE-14 CE). All versions reflect the religious significance of divination, the marking of boundaries and the danger of infringing upon them.

Livy tells the story of the foundation of Rome, in which Romulus and Remus employ divination by observing signs in the heavens to decide which of them should rule and give his name to the newly founded city. Both men received auguries,[2] but a quarrel arose over the question of priority or superiority in number of signs. In the more popular patriotic myth, Remus was slain by Romulus; in another version, however, the killer is not named. The city was named after Romulus who then fortified the Palatine hill.[3]

2.1 LIVY 1.6.3-7.3. Romulus and Remus were seized by a desire to found a city in the area where they had been exposed and reared.... Since the brothers were twins and respect for age could not determine between them, Romulus took the Palatine as his augural station and Remus the Aventine in order that the gods who protected those places should decide by augury who should give his

---

[1] 'All divination stems from the belief that gods send meaningful messages.' (Linderski, *OCD* 3. 488)

[2] *augury*: auspices or signs that pertained to both substance and time.

[3] *Palatine*: one of the seven hills of Rome, reputedly the oldest settlement. It came to be the most desirable residential area, and thus was inhabited by the emperors. English 'palace' derives from *palatium*.

name to the new city and who should rule over it when it was established.[4]

The story is that Remus was the first to receive an augury, the flight of six vultures. This augury had already been announced when twice that number appeared to Romulus. Whereupon each was hailed as king by his own supporters, the former group claiming the kingship on the principle of priority, the latter because of the number of birds. They engaged in a battle of words, anger led to bloodshed and, amidst the disturbance, Remus was struck and killed. The more common story is that Remus leaped over the new walls in mockery of his brother and was killed in anger by Romulus with the words, 'So perish anyone else who shall leap over my walls.' Thus Romulus obtained sole power, and the city was founded in the name of its founder. His first act was to fortify the Palatine where he himself had been reared.

> Ovid in the *Fasti*, a poem about the festivals of the Roman calendar, gives yet another version of the story, naming a new character, Celer, as the killer, thus avoiding any mention of the fratricide. Like Livy, however, Ovid emphasises, albeit briefly, the use of divination to decide who should be the founder and ruler of Rome.

2.2 OVID, *FASTI* 4. 807-859. We have reached the foundation of the city. Great Quirinus, stand by me as I sing your deeds.[5] Already the brother of Numitor had suffered punishment and all the shepherd folk were under the leadership of the twins.[6] They agreed to concentrate the scattered country folk and found a city. The question was: which of the two should found it? 'There is no need of a contest,' said Romulus, 'Great faith is put in birds. Let us try the bird omen.' This was approved. One went to the rocks of the wooded Palatine. The other in the morning approached the top of the Aventine. Remus saw six birds, Romulus twice that number, one after another. They stood by their agreement and Romulus had control of the city.

A suitable day was chosen for him to mark out the line of the walls with a plough. The festival of Pales was at hand. On that day the work began.[7] A trench was dug down to the solid rock and fruits were thrown to the bottom and earth brought from the neighboring soil. The ditch was filled up with earth. When it was full, an altar was placed on top and a new hearth enjoyed the kindled fire. Then pressing the plough handle, he marked out the line of the walls with a furrow. A white heifer and a white ox bore the yoke. The king spoke as follows: 'Jupiter, and father Mars and mother Vesta, stand by me as I found the city! Pay attention all you gods that piety bids be summoned. Under your auspices

---

[4]   *Aventine*: one of the seven hills of Rome, that lay outside the pomerium or sacred boundary of Rome. This area is later associated with the lower classes or plebeians.

[5]   *Quirinus*: the name of the deified Romulus.

[6]   *brother of Numitor*…: Amulius had deposed his brother Numitor from the kingship of Alba and had Numitor's infant grandsons, Romulus and Remus, exposed to die by the Tiber. They were suckled by a wolf, rescued by a shepherd and grew up to take revenge and kill Amulius.

[7]   *Pales*: a pastoral god or goddess (both genders occur) honored at the *Parilia*, a festival celebrated in the late republic on April 21 as the birthday of Rome; see 6.7-6.9.

may this project of mine rise! May the life and power of the city's dominion long endure! May East and West be subject to her!' This was his prayer. Jupiter sent omens with thunder on the left and flashes of lightning appeared in the left of the sky. Joyful at the augury, the citizens laid the foundations and in a short time there was a new wall.

The work was urged on by Celer whom Romulus himself had summoned and said 'Let this be your concern, Celer, that no one cross either the walls or the ditch made by the plough. Any man who dares to do this, put him to death.' Unaware of this, Remus began to show contempt for the lowly walls, saying, 'Will these protect the people?' Without delay, he leaped over them. For his daring Celer struck him with a shovel. Covered with blood, he fell to the hard ground. When the king learned of this, he suppressed his welling tears and kept his wound locked up in his breast. He refused to weep openly, setting an example of fortitude with the words, 'This is what will befall any enemy that crosses my walls.' Yet he granted him funeral honors and could no longer bear to hold back his tears. The affection that he had concealed was evident. When they set down the bier, he gave it a last kiss, saying, 'Farewell brother, snatched from me against my will.' He then anointed the body before committing it to the flames. Faustulus and Acca, her hair loosed in mourning, did the same.[8] Then the Quirites, though not yet known by that name, wept for the youth.[9] Finally a flame was put to the pyre, wet with their tears.

A city arose that was destined to plant its victorious foot on the neck of the world. But who at that time could have believed it? Rule the world, Rome, and may you be always subject to great Caesar.[10]

> The biographer Plutarch (c. 50 – 120 CE) describes how Romulus established the *pomerium*, the sacred boundary of the city.

2.3 PLUTARCH, *LIFE OF ROMULUS* **11.1-3.** Romulus then buried Remus ... and set to work building his city, summoning men from Etruria who prescribed the details according to certain sacred laws and writings, and taught them to him as in a religious ritual. A circular pit was dug around what is now the Comitium,[11] and in this were placed the first fruits of all things whose use is thought good by custom and necessary by nature. Finally, each man threw in a small share of the soil of his native land and they mixed it all together. They call this pit the *mundus*, the same word they use for the heavens.

Then, taking this as the center, they marked out the city around it. Next the founder (Romulus), fixing a bronze blade on a plough and yoking a bull and a cow, himself drove a deep furrow for the boundary lines, while those who followed behind him had the task of turning back inside the city all the clods that the plough threw up, allowing no clod to lie turned outwards.

---

[8] *Faustulus*: the shepherd who found the twins and brought them home to be reared by his wife, Acca.

[9] *Quirites*: the name by which the Roman citizen body was frequently addressed.

[10] *great Caesar*: Augustus, who had been adopted as the son of Julius Caesar.

[11] *Comitium*: the chief place of political assembly, in the Roman Forum near the Senate House.

With this line they marked out the course of the wall. By contraction it is called the *pomerium*, that is, *post murum*, behind or next to the wall. And wherever they intended to put a gate, they removed the ploughshare from the ground, lifted the plough over, and left a space. And this is why they regard all the wall as sacred except for the gates. For if they regarded the gates as sacred, it would not be possible without religious scruples to import and export from the city things that are necessary but impure.[12]

> Numa Pompilius, a Sabine, succeeded Romulus as king.[13] Livy introduces Numa as having a reputation for justice and *religio* (1.18.1). When offered the kingship, Numa insisted on following the precedents set by Romulus in consulting the gods. Livy describes the ritual of augury by which Numa was 'inaugurated' as king.

2.4 LIVY 1.18.6-10. When summoned, Numa ordered that, just as Romulus had obtained the kingship by taking augury concerning the foundation of the city, so too the gods should be consulted in his own case. Therefore an augur (who thereafter, as a mark of distinction, was made a state priest permanently in charge of that function) led him to the citadel and seated him on a stone facing the south. The augur seated himself on Numa's left; his head was covered and in his right hand he held a crooked staff without a knot which they call a *lituus*.[14]

Then, looking out over the city and the countryside beyond, he prayed to the gods and marked off the regions from east to west, the areas to the south were designated as 'right', those to the north as 'left'. He fixed in his mind a

Roman augur with *lituus*.

---

[12] *religious scruples*: the Greek word here is a cognate of *deisidaimonia*.

[13] *Sabines*: an Italic tribe, near neighbors of the Romans. In the story of the rape of the Sabines, the Romans, led by Romulus, are said to have forcibly taken Sabine women to be their wives.

[14] *covered head*: Romans usually sacrificed with the head covered, except for certain cults which required the Greek ritual, with the head uncovered; see illustrations on pp. 3, 24, 36.

sign opposite to him and as far away as the eye could see. Then, transferring the crook to his left hand and placing his right on Numa's head, he prayed as follows: 'Father Jupiter, if it is right *(fas)* that his man Numa Pompilius whose head I hold, be king in Rome, I beg that you reveal to us clear signs within those limits that I have set.' He then specified the auspices that he wished to be sent. Sent they were. Thus Numa was declared king and descended from the augural station.

> To Numa are attributed many religious institutions, including the foundation of the temple of Janus, various rituals, a lunar calendar with intercalation, and several priesthoods. In order to create a fear of the gods, Numa fabricates a story that a goddess, Egeria, had communicated to him the gods' wishes concerning their rituals and his innovations. Setting up an altar to Jupiter Elicius (the one who elicits), Numa used augury to determine what signs from the gods were to be accepted.

2.5 LIVY 1.19.1-7. After Numa had obtained the kingship in this way, he prepared to refound this new city, founded by force of arms, with a new foundation in law, statutes and customs. When he perceived that men could not become accustomed to such things in the midst of wars because their minds had become brutalized by warfare, he thought that his fierce people needed to be softened by the disuse of arms. So he built the temple of Janus at the bottom of the Argiletum,[15] as an indicator of peace and war, so that when open it would signify that the state was at war; and when closed that all the surrounding peoples were pacified....

Numa closed the temple after first securing the goodwill of all the neighboring peoples by alliance and treaties. Fearing that relief from the anxieties of foreign dangers might lead men who had been restrained by fear of their enemies and military discipline into extravagance and idleness, he thought the first thing that needed to be done was to instill into them a fear of the gods *(deorum metus)*. This he considered was most efficacious in the case of a populace that was ignorant and, in those days, uncivilized. Since he could not get this into their minds without fabricating a miraculous story, he pretended to have nightly meetings with the goddess Egeria. On her advice, he said, he was instituting the religious rituals *(sacra)* that were most approved by the gods and appointing the special priests for the service of individual gods.[16]

First of all, he divided the year into twelve months, according to the revolutions of the moon. But since the moon does not fulfill thirty days for each month, and eleven days are lacking for the full complement of the solar year, he inserted intercalary months so that every twenty years the cycle should be completed and the days come round again to the same position of the sun from which

---

[15]   *Janus*: god of doors and gates, that is, openings and also beginnings. Like a door, he faced two ways and so was represented with two faces or double-headed.
   Argiletum: an area at the foot of the Capitoline, close to the river Tiber.

[16]   Note how Livy indicates his own disbelief in the stories he is relating by remarking that this is a 'miraculous story' fabricated by Numa and by reporting Numa's alleged words with the interpolation 'he said'.

they had started. He also fixed days when it was lawful or unlawful to enact public business, since it would sometimes be useful that no measures be brought before the people.[17]

2.6 LIVY 1.20.1-7. Numa then turned his attention to the appointment of priests, although he himself performed very many rituals, especially those that now belong to the *flamen Dialis*.[18] ... To him he added two other flamens, one for Mars, the other for Quirinus.[19] He chose virgins for the service of Vesta, a priesthood that derives from Alba and so not inappropriate to the race of the founder.[20] So that they might be permanent priestesses of the temple, he assigned them a stipend from the public treasury, investing them with awe and sanctity because of their virginity and other religious observances....

He then chose as pontifex[21] Numa Marcius, son of Marcus, one of the senators, and entrusted to him written instructions for all the sacrifices: with what victims, on what days, in what temple, sacrifices should be made, and from what source the funds should be raised for these expenses. All the rest of the sacrifices, both public and private, he made subject to the decrees of the pontifex, so there might be someone to whom the people might come for advice in the event of political strife concerning divine law through neglect of the ancestral rites and the adoption of foreign ones.[22] The same pontifex was to teach not only the ceremonies relating to the gods above but also the proper funeral rites, propitiation of the spirits of the dead *(manes)*, and also what prodigies sent by lightning or other manifestation were to to be taken up and attended to.[23] To elicit this information from the minds of the gods, Numa dedicated an altar on the Aventine to Jupiter Elicius and consulted the god by augury so that he might learn what signs were to be accepted.

> To Tullus Hostilius, the next king of Rome (672-640 BCE), is attributed the earliest tradition regarding the procedure for making a treaty. This task was entrusted to fetials, special priests who were also concerned with the declaration of wars and advising the Senate concerning such ritual tradition.[24]

2.7 LIVY 1.24.3-9. One treaty differs from another in its terms, but the same

---

[17] *days when it was lawful or unlawful...*: the Latin epithets (*fastus* and *nefastus*) contain the word *fas*, action that is lawful in the eyes of the gods.

[18] *flamen Dialis*: priest of Jupiter; on the taboos imposed by this office, see 5.9.

[19] *Quirinus*: originally a Sabine god whose functions resembled those of Mars, later assimilated to the deified Romulus.

[20] *Vesta*: Roman goddess whose temple was in the Roman forum.
Alba: Alba Longa, a town outside of Rome.

[21] *pontifex*: one of the two major priesthoods, see chapter 5.

[22] On the adoption of foreign religious practices, see chapters 8 and 9.

[23] *prodigy*: an unusual or unnatural occurrence that was considered to have been sent by the gods as an indication of a future event. On the process of dealing with a prodigy, see chapter 7.

[24] Livy attributes the fetials' ritual declaration of war to the next king, Ancus Marcius; see 7.2.

procedure is always followed. We hear that the following was done in this case, and tradition has not preserved any treaty that is more ancient.[25] The fetial asked King Tullus, 'Do you order me, O King, to make a treaty with the *pater patratus* of the Alban people?'[26] When the king ordered him to do so, he said, 'I demand of you, king, a tuft of sacred grass.' The king replied, 'You shall take it untainted.' The fetial brought from the citadel an untainted tuft of grass. After this he asked the king, 'Do you make me the royal spokesman of the Roman people of the Quirites, with my implements and companions?' The king answered, 'I do this in as much as it may be done without harm to myself and the Roman people of the Quirites.'[27]

The fetial was Marcus Valerius. He made Spurius Furius *pater patratus,* touching his head and his hair with the sacred plant.[28] The *pater patratus* is appointed to administer the oath, that is, to make the treaty inviolable. This he does with many words expressed in a long metrical formula that is not worthwhile quoting. When the terms are read aloud, he says, 'Hear, Jupiter; hear, *pater patratus* of the Alban people; hear, people of Alba. The Roman people will not be the first to depart from these terms, as they have publicly been read out without malice aforethought from beginning to end from these tablets or from wax and as they have been fully understood today. If they should be the first to depart from them with malice aforethought by public consent, then great Diespiter,[29] so strike the Roman people as here today I will strike this pig. And, insofar as your power and might are greater, do you strike them so much the harder.' When he had spoken these words, he struck the pig with a flint.

> With the last three kings of Rome, Tarquin the Elder, Servius Tullius and Tarquin the Proud, we are dealing with more secure historical material. The building of the temple of Jupiter on the Capitoline is attributed to Tarquin the Elder and his son, Tarquin the Proud, a tradition that is confirmed by the extant remains. But first the existing shrines had to be removed. Divination sanctioned the removal of all but one, the shrine of Terminus, the god of boundaries.

2.8 LIVY 1.55.1-7. Tarquin next turned his attention to affairs in the city. Here his first aim was to leave the temple of Jupiter on the Tarpeian rock as a memorial of his reign and of his name:[30] of the two Tarquinii, the father vowed the temple and the son fulfilled it.[31] In order that the site be free from all other religious

---

[25] *in this case*: the combat between the Horatii and Curiatii in the reign of Tullus Hostilius.

[26] *pater patratus*: an ancient title. The exact meaning of the epithet *patratus* is disputed.

[27] *Quirites*: an ancient title of the Romans, perhaps to be connected with *Quirinus*, see n. 19.

[28] By touching the head of the *pater patratus* with the sacred plant which retained soil from the Capitol and carrying it with them, the fetials maintained contact with Rome and thus their inviolability which they transmitted to the treaty.

[29] *Diespiter*: an alternative form of Jupiter, found in old religious formulas.

[30] *Tarpeian rock*: part of the Capitoline hill from which traitors and murderers were thrown.

[31] *the son fulfilled it*: although Livy states that the son completed his father's vow, the actual dedication was not made until the beginning of the republic (Livy 2.8.6-8). It was built in the Etruscan style and was dedicated to three deities — Jupiter, Juno and Minerva — in 509 BCE. The original platform of the temple still exists.

claims and belong entirely to Jupiter and his temple, he decided to annul the consecration of the various shrines and sacred areas that had originally been vowed by king Tatius in the crisis of the battle against Romulus, and had afterward been consecrated and inaugurated.[32]

At the beginning of this project, tradition has it that the gods exercised their power *(numen)* to show the might of this great empire.[33] For although the birds gave their assent to the deconsecration of all the shrines, they refused it in the case of the shrine of Terminus (Boundary). This was taken as an omen and augury: the fact that the seat of Terminus was not moved, and that he alone of all the gods was not summoned forth from the place consecrated to him, was a portent of endurance and stability.

When this auspice of permanence had been received, another prodigy portending the greatness of the empire followed. It is said that a human head with its features intact was discovered by the men who were digging the foundations of the temple. This manifestation clearly foretold that here would be the citadel of empire and the capital of the world. This was the interpretation of the soothsayers *(vates)*, both those who were in the city and those who were called in from Etruria to consider the matter.

> The Greek historian Dionysius of Halicarnassus writing in the time of Augustus tells the story of how Tarquin the Elder (616-579 BCE) acquired the Sibylline oracles.[34] Throughout the republic these oracles were kept in the temple of Jupiter on the Capitoline and were consulted in times of crisis. They were later transferred by Augustus to his newly built temple of Apollo on the Palatine.

2.9 DIONYSIUS OF HALICARNASSUS, *ANTIQUITIES* **4.62.1- 5.** It is said that another wonderful piece of good fortune befell the Roman state during Tarquin's reign,

Reconstruction of temple of Jupiter the Best and Greatest on the Capitoline hill in Rome.

---

[32] *Tatius*: a Sabine who fought with Romulus after the rape of the Sabine women. The battle was stopped by the intervention of the women who had become wives of the Romans. Tatius ruled jointly with Romulus for several years.

[33] *tradition has it*: here Livy distances himself from his anonymous source.

[34] The Sibyl of Cumae, a former Greek colony near Naples, was the prophetess of Apollo who is said to have been consulted by Aeneas before his descent into the underworld; see Vergil, *Aeneid* 6.42–155.

a gift of some god or divine power. This was not just a benefit of short duration, but one that has many times saved Rome from great disasters throughout her entire existence. A foreign woman approached the tyrant wishing to sell him nine books filled with Sibylline oracles. When Tarquin refused to buy the books at the price she asked, she went away and burned three of them. Not long after she brought the six remaining books and offered them at the same price as before. They thought she was crazy and laughed at her for asking the same price for the smaller number that she had been unable to get even for the larger number. She went away again and burned half those that were left. Then, bringing the three remaining books, she asked the same price.

Tarquin, marvelling at the woman's purpose, sent for the augurs, explained what had happened and asked what he should do. From certain signs they realized that what he had rejected was a blessing sent by the gods. Declaring that it was a great misfortune that he had not bought all the books, they ordered him to pay the woman all the money that she asked and get the oracles that were left. The woman delivered the books, told him to take care of them and disappeared from human sight.

Tarquin chose two distinguished citizens and appointed two public slaves as their assistants, entrusting them with the guarding of the books.[35] When one of these men, Marcus Atilius, seemed to have betrayed his trust and was informed on by one of the public slaves, Tarquin ordered him to be sewn up in a leather bag and thrown into the sea as a parricide.[36]

> After the expulsion of Tarquin the Proud and the abolition of the monarchy, Livy reports the establishing of the Republic under two annually elected magistrates, the consuls. He then notes the religious changes that were made now that Rome no longer had kings.

2.10 Livy 2.2.1-2. Matters of religion then received attention. Since certain public sacrifices had been usually performed by the kings in person, they appointed a king of sacrifices so that kings would not be missed. This priesthood was made subordinate to the pontifex, in case the honor attached to the title should somehow pose a obstacle to the liberty which was at that time their primary concern.

---

[35]   *two distinguished citizens...*: an allusion to the *duumviri* who number increased to sixteen by the end of the republic; see *quindecimviri* in Glossary.

[36]   *parricide*: literally father-slayer, but the word refers to treasonous behavior that is tantamount to 'killing' the fatherland. See 5.7 for the continuation of this excerpt which discusses the *quindecimvirs'* supervision of the sacred books.

Bronze figurine of a Roman worshipper with veiled head who is holding an incense box. This figure perhaps represents the Genius depicted as the *pater familias*. Photo Ch. Thioc. Courtesy of Musée de la civilisation gallo-romaine, Lyon, France

THE RELIGION OF THE FAMILY

3.1 CICERO, *ON THE LAWS* 2.22. The sacred rites of families *(sacra privata)* shall endure for ever.

> The word *familia* embraces both 'family' and 'household,' that is, all living creatures on the property of an individual. Thus included were slaves and farm animals. Each Roman family had its own tutelary deities, the Lar (plural, Lares) that protected the entire household and were kept in the Lararium, a small shrine; the Penates that protected the store-cupboard or pantry *(penus)* in the inner part of the house; Vesta, goddess of the hearth; and the Genius of the house.[1] It was the task of the male head of the family, the *pater familias*, to tend these deities, keep their favor and so ensure the prosperity of the family, as is indicated by the Lar in the prologue of Plautus' *Pot of Gold*.[2]
>
> In prescribing laws for his ideal state, Cicero emphasizes the importance of maintaining the integrity of traditional family cults.

3.2 CICERO, *ON THE LAWS* 2.19. No one shall have gods for himself, either new gods or alien gods, unless they have been recognised by the state. Privately they shall worship those gods that they have duly received from their ancestors. In cities they shall have shrines; in the country they shall have groves and places for the Lares. They shall preserve the rites of the family and their ancestors.

> In Plautus' comedy *Merchant*, a young man melodramatically bids farewell to his father's home, announcing that he is going to live elsewhere because of the vice inherent in the city. Although the scene is set in Athens, the details are essentially those of Roman family cultic worship.

---

[1] *Genius*: a divine 'double,' as it were, or guardian spirit of an individual, usually a male that is often represented as a bearded snake. The Genius of the *pater familias* was thus a part of family religion, and the whole household came to have its own Genius. The latter Genius protected family and clients (individuals dependent on the *pater familias*).

[2] See 1.7.

3.3 PLAUTUS, MERCHANT 830-37. Lintel and threshold, hail and, at the same time, farewell. Today for the last time I lift this foot from my paternal home. The use, enjoyment, support and nurture of this dwelling are now cut off from me, estranged and dead as far as I am concerned. Divine Penates of my parents, paternal Lar of the family, to you I entrust the fortunes of my parents; protect them well. For myself I shall seek other household gods, another Lar, another city, another country.

> The poet Martial expresses his devotion to the various deities of his farm that he is about to leave. He entrusts the sacred observances to the new occupant, but also wishes to participate in the worship, despite his absence.

3.4 MARTIAL, EPIGRAMS 10.92. Marius, cultivator and companion of the quiet life, citizen of ancient Atina that glories in you, I entrust to your care these twin pines that adorn the rough grove, these holm oaks of the Fauns, the altars of Jupiter the Thunderer and of shaggy Silvanus that were built by the half-skilled hands of my farm manager.[3] The blood of many a lamb and kid has often stained these altars. I also entrust to your care the virgin goddess, mistress of her sacred shrine, and him whom you see as guest of his chaste sister, Mars, who initiates the month of my birth;[4] and the laurel grove of dainty Flora into which she fled when pursued by Priapus.[5] Whether you propitiate all the kindly deities of my tiny little farm with a blood sacrifice or with incense, you shall say: 'Wherever your Martial is, behold, by this right hand, though an absent priest, he is here with me sacrificing to you. Deem him present and grant to each of us whatever we may pray for.'

Birth, marriage and death

> Birth, marriage and death for the Romans were essentially the concern of the family, and did not involve state religion or require the intervention of a public official. Because the rituals surrounding birth, marriage and death were performed within the family and generally unrecorded, the evidence is extremely scanty and we have to rely on isolated references in a variety of disparate sources.
>
> The male head of the family (*pater familias*) was responsible for maintaining the worship of the family gods, as we saw in the prologue to Plautus' *Pot of Gold*.[6] Under his control (*potestas*) were all members of his household, including animals and slaves. A father symbolically acknowledged his paternity by 'taking up' a newly-born infant. From a legal point of view, sons did not

---

[3] *Fauns*: deities of woodland areas.
    Silvanus: a deity of uncultivated land, pastures and woodland areas, depicted as shaggy because he lived in the wild.

[4] *virgin goddess*: Diana, who was the stepsister of Mars because both were children of Jupiter.

[5] *Flora*: goddess of flowers.
    Priapus: guardian deity of flocks of sheep and goats, especially concerned with their fertility, hence he is frequently represented with an enormous phallus.

[6] See 1.7.

attain independence from their father but remained under his control until his death.

The fourth of the Laws of the Twelve Tables illustrates the extent of *patria potestas*.[7]

3.5 ROL 3.440-441. Quickly kill ... a dreadfully deformed child.

3.6 ROL 3.442-443. If a father surrenders his son for sale three times, the son shall be free from the father.[8]

3.7 ROL 3.442-443. A child born ten months after the father's death will not be admitted into a legal inheritance.

A letter from a man who was working away from home in Alexandria and sending money home to his pregnant wife indicates the practice of exposing babies, particularly girls, usually for economic reasons. This letter is preserved on a first century BCE papyrus from Egypt.

3.8 *OXYRHYNCHUS PAPYRI* 744. I send you my warmest greetings. I want you to know that we are still in Alexandria. I beg and beseech you to take care of the child and, if I receive my pay soon, I will send it to you. If you have the baby before I return, if it is a boy, let it live; if a girl, expose it. You sent a message with Aphrodisias, 'Don't forget me.' How can I forget you? Please don't worry.

The fifth of the Twelve Tables indicates the control exercised over women by men, either their fathers, guardians, or husbands.

3.9 ROL 3.444-445. Females shall remain in guardianship even when they have attained their majority... except Vestal Virgins.[9]

The jurist Gaius, writing in the second century CE, writes of a provision of the Twelve Tables whereby wives could avoid coming under the control of their husbands.

3.10 GAIUS, *INSTITUTES* 1.111. A woman came into the control [of her husband] if she remained married for a continuous year because she was, as it were, acquired by *usucapio* as a result of the year's occupancy (*usus*) and went over into the family of the husband, obtaining the position of a daughter.[10] Therefore it was prescribed by a law of the Twelve Tables that if a woman did not wish to come into the husband's control in that manner, she should absent herself for three nights each year and so interrupt the *usus* of each year. But this whole rule has partly been abolished by statutes and partly wiped out by lack of use.

---

7   *Laws of the Twelve Tables*: a collection of statutes divided into twelve 'tables,' traditionally said to have been made in 451/0 BCE. This collection is the foundation of Roman law. Cicero tells us that as a schoolboy he and his brother had to learn the Twelve Tables by heart.

8   *surrenders his son*: at the time the law was enacted, fathers were apparently selling their sons into slavery during times of hardship and buying them back when they had the means to do so.

9   *Vestal Virgins*: see 5.10-5.12.

10   *usucapio*: literally a taking (*capere*) by use or occupancy (*usus*).

Marriage

The ancient testimony for marriage ceremonies is scanty, the extant literary sources being mainly concerned with the legal aspects of marriage. Arrangements for and the enactment of a marriage were the responsibility of the family. A marriage would be arranged by the father of the bride or by her guardian with the parents of the groom, or with the groom himself in the case of an older man or one who was already a *pater familias*. The religious aspects of marriage came within the purview of family religion and would thus have varied widely in both their social and religious significance. An incidental reference by Cicero indicates that before the wedding itself private auspices would be taken, presumably by the *pater familias* of each family.[11]

Of the ceremony of *confarreatio*[12] Pliny the Elder (23/24-79 CE) writes:

3.11 PLINY, *NATURAL HISTORY* 18.10. Among religious rites, there was none more sacred.

That marriages could only be celebrated at certain times is an indication of their sacredness. In the *Fasti*, a poem about the Roman calendar year, Ovid records a prohibition on marriage in May, especially on the festival of the dead, the Lemuria.[13]

3.12 OVID, *FASTI* 5.485-490. The ancients shut the temples during these days, just as now you see them closed during the season sacred to the dead. The times are not suitable for either a widow or a maid to marry. For the same reason, if you are influenced by proverbs, the common folk say that it is bad to marry in May.

The beginning of March was also not recommended for marriage.

3.13 OVID, *FASTI* 3.393-396. If, woman, you wish to wed, although you both are in haste, put it off; short delays have great advantages. Weapons arouse battles and battle is no friend to married couples. When the weapons have been stored away, the omens will be more favorable.

The jurist Gaius gives an account of what was probably the most ancient form of Roman marriage, *confarreatio*, a ceremony that was only open to a select few since it involved the participation of an official priest.

3.14 GAIUS, *INSTITUTES* 1.112. Women come into *manus* by *farreum*, a type of sacrifice which is made to Jupiter Farreus.[14] A loaf of emmer is used in this, and the *confarreatio* is said to derive from it. Several acts and rituals are involved in performing this procedure in due order. There are prescribed and solemn words, and ten witnesses are present.

---

[11] Cicero (*On divination* 1.28) notes that private auspices fell into disuse, except for weddings.

[12] *confarreatio*: the name of a particular religious ceremony deriving from *far* (spelt) and *con-* (with), apparently because it involved a sacramental loaf.

[13] See 3.23 for a further example of a ban on marriages during the Feralia and Parentalia, festivals of the dead that were observed in February.

[14] *farreum*: a type of sacrificial cake made of *far*, emmer or spelt (Festus 78 L).

This procedure is still in existence today. The greater *flamines* (priests), that is, those of Jupiter, Mars, and Quirinus, and also the *rex sacrorum*, are picked only from sons of parents married by *confarreatio*, and they themselves cannot hold their priesthoods unless they have been married in this manner.[15]

In Plautus' *Pot of Gold* the miserly *pater familias*, Euclio, brought an offering of incense and some floral headdresses to the Lar.

3.15 PLAUTUS, *POT OF GOLD* 386-387. We will lay these on the hearth as offerings to our Lar, so that he may grant my daughter a happy marriage.

A wedding song by the poet Catullus, though obviously a literary construct, combines the atmosphere of a Greek feast with the Roman ceremony of the arrival of the bride at the home of her new husband. The poem is in the form of a choral competition between the young men and the maidens who have feasted at separate tables while awaiting the bride's arrival.

3.16 CATULLUS 62.1-5. [Young Men:] The evening star is here; arise, young men.[16] At long last the evening star has just raised his long awaited light in the heavens. Now it is time to arise, now time to leave the rich tables. Now the bride will come, now the wedding song will be sung.[17] Hail, Hymen Hymenaeus![18] Come, Hymen Hymenaeus!

3.17 CATULLUS 62.6-10. [Maidens:] Maidens, do you see the young men? Arise to meet them! Surely the Bringer of Night shows his Oetaean fires.[19] Yes, it is time. See how swiftly they have sprung to their feet. Not for nothing have they sprung to their feet. Their song will be worth beating. Hail, Hymen Hymenaeus! Come, Hymen Hymenaeus!

At the end of the poem, Catullus defines for the bride the essence of marriage.

3.18 CATULLUS 62.57-66. When in the fullness of time a maiden has made a fitting marriage, she is more dear to her husband and less hateful to her father. And you, maiden, do not fight against your husband. It is not just to fight against the man to whom your father gave you, your father together with your mother, whom you must obey. Your virginity is not entirely yours, but partly your parents'. A third belongs to your father, a third is allotted to your mother,

---

[15] *greater flamines* (singular *flamen*): special priests assigned to the cult of an individual deity. The presence of these priests suggests that this type of marriage ceremony was only available to the upper classes of Roman society; see Treggiari (1991) 22-3. The other two forms of marriage were by *coemptio*, the fictitious purchase of the bride from her father, or by *usus*, cohabitation.
rex sacrorum: also known as the *rex sacrificolus*, an office said to have been initiated after the abolition of the monarchy.

[16] *arise*: the young men are to get up from the couches on which they were reclining while feasting.

[17] *the bride will come*: a reference to the bringing of the bride from the home of her parents to her new home (*deductio*).

[18] *Hymen Hymenaeus*: a ritual invocation of the Greek god of marriage.

[19] *Oetaean fires*: a reference to Mount Oeta in Greece which is conventionally associated in poetry with the rising of the evening star, the planet Venus.

and only a third is yours. Do not fight against your parents who have given to their son-in-law their rights over you, together with a dowry. Hail, Hymen Hymenaeus! Come, Hymen Hymenaeus!

> The purpose of marriage was the procreation of legitimate children, the continuation of the family. The man took his bride to his home, thus leading her into marriage (in matrimonium ducit), and keeping her thereafter in marriage (in matrimonio habet). As Susan Treggiari has observed, 'The Romans saw marriage as a matter of human practice, varying in different cultures, but in Roman law accompanied by precise legal results. Its purpose was clear and pragmatic: the production (and consequent rearing) of legitimate children. A union could be defined as a Roman marriage if certain legal conditions were met and if both partners intended marriage. Their intention could often be proved if they produced children and the man acknowledged them.'[20]

> In his account of the rape of the Sabines, Livy has Romulus relate the benefits that marriage will bring to the Sabine women who have just been abducted by the Roman youths.

3.19 LIVY 1. 9.14. You will be in marriage and will enjoy partnership of all our fortunes, of citizenship and of children, the dearest thing that there is for human beings.

> Prior to the above excerpt, Livy tells a story of the origin of the ritual cry 'Talassio' that was uttered at Roman weddings by those who were taking the bride to her new home.

3.20 LIVY 1.9.10-13. At a given signal, the Roman youths ran in all directions to seize and carry off the maidens. Most of them were taken by the men in whose path they happened to be.... One who far excelled the rest in appearance and beauty, was seized, as the story goes, by the gang of a certain Thalassius. When asked to whom they were taking her they repeatedly cried out that she was being taken to Thalassius so that no one should touch her.[21] This was the origin of the wedding cry.

> After relating the same story, Plutarch comments on two Roman wedding customs.

3.21 PLUTARCH, ROMULUS 15. And it prevails to the present day that the bride shall not of herself cross the threshold into her new home, but be lifted up and carried in, because the Sabine women were forcibly carried in and did not enter of their own accord. Some also say that the custom of parting the bride's hair with the head of a spear symbolises the fact that the first marriage was in context of fighting and war.[22]

---

[20] Treggiari (1991) 13 and 5: '*Matrimonium* is an institution involving a mother, mater.'
[21] *to Thalassius*: Talassio is the dative of the name Thalassius.
[22] *spear*: see n. 28 on the combing of the hair as a metonym for marriage.

Death

In prescribing laws for his ideal state, Cicero writes:

3.22 CICERO, *ON THE LAWS* **2.22.** The rights of the gods of the dead shall be sacred. Consider dead kinsfolk as gods; the expenditure and mourning for them shall be limited.

Ovid describes two festivals in honor of the dead, the Parentalia and Feralia, that were celebrated from 18 to 21 February. He reports the reputed origins of these practices, while also recounting several rituals that involve sympathetic magic. Also included are some taboos that applied during this period, including one on celebrating weddings.[23]

3.23 OVID, *FASTI* **2. 533-570.** The tombs also are honored. Appease the spirits (*animae*) of your fathers and bring small gifts to the extinguished funeral pyres. The shades (*manes*) ask but little: rather than an expensive gift, piety (*pietas*) is what is welcome. The gods that inhabit the depths of the Styx are not greedy.[24] A tile covered with a wreath of garlands, a sprinkling of grain, a small pinch of salt, bread soaked in wine, and some loose violets, these are enough. Put these in a potsherd and leave it in the middle of the road.[25] I do not forbid larger offerings, though even by these a shade (*umbra*) is appeased. Add prayers and the appropriate words at the hearths that have been set up. This custom was introduced into your lands, righteous Latinus,[26] by Aeneas, appropriate instigator of piety. He brought solemn offerings to his father's spirit (*Genius*).[27] From him the people learned the rituals of piety.

But while waging long wars with aggressive arms, they once neglected the days of the Parentalia. This negligence did not go unpunished. For it is said that as a result of that omen Rome glowed with funeral fires burning outside the city. The story is, though I can hardly believe it, that in the silence of night the ancestors came forth from the tombs, lamenting. Hideous ghosts, a shadowy crowd, howled throughout the city streets and wide fields. Afterwards the honors that had been omitted were again paid to the tombs, and so an end came to the prodigies and deaths.

But while these rites are being performed, women, do not change your widowed state. Let the marriage torch wait for the days that are pure. You, O girl, who to your eager mother seem ripe for marriage, let not the bent spear comb your virgin locks.[28] Hymen, hide your torches and take them away from the black

---

[23] See also 3.12 and 3.13.

[24] *Styx*: a river of the Underworld.

[25] *in the middle of the road*: here, it was thought, they would be picked up by Hecate, one of the underworld deities who haunted the roads by night.

[26] *Latinus*: king in Latium at the time Aeneas arrived in Italy.

[27] *Genius*: A divine 'double', as it were, of an individual, usually a male. The *Genius* of the *pater familias* was a part of family religion and protected the whole household. See 3 n.1.

[28] *bent spear...*: a metonym for marriage; see 3.21 with text for an explanation of this marriage ritual.

fires.[29] Far different are the torches of the doleful graves. Let the gods also be hidden by the closing of the temple doors. Let the altars be free of incense and let there be no fire on the altars. Now the insubstantial spirits (*animae tenues*) and the buried dead wander, and the ghost feeds upon the food that has been provided. But this only lasts until there are left as many days in the month as there are feet in my verses.[30] That day they call the Feralia, because they carry (*ferunt*) to the dead their dues. It is the last day for propitiating the spirits of the dead (*manes*).[31]

> In explaining the origin of the name of the Feralia, the antiquarian Varro describes its essential features.

3.24 VARRO, *ON THE LATIN LANGUAGE* **6.13.** The Feralia is so called from the *inferi*, spirits of the underworld, and from *ferendo*, bearing or carrying, because at that time they bear a meal to the tomb of those to whom it is right that they pay ancestor worship.

> Ovid describes the Lemuria, another festival in honor of the dead, enacted in May.

3.25 OVID, *FASTI* **5.421-6.** An ancient rite, the nocturnal Lemuria, will be celebrated, bringing offerings to the silent ghosts... Yet even then (in earliest times) people brought offerings to the ashes of the dead, as their due. The grandson paid his respects to the tomb of his buried grandfather.[32]

> Polybius describes the funeral of a Roman noble, noting how such an occasion was used by the family to advertise the history of their ancestors' political achievements both to younger family members and to the Roman people at large. Images (*imagines*) of the departed and his ancestors were kept in a special area of the family home, displayed at public sacrifices, and worn by family members at funerals of distinguished members of the family. Thus at funerals the living literally impersonated their illustrious ancestors.[33]

3.26 POLYBIUS **6.53-54.3.** Whenever one of their distinguished men dies, in the course of the funeral procession he is carried with every kind of honor into the Forum to the so-called Rostra; often the body is prominently upright, more rarely recumbent.[34] All the masses stand around, as his son, if he has left one of adult age who can be present, or if not some other relative, mounts the Rostra and speaks about the virtues of the deceased and the successful achievements of his life. By this means, the people, not just those who had a part in these achievements but also those who had none, are moved to such sympathy when recalling and visualising the career of the dead man that the loss seems to affect the whole people, and not be just confined to the mourners.

[29] *torches*: an allusion to the torches that were carried at wedding ceremonies.
[30] *feet in my verses*: eleven feet, since Ovid was writing in elegiac couplets, one line of hexameter verse, followed by an iambic pentameter.
[31] See 12.8 for the magic rites described in the continuation of this passage.
[32] See 12.9 for the magic rites described in the continuation of this passage.
[33] *impersonated*: the Latin *persona* means a mask, assumed character or part.
[34] *Rostra*: the speakers' platform in the Comitium, the people's place of assembly, in the Roman Forum.

Then, after the interment and performance of the customary rites, they place the image of the departed in the most conspicuous position of the house, enclosed in a wooden shrine. The likeness is a mask, which reproduces with a remarkable fidelity both his features and complexion. On the occasion of public sacrifices, these masks are displayed and decorated with much care. When any distinguished member of the family dies, the masks are taken to the funeral and are worn by men who are considered most closely to resemble the original ancestor both in height and general bearing. These men also dress according to the rank of the deceased, a toga with a purple stripe if he was a consul or praetor, full purple if he was a censor, and embroidered with gold if he had celebrated a triumph or performed some similar exploit. They also ride in chariots, preceded by the *fasces*, axes and other insignia, according to the dignity of the offices held by each during his life.[35]

When they arrive at the Rostra, they all seat themselves in a row on ivory chairs. There could not easily be a more ennobling spectacle for a young man who aspires to win fame and practice virtue. For who would not be inspired by the sight of the images of men renowned for their excellence, all together as if alive and breathing? What spectacle could be more glorious than this? Moreover, the speaker who delivers the oration on the deceased, after finishing that speech, goes on to relate the successes and achievements of each of the others whose images are present, beginning with the oldest.

By this constant renewal of the famed excellence of brave men, the renown of those who performed noble deeds is immortalized and the glory of those who have served their country is a matter of common knowledge and a legacy for future generations. But the most important result is that young men are inspired to undergo every extreme for the common good in the hope of winning the glory that attends upon the brave.

Some epitaphs

Roman epitaphs, inscribed on tombs by the roadside outside the city, often address the passerby, purporting to give a message from the dead to the living. Generally they give a brief biographical note, occasionally referring to religious matters or ideas about what happens after death.

A freedwoman commemorates her husband, begging the Manes to care for his shade so that he may visit her in her dreams.[36] She also expresses the wish that she will soon join him.

3.27 *CIL* 6.18817. Furia Spes, freedwoman of Sempronius Firmus, provided this memorial, for her dearly beloved husband. When we were still boy and girl, we were bound by mutual love as soon as we met. I lived with him for too brief a time. We were separated by an evil hand when we should have continued to

---

[35] *fasces*: a bundle of rods that was carried by a magistrate such as the consul, symbolizing his power to scourge or execute transgressors.

[36] *Manes*: spirits or shades of the dead in the underworld. Often inscribed on a tomb are the letters D M, acronym for *dis manibusque*: to the spirits of the dead.

live in happiness. I therefore beg, most sacred Manes, that you look after the loved one I entrusted to you and that you will be well disposed and very kind to him during the hours of night, so that I may see him,[37] and so that he, too, may wish to persuade fate to allow me to come to him, sweetly and soon.

> An anonymous donor invokes the powers of the underworld, lamenting the premature death of a seven-year-old girl.

3.28 *CIL* 6.21846. O serene peace of the inhabitants of the underworld and you renowned spirits of the pious who dwell in the sacred areas of Erebus, conduct innocent Magnilla through the groves and the Elysian fields directly to your resting places.[38] She was snatched away in her eighth year by the unkind fates while she was enjoying the time of tender youth. She was beautiful and sensitive, wonderful and elegant, sweet, charming and learned far beyond her years. This unfortunate child who was deprived of her life so quickly must be mourned with perpetual tears and lamentation.

> A plasterer, living in Gaul near the river Seine, commemorates his young wife, giving her precise age and the exact length of their union. Such exactitude indicates an acute awareness of the preciousness of life. The concluding line reflects his loss, as he addresses the reader who would have been en route to the baths that he and his wife had frequented. He apparently entertains no hope of reunion after death.

3.29 *CIL* 13.1983. To the everlasting memory of Blandinia Martiola, a most faultless girl, who lived eighteen years, nine months, five days. Pompeius Catussa, a Sequanian and a Roman citizen,[39] a plasterer, dedicates to his wife, who was incomparable and most kind to him, who lived with him five years, six months, eighteen days without any breath of scandal, this memorial which he had erected in his lifetime for himself and his wife and which he consecrated while it was still under construction. You who read this, go bathe in the baths of Apollo, as I used to do with my wife. I wish I still could.

> A freedman who had been an auctioneer is anxious to memorialize his upright character.

3.30 *ROL* 4.20-21, FROM ROME C. 100 BCE. This silent stone asks you, who pass by, to stop while it reveals what he, whose shade it covers, entrusted it to reveal. Here lie the bones of Aulus Granius, an auctioneer and herald, a man of integrity, and great trustworthiness. He wanted you to know this. Aulus Granius, auctioneer and herald, freedman of Marcus.

> That there is nothing after death is reflected in the following epitaph on a third century CE tomb with a represention of the deceased reclining at a banquet

---

[37] *see him*: evidently in a dream.
[38] *Erebus*: the underworld where the shades of the dead were thought to go. Erebus was a god of darkness, son of Chaos and the brother of Night.
Elysian fields: an area in the underworld, thought to be reserved for the more fortunate shades.
[39] Note the boast that he, a Sequanian Gaul, has Roman citizenship.

or feast. The same skepticism is expressed in acronymic form on numerous tombstones: NF F NS CN (*non fui, fui, non sum, non curo*), meaning 'I didn't exist, I did exist, I don't exist, I have no cares.'

3.31 *CIL* **6.17985A.** My home was at Tibur; I was called Flavius Agricola. I am the one you see reclining here, just as I used to do at dinner, carefully looking after myself for all the years that Fate granted me. Nor was I ever sparing with the wine. My beloved wife, Flavia Primitiva, died before me, a chaste and attentive worshipper of Isis.[40] With her I spent thirty years of happiness. For consolation, she left me the fruit of her body — Aurelius Primitivus, who will tend our grave with piety and preserve our resting place forever. Friends who read this, pay attention to what I say: mix the wine, bind the festive garland around your brow, drink far from here [the tomb]. And do not refrain from the pleasures of love with beautiful women. When death comes, everything will be consumed by earth and fire.

---

[40]   Since the cult of Isis offered hope of an after-life (see chapter 9), Flavius Agricola evidently did not share his wife's devotion to this goddess.

Panel from triumphal arch of Marcus Aurelius, Rome, 176 CE. Beside the veiled emperor offering a libation at the altar in front of a temple are a young male attendant (*camillus*) holdling an incense box, and a musician who is playing to exclude any extraneous sounds. The bare-chested individuals are slave attendants whose task it was to lead the animals and later kill them. Nimatallah/Art Resource, NY.

Ritual (*sacra*): Prayer and Sacrifice

4.1 PLINY THE ELDER, *NATURAL HISTORY* **28.11.** Sacrificing or consulting the gods without also making a prayer apparently does no good.

> Cato the Elder, writing in the first part of the second century BCE, gives instructions for the purification of the farmland of a private individual by means of the blood-sacrifice of a pig, sheep and bull (*suovetaurilia*), on behalf of himself and his family. This excerpt illustrates the integration of the prayers with the sacrificial procedure. Note also the precise all-encompassing details in the prescription for the different prayers.

4.2 CATO THE ELDER, *ON AGRICULTURE* **141.** The following is the formula for purifying your farm land. Order a pig-sheep-bull procession to be led around the land, while the following words are spoken: 'With the benevolence of the gods and the prayer that everything may turn out well, I entrust to you the responsibility of purifying my farm, field and land with this pig-sheep-bull procession, wherever you decide the animals ought to be driven or carried.'

Invoke Janus and Jupiter with an offering of wine;[1] then speak these words: 'Father Mars,[2] I pray and beseech you to be benevolent and well disposed toward me, my home and my family. With this intent I have ordered a pig-sheep-bull procession to be led around my field, land and farm, so that you will keep away, ward off, and avert diseases, both seen and unseen, barrenness, crop losses, disasters and unseasonable weather; and so that you will allow the harvests, the grain crops, the vineyards, and the orchards to flourish and achieve a productive maturity; and so that you will protect the shepherds and the flocks and bestow good health and strength upon me and my home and my family. To this end, therefore, because of the purifying of my farm, land and field, and the offering of a sacrifice for purification, as I have prayed, be honored by the sacrifice of the suckling pig-sheep-bull. For this reason, therefore, Father Mars, be honored by the sacrifice of the suckling pig-sheep-bull sacrifice.'

---

[1]   *Janus* is here invoked as the god of beginnings.
[2]   *Mars* here is invoked as an agricultural deity.

So also pile up the offerings with the knife and see that the sacrificial cake is at hand;[3] then bring up the victims. When you sacrifice the pig, lamb and calf, the formula is as follows: 'In respect of these things, be honored by the sacrifice of the *suovetaurilia*.'

Prayer

Two basic categories of prayer can be discerned: the petitionary and the laudatory. Of the many prayers preserved in Roman literature the former are by far the most common. These include vows, oaths and prayers of propitiation, both by private individuals and state officials. The *supplicatio* 'collective prayer' was performed on behalf of the citizen body in order to elicit the favor of the gods, expiate a prodigy or give thanks for the fulfilment of an earlier petitionary prayer. This ritual, in which the whole populace would participate by visiting all the *pulvinaria* (couches or platforms on which the statues of the gods were placed), was apparently of Greek origin and adopted during the fifth century. Other kinds of prayer are thanksgiving, expiation, dedication, lamentation, adoration and confession, of which the last three are rare in the extant sources.

The following prayer to Mars as god of agriculture, chanted by the Arval Brethren,[4] is preserved on an inscription of the early third century CE and is probably the oldest extant Roman prayer, dating perhaps to the end of the regal period. In some places the text is disputed and the meaning unclear. The correct repetition of these formulaic phrases served as a password to open communication with the gods. If there was an error (*vitium*) as the prayer was uttered, the prayer had no chance of succeeding.

4.3 *CIL* 6.2104.

Help us Lares! Help us Lares! Help us Lares![5]

Marmar, let not plague or ruin assail more folk.[6] Marmar, let not plague or ruin assail more folk. Marmar, let not plague or ruin assail more folk.

Be full satisfied, fierce Mars. Leap the threshold. Halt. Beat the ground. Be full satisfied, fierce Mars. Leap the threshold. Halt. Beat the ground. Be full satisfied, fierce Mars. Leap the threshold. Halt. Beat the ground.

By turns call on all the gods of Sowing.[7] By turns call on all the gods of Sowing. By turns call on all the gods of Sowing.

Help us, Marmor![8] Help us, Marmor! Help us, Marmor!

Bound, bound, and bound again, bound and bound again!

---

[3] For Cato's recipe for a sacrificial cake, see 4.12.

[4] *Arval Brethren*: an ancient college of priests that ceased to function in late republican times, but was revived by Augustus.

[5] *Lares*: see Glossary.

[6] *Marmar*: a variant reduplication of the name *Mars*.

[7] *gods of Sowing*: the interpretation of the text is here disputed. Some read 'half gods.'

[8] *Marmor*: another variant reduplication of the name Mars.

In response to the question, do ritual words and incantations possess any power?, the Elder Pliny (23/4–79 CE) discerns different objectives of prayer, describing some of the elaborate rituals that accompany prayer to ensure that the ritual is not invalidated by a mistake (*vitium*) in performance.

4.4 PLINY THE ELDER, *NATURAL HISTORY* 28.11. Some words, moreover, are appropriate for seeking favorable omens, others for averting evil, and still others for praise. We observe, for example, that our highest magistrates appeal to the gods with set prayers. One attendant dictates the prayer in advance from a script, another is assigned to keep a close check on it, a third is appointed to enforce silence, all this in order that no word be omitted or spoken out of place.[9] In addition, a flutist plays so that nothing but the prayer is heard.[10] Remarkable cases of two kinds are recorded, where either ill-omened noises have ruined the ritual or a mistake has been made in the prayer itself.

In a satire, Horace alludes to the audibility of prayers.

4.5 HORACE, EPISTLES 1.16.57–62. The so-called good man who is the cynosure of every forum and speaker's platform cries out in clear tones, whenever he is propitiating the gods with a pig or an ox, 'Father Janus', then again in clear tones, 'Apollo'. But when he is afraid of being heard, he moves his lips, 'Fair Laverna,[11] grant me to escape detection; grant me to appear just and upright. Cover my wrongdoing with night and my cheating with clouds.'

As noted in the introduction, Roman magistrates would make a formal prayer to the gods before enacting any public business. In the preface to his speech in defense of the consul Murena, Cicero quotes the prayer that he himself had recited as the retiring consul who had presided at Murena's election.

4.6 CICERO, *ON BEHALF OF MURENA* 1. On that day on which, after taking the auspices,[12] I announced the election of Lucius Murena to the People's Assembly, I prayed, gentlemen of the jury, to the gods according to the traditional usage of our ancestors that his election would bring every good fortune to me, my good name, my office, and to the people and commons of Rome.

And so today I pray again to the same immortal gods that Murena may obtain both his acquittal and his consulship.[13] I pray that your opinion and verdict may be in accordance with the wishes of the Roman people that were expressed in their vote for his election, and that this agreement may bring to you and the Roman people peace, tranquillity, calm and concord.

But if that customary election prayer, consecrated by the auspices taken by a consul, has the force and religious power that the dignity of the state demands,

---

[9] See 1.29 for an instance of a festival having to be repeated because of an omission in a prayer.

[10] See illustration, page 36.

[11] *Laverna*: a minor goddess, protector of thieves.

[12] The taking of auspices was an essential preliminary to the conduct of elections.

[13] Murena was being prosecuted on a charge of electoral bribery. If convicted, he would have been debarred from assuming the office of consul to which he had been elected.

I prayed too that the election over which I presided should bring all good fortune and success to the elected candidates.

> As magistrates offered prayers before initiating civil actions, so generals prayed before military action. Livy attributes a prayer to the general Scipio as he set out from Sicily to invade Africa in the final years of the Hannibalic War.

4.7 LIVY 29.27.2-4. Gods and goddesses who watch over the seas and lands, I pray and beseech you that whatever has been done, is being done and will be done under my command, may prosper for me, for the Roman people and commons, for the allies and Latins who by land, sea and rivers follow the lead, authority and auspices of the Roman people and of myself; that you lend your kind aid to all those acts and make them bear good fruit.

I pray that, when the enemy has been conquered, you bring the victors home with me, safe and sound, decorated with spoils, laden with booty and in triumph; that you give me the power to take vengeance on opponents and enemies; and that you grant to me the opportunity to inflict upon the state of Carthage the penalties that the people of Carthage have tried to inflict upon our state.

> In Plautus' *Persian*, a bumptious slave parodies the traditional prayer of thanksgiving offered by a victorious general.

4.8 PLAUTUS, *PERSIAN* 753-756. Now that the enemy is vanquished, our citizens safe, peace made, war terminated and everything brought to a successful conclusion, with the army and garrisons intact, I do thank you, Jupiter, for your good help. To all the other dwellers in heaven I offer thanks because I have wrought glorious vengeance upon my foe. Wherefore I shall divide the booty among my fellow soldiers and share in the spoils.

Sacrifice

> The Romans usually sacrificed with the head covered (see illustrations, pp. 3, 24 and 36). There were two kinds of sacrifice: blood and bloodless.[14] The latter could consist of garlands of flowers, offerings of grain, sacrificial cakes, or wine. In the former category, the sacrificial victims were usually animals – pigs, sheep, goats, and cattle – and a distinction was made between full-grown and younger animals.[15] Exceptions to animal sacrifice are the *devotio* of a general and a human sacrifice after the Roman defeat at Cannae.[16]
>
> There are six main stages in the lengthy and elaborate ritual of animal sacrifice. First the animal victims were led in a procession (*pompa*) by slave attendants (illustration, p. 41) to an altar which was often situated in front of a temple (illustration, p. 36). The worshipper would have invited friends and family to attend the ceremony, and precautions were taken to exclude intruders who might contaminate the sacred rites. The priests and officiants would wash

---

[14] The illustration on the following page shows officiants of a bloodless sacrifice, who precede a procession of animals destined for sacrifice.

[15] See Lucretius' exaggerated description in 1.9.

[16] On *devotio*, see below 4.18, and on the sacrifice after Cannae, see 7.15.

Small frieze from the inner altar of the Augustan Ara Pacis (9 BCE). Procession (*pompa*) of victims, a ram, steer and heifer, led by half-naked slave attendants (*victimarii*) who will kill the victims. The procession is headed by a young male attendant (*camillus*) carrying the materials for a bloodless sacrifice. He looks over his shoulder toward the priest immediately behind him, and is followed by two attendants, one of whom is a lictor who accompanied every priest. Alinari /Art Resource, NY

their hands with water from a special vessel, to ensure ritual purity. Silence would then be commanded with the ritual cry, 'check your tongues' (*favete linguis*).

The main officiant, with his toga pulled over his head like a veil, made a prayer, offering wine and incense as a libation at the altar. Meal was then poured over the animal's head (*immolatio*) which was held by an attendant (*camillus*), often a young man (illustration, p. 3). Then the victim was killed by the slave attendants who had led the animals in the procession. First the animal was stunned by a blow to the head, causing it to fall to its knees. Then its throat was cut and the carcass opened up. The entrails were examined to see whether the sacrifice was acceptable to the gods (illustration, p. 57).[17] Parts of the animal were burned on the altar. The normal practice was for the participants in the sacrifice to end with a banquet using the rest of the meat. Occasionally, however, the whole animal would be given to the gods.

Less apparent in both the literary texts and the iconography are the sordid details of animal sacrifice. The actual killing would literally have been a bloody business, requiring considerable skill and brute force. Note in the illustrations how the slave attendants who did the actual killing are naked from the waist up (pp. 36 and 41). Particularly awful would have been the stench of blood, guts and excrement which would hardly have been disguised by incense. Neither the literary sources nor the iconography clarify how the blood was dealt with, though some of it may have been caught in ritual vessels and poured on the altar.

Dionysius of Halicarnassus describes the details of a public sacrifice.

4.9 DIONYSIUS OF HALICARNASSUS, *ANTIQUITIES* 7.72.15-16. After the procession was ended, the consul and the priests whose function it was sacrificed the oxen.

---

[17]   See 1.28 for a victim that was found to be flawed because the head on the liver was missing.

Their manner of performing sacrifices was the same as ours (that is, Greek). After washing their hands they consecrated the victims with pure water and sprinkled the fruits of Demeter (Ceres) on their heads. Then they prayed and ordered the attendants to sacrifice them. Some of the attendants struck the victim on the temple with a club while it was still standing, and others wielded their sacrificial knives as it fell. Then they skinned and cut it up, taking off a piece from each of the entrails and also from every limb as a first-offering. On these they sprinkled spelt with barley and carried them in baskets to the officiating priests. They placed the offerings on the altars, lighting a fire under them and pouring wine over them while they were burning. It is easy to see from Homer's poems that every one of these ceremonies was performed according to the customs established for sacrifice by the Greeks.[18]

> In Plautus' humorous account of a sacrifice by a pimp, the sacrificant boasts that, since he can't appease the gods' anger, he himself has become so angry that he has denied the gods their share of the meat.

4.10 PLAUTUS, *LITTLE CARTHAGINIAN* **449-66.** May the gods, one and all, damn the pimp who after this day sacrifices a single victim to Venus, or offers her a single grain of incense. For here I am, damned in the eyes of my gods who are angry at me. Six times today I've sacrificed a lamb, yet not one sign of favor could I get from Venus. So, seeing I can't get good omens, I've gone off in anger myself — forbidding them to cut off the gods' share of the meat.

That's the neat way I've caught her out, that greedy Venus. She wasn't willing to let enough be enough — so I called a halt myself. That's the way I take action. That's my style. I'll bet it makes the rest of those gods and goddesses easier to please, and less greedy — when they learn how the pimp caught Venus out. And that *haruspex* — not worth a cent — he was really worthy of his job when he said that all the entrails foretold disaster for me, bankruptcy and the gods angry at me. How could you believe such a man in anything, divine or human?

> The poet Ovid visualises a time before animals were sacrificed, suggesting the origin of blood sacrifice, while also offering a reason for the practice of sprinkling wine on the horns of a sacrificial animal.

4.11 OVID, *FASTI* **1.337-61.** Long ago it was grain and the sparkling pinch of pure salt that served to win the goodwill of the gods for man. As yet no foreign ship had brought bark-distilled myrrh cross the blue seas; the Euphrates had sent no incense, India no spice; nor were the threads of red saffron then known to man. The altar would smoke, content with Sabine herbs,[19] and the laurel would burn up, crackling loud. Anyone who could add violets to the garlands made from meadow flowers was rich indeed. And the knife that now lays bare the entrails of the stricken bull then had no work to do in sacred rites. The first to

---

[18] See Homer, *Odyssey* 3.417 ff.

[19] *Sabine*: an allusion to an area close to Rome, as opposed to the exotic products from the distant Euphrates and India. The Sabine herb is juniper.

rejoice in the blood of the greedy sow was Ceres,[20] avenging with just slaughter the harm that the guilty beast had done to her crops. For she discovered that in early spring a bristly sow with its snout had uprooted the milky seedlings from their soft furrows. The swine paid the penalty.

Terrified by her example, he-goat, you should have spared the vine-shoot. Watching a he-goat nibbling at a vine, somebody vented his anger with these words: 'Gnaw the vine, he-goat. Yet when you stand at the altar, the vine will be what is sprinkled on your horns.' The words came true. Your enemy, Bacchus,[21] is surrendered to you for punishment, as its horns are sprinkled with a draught of wine. The sow suffered for her crime, the he-goats suffered for theirs.

> Cato the Elder gives a recipe for sacrificial cakes.

4.12 CATO THE ELDER, *ON AGRICULTURE* 75. Crush two pounds of cheese in a mixing bowl; when that is thoroughly mashed, add a pound of wheat flour or, if you want the cake to be lighter, just half a pound of fine flour and mix thoroughly with the cheese. Add one egg and mix together well. Make it into a loaf, place it on leaves and bake slowly on a warm hearth under a crock.

Vows

> Vows are defined as 'prayers in which the petitioner, while making a request of a deity, also promises to give something to the deity if that request is granted. Normally the offering is made only after the granting of the request.'[22]
>
> At a critical moment in a battle against two long-standing foes, the Etruscans and Samnites, the consul Appius Claudius vowed a temple to Bellona, goddess of war (296 BCE).

4.13 LIVY 10.19.17-18. It is said that in the midst of the battle crisis Appius uttered a prayer in such a way that he might be conspicuous in the very forefront of the standards as he lifted up his hands to the sky: 'Bellona, if today you grant victory to us, then I vow you a temple.' With this prayer, as if the goddess were inspiring him, he equalled the valor of his colleague and the army equalled his.

> In a battle against the Samnites later in the following year the consul, Lucius Papirius Cursor, vowed to offer a libation, an offering of wine, to Jupiter Victor if he should be successful. This excerpt shows that, at least in this case, the unusual vow of a libation had the same effect as that of a more grandiose offering.

4.14 LIVY 10.42.7. In the very moment of crisis, when it was customary to vow temples to the gods, the consul made a vow to Jupiter Victor that if he routed the legions of the enemy he would present him with a small cup of mead before he drank strong wine himself. This vow was pleasing to the gods and

---

[20] *Ceres*: the Roman goddess of grain.

[21] *Bacchus*: god of the vine, also known as Dionysus.

[22] Hickson (1994) 91.

they granted good auspices.

> After the Roman defeat at Trasimene during the war against Hannibal (218-201 BCE), the Sibylline books recommended that the Roman people should celebrate a Sacred Spring, the killing of all the animals born in a particular spring.[23] Such a vow promised an action that would inhibit the size of the flocks for several years and so represented an enormous 'sacrifice.' We should, however, note the conditional nature of the vow: it would only be fulfilled 'if the Romans should prove victorious and the state remained as it had been before the outbreak of hostilities' (Livy 22.9.10).

4.15 Livy 22.10.1-5. After these resolutions by the Senate, the praetor consulted the college of *pontifices*. Lucius Cornelius Lentulus, the *pontifex maximus*, gave his opinion that first of all the People's Assembly should be consulted on the question of a Sacred Spring; for it could not be vowed unless the people ordered it.

The question was put to the assembly in the following form: 'Do you wish and so order that this action be carried out as follows? If the Republic of the Roman people, the Quirites, is preserved for the next five years (as I would wish it to be preserved) in these wars — that is, the war of the Roman people with the Carthaginian people and the wars with the Gauls on this side of the Alps — let the Roman people, the Quirites, offer to Jupiter, as an unalterable sacrifice, the spring produce from the flocks of swine, sheep, goats, cattle, whatever is not already consecrated, beginning with the day that the Senate and people shall have designated.[24]

Let him who makes this sacrifice do so at such a time and by such a ritual as he wishes. However it is done, let it be accounted as duly done. If an animal that ought to be sacrificed dies, let it be deemed outside the vow and let no guilt attach to the sacrificer. If anyone harms or kills an animal unawares, let it not be a crime...' [25]

> At the beginning of 191 BCE, the new consuls sacrifice and pray for success in the projected war against Antiochus the Great of Syria. After the vote for war had been passed, a vow was made to celebrate games in honor of Jupiter on the successful completion of the war. The legalistic formulae stipulating the conditions under which the vow would be fulfilled are again apparent.

4.16 LIVY 36.1.1-6. Publius Cornelius Scipio, the son of Gnaeus, and Manius Acilius Glabrio were inaugurated as consuls; the Senate directed them before they took up the business of the provinces to perform sacrifices with full-grown victims at all the shrines at which the *lectisternium* was customarily celebrated

---

[23] For the preceding part of the text, see 7.11.

[24] Although the vow stipulated Rome's preservation for the next five years, it was not fulfilled until 195 BCE, more than six years after the war with Hannibal had ended. It had, moreover, to be repeated the following year because of a flaw in the performance of the ritual (Livy 33.44.2 and 34.44.1-3).

[25] These provisos were evidently to guard against the fulfilment of the vow being invalidated by a flaw (*vitium*).

throughout the major part of the year, and to offer a prayer that the Senate's intentions for a new war might turn out well and successfully for the Senate and the Roman people.

All these sacrifices were favorable and good omens were obtained from the first victims. The *haruspices* reported that by means of this war the boundaries of the Roman people were being enlarged and that victory and a triumph were forecast.[26] This report freed the senators' minds from religious fears, and so they directed that the question be put to the people whether they wished and ordered the initiation of war with King Antiochus and those who followed his path....

4.17 LIVY 36.2.2-5. The Senate passed a decree advising that, since the Roman people had at that time ordered that there be war with Antiochus and those who were under his dominion, the consuls should proclaim a period of public prayer (*supplicatio*) for the success of this undertaking, and that the consul Manius Acilius should vow great games to Jupiter and gifts at all the festal couches (*pulvinaria*).

The consul made this vow, reciting after the pontifex maximus, Publius Licinius, the following words: 'If the war which the people has ordered be undertaken with King Antiochus is brought to a conclusion that is in accordance with the wish of the Senate and Roman people, then the Roman people will hold great games in your honor, Jupiter, and for ten consecutive days gifts will be offered at all the festal couches from a sum of money that the Senate will prescribe. Whatever magistrate shall celebrate these games, at whatever time and place, these games shall be duly celebrated and the gifts duly offered.' Then a period of public prayer (*supplicatio*) for two days was proclaimed by both consuls.

The ritual of *devotio*

> Livy describes the ritual of *devotio*, in which a general dedicated and gave his own life in return for victory. In the press of a battle against the people of the Latin League who had revolted against Rome in 340 BCE, the consul Decius Mus decided to sacrifice himself to save his troops.

4.18 LIVY 8.9.1-11. Before leading their troops into battle, the Roman consuls offered sacrifice. It is said that the *haruspex* pointed out to Decius that the liver was damaged on the side that related to his fortunes, but that the victim was in all other respects acceptable to the gods. Manlius' (the other consul) sacrifice, however, had been exceptionally successful. 'It is good enough,' said Decius, 'if my colleague has received favorable omens.' They advanced into the field....[27]

At first the battle was fought with equal strength and ardor on each side. But after a while the first line of Roman soldiers on the left failed to withstand

---

[26] *haruspices*: (singular *haruspex*) priests who specialized in the art of divination.
[27] Although there was clearly a flaw (*vitium*) in the sacrifice, Decius decided to disregard it.

the Latin attack and fell back on the second line. In this confusion the consul Decius called out to Marcus Valerius in a loud voice: 'We have need of the gods' help, Marcus Valerius. So come, state pontifex of the Roman people, dictate the words so that I may vow my life to save the legions.'[28]

The *pontifex* ordered him to put on the purple-bordered toga and, with veiled head and one hand thrust out from his toga, touching his chin and standing upon a spear that was laid under his feet, to recite the following words:[29] 'Janus, Jupiter, Father Mars, Quirinus, Bellona, Lares, divine Novensiles, divine Indigites, who have power over both us and our enemies, and you divine Manes — I invoke and worship you, I beseech and beg your indulgence, that you prosper the might and victory of the Roman people of the Quirites, and send fear, shuddering, and death upon the enemies of the Roman people of the Quirites. Just as I have pronounced the words, even so on behalf of the republic of the Roman people of the Quirites, and of the army, the legions, the auxiliaries of the Roman people of the Quirites, do I devote the legions and auxiliaries of the enemy, together with myself, to the divine Manes and to Earth.'[30]

Having uttered this prayer he ordered the lictors to go to Titus Manlius and lose no time in announcing to his colleague that he had vowed his own life on behalf of the army.[31] He himself, tying his toga in the Gabinian knot,[32] leaped fully armed onto his horse and plunged into the midst of the enemy. He could be clearly seen by both sides, a sight to be revered as almost superhuman, as if he had been sent from heaven to expiate all the anger of the gods and turn destruction away from his own men and bring it upon their adversaries.

---

[28] It may have been customary for a *pontifex* to accompany the army in the field to give advice on ritual.

[29] *veiled head*: the regular dress for one conducting a sacrifice.

[30] *Novensiles, Indigites*: deities whose functions are obscure.
Manes: deities of the underworld.

[31] *lictors*: attendants who carried the rods of office (*fasces*) for the magistrates, accompanying them at all times.

[32] *Gabinian knot*: a distinctive way of wearing the toga firmly tied around the waist. The Romans are said to have worn their togas in this style in a battle against the people of Gabii, a town in Latium.

PRIESTS AND RELIGIOUS AUTHORITY

5.1 FESTUS 284 L. Rituals of the state are celebrated at the expense of the state for the people.

> With the exception of the Vestal Virgins, priests of the state religion were male. They were organized into colleges or brotherhoods, holding office for life. There were four major colleges of male priests: *pontifices*, augurs, the board for the performance of sacred rites (*quindecimviri sacris faciundis*), and the *tresviri epulones*, three men in charge of feasts, a number later raised to seven. In the late Republic, Sulla raised the number in the first three colleges to fifteen, Caesar to sixteen. After the admission of plebeians to priesthoods under the Ogulnian law of 300 BCE, the only official requirements for selection were Roman citizenship, free birth and the absence of physical defects.
>
> Rather than being attached to particular deities or temples, most priests were connected with festivals (e.g., the Luperci with the Lupercalia) or with particular religious duties (e.g., the augurs with augural law and the taking of auspices, and the fetials with the making of treaties and declaration of war).[1] Three exceptions, however, should be noted: the *flamen Dialis* (priest of Jupiter), *flamen Martialis* (of Mars) and *flamen Quirinalis* (of Quirinus).[2] Unlike the Vestals who served full-time, male priests were only engaged part-time in their priestly duties, and frequently had active political and military careers. Indeed most prominent political figures held a priesthood. For example, Julius Caesar became *pontifex maximus* and among the priesthoods held by Augustus were those of *pontifex maximus*, augur, quindecimvir (member of the board for conducting the rites), member of the board of seven for feasts, and fetial.
>
> The method of selecting men to these priesthoods changed from time to time, varying between cooptation (selection by the surviving members of the college to fill a vacancy) and a form of popular election. The ancient sources indicate

---

[1]   On the fetial priests, see 2.7 and 7.2.

[2]   For Numa's institution of these *flamines*, see 2.6.
     Quirinus: originally a Sabine god, later assimilated to the deified Romulus.

that *pontifices* and augurs came from leading noble families, were generally selected at the beginning of their political career and held office for life. Since the Senate was composed of ex-magistrates, many priests would have been members of that body and thus would have been consulted in both capacities when religious matters were referred to the Senate, a further indication of the intertwining of 'politics' and 'religion'. During the Republic, the Senate had control over religious matters, including the financing of state religion.

College of pontifices

5.2 CICERO, *ON THE NATURE OF THE GODS* 1.122 The *pontifices* are in charge of the rituals (*sacra*).

5.3 DIONYSIUS OF HALICARNASSUS, *ANTIQUITIES* 2.73.1 - 2. The *pontifices* have authority over the most important matters. They give judgments on all religious cases involving private citizens, magistrates and religious officials. They make laws for the observance of any religious rites that are not established either in writing or by custom, but which seem to them suitable to receive the sanction of law and custom. They scrutinize all the magistracies that have duties involving any sacrifice or religious duty and also all the priests, taking care that the subordinates and officials whom they employ in the rituals commit no error in regard to the sacred laws. For private citizens who are not knowledgable about worship of the gods and divine spirits, the *pontifices* are explainers and interpreters.

The *pontifices* had general oversight over the state cult, including control of the calendar and thus religious festivals.[3] They were an advisory body of religious experts whose rulings were requested by the Senate and put into effect by magistrates or the assemblies. Thus, they had both secular and religious duties and became, as it were, the repository of both divine and human law. They published 'the great events' of each year (the *annales maximi*) on a whitened board that was displayed in public. Such events included battles, grain shortages, pestilences and prodigies. They were also concerned with adoptions, wills and inheritances.

The college of pontifices consisted of *pontifices*, the *pontifex maximus* and *rex sacrorum* (king of sacred matters), *flamines* of Jupiter, Mars and Quirinus, Vestal Virgins, scribes of the *pontifices* and the twelve lesser *flamines*. Originally there were three pontifices, all from patrician families until the lex Ogulnia, when the number was increased to six in order to admit plebeians. The *pontifex maximus* (Chief Priest) was originally selected by fellow members of the pontifical college. From the third century, however, he was elected by a special form of popular election, which in 104 BCE was extended to all other priesthoods of the major colleges. Julius Caesar became a *pontifex* in 73 BCE and was elected *pontifex maximus* in 63 BCE before he had held a senior magistracy. When Augustus became *pontifex maximus* in 12 BCE, the

---

[3]   See 2.5 and 2.6 for Livy's description of Numa's institution of the pontificate and calendar.

position came to resemble that of a high priest and was automatically held by subsequent emperors.

College of augurs

5.4 CICERO, *ON THE NATURE OF THE GODS* **1.122.** The augurs are in charge of the *auspicia*.

> In the prescriptions for his ideal state, Cicero retains the division into three major colleges, detailing the functions of the augurs.[4]

5.5 CICERO, *LAWS* **2.20-1.** There shall be three kinds of state priests: one to be in charge of ceremonies and sacred rites (*sacra*), another to interpret the obscure utterances of soothsayers and prophets, and the state augurs, the interpreters of Jupiter the Best and Greatest who shall foretell the future from signs and auspices, and shall maintain their discipline.[5]

And the augurs shall observe the omens in regard to vineyards and orchards and the welfare of the people; those who conduct war or civic matters shall be informed by them beforehand of the auspices and shall obey them; the priests shall foresee the anger of the gods and shall give way to it; they shall observe lightning in fixed regions of the sky and shall keep free and demarcated the city, fields and places of observation. Whatever an augur shall declare to be unjust or unlawful, pernicious or ill-omened, shall be null and void.

> Since auspices were sought before all state actions, the functions of the augurs are a striking demonstration of the interconnection of religion and politics. Augurs were both experts and priests. In their latter capacity they celebrated rites known as *auguria*, auspices that pertain to both substance and time and could only be conducted by augurs. As experts, they maintained records of past decisions, the 'augural law' (*ius augurale*). When questions about auspices arose, the college as a whole had to decide. Their findings would then be submitted to the Senate which was free to accept or reject their advice. They also oversaw the designation of sacred space. Thus one of their duties was the assigning and marking out of an area for a temple, hence the 'inauguration' of a temple, as opposed to the subsequent dedication of the completed building. They also inaugurated priests and conferred on magistrates the right to take auspices.
>
> The first augury is said to have been conducted by Romulus who was granted a flight of twelve birds, as opposed to Remus' six.[6] When the Romans were considering leaving Rome and migrating to Veii, Livy has the dictator Camillus refer to Rome as 'founded with due observance of auspice and augury. There is no part of the city that is not permeated by feelings of awe and by the gods' (Livy 5.52.2). In the Hannibalic War, Scipio, confronted by mutiny among his

---

[4]   Cicero himself was an augur (for augur with *lituus*, see illustration, p. 18).

[5]   *auspices*: signs that were considered to indicate the favor or disfavor of the gods towards an action already in progress or one that was under consideration; see chapter 1 for the five categories of signs.

[6]   See 2.1 and 2.2.

troops, reminds them that Rome was 'founded with due auspices and with the support of the gods to endure forever' (Livy 28.28.11).

Livy relates the story of Attus Navius, an early augur. When King Tarquin the Elder wanted to add more units of cavalry to the three established by Romulus, Attus Navius insisted that the king follow the precedent established by Romulus and take the auspices.[7] Thereafter, auspices were always taken before any political or military undertaking.

5.6 LIVY 1.36.3-7. Since this was a matter in which Romulus had obtained the sanction of augury, Attus Navius, a famous augur at that time, said that no change or innovation could be made unless the birds had signified their approval. This moved the king to anger; mocking the skill (*ars*) of augury, he is reported to have said, 'Come now, god-inspired seer! Inquire of your augury if what is now in my mind can be done.' Attus took the auspices, and replied that it would surely come to pass. Whereupon the king said, 'I was thinking of cutting a sharpening-stone in half with a razor. Get these things and perform what your birds declare can be done.' Without delay, they say, he cut the stone in two.

There was a statue of Attus with veiled head on the spot where the event happened, in the Comitium on the very steps on the left hand side of the senate house.[8] It is also said that the sharpening-stone was placed in the same spot, to be a memorial of that miracle for posterity. However this may be, such great honor was accorded to augury and the priesthood of the augurs that nothing thereafter was done, in war or domestic politics, without the auspices first being taken. For example, assemblies of the people and levies of troops, such matters of the utmost importance were postponed when the birds refused their consent.

Quindecimvirs as interpreters of prophecies

The quindecimvirs was a board of priests responsible for the performance of sacred rites. Originally the board consisted of two (*duoviri*), then ten (*decemviri*), fifteen (*quindecimviri*) and finally sixteen men, although the title *quindecimviri* was maintained. Their principal task was to guard the Sibylline books, a collection of oracles and ritual texts that were written in Greek. This collection was said to consist of utterances of the Sibyl of Cumae that had been acquired by Tarquin the Elder (616-579 BCE), and later placed in the temple of Jupiter on the Capitoline.[9] In times of emergency that were often signalled by prodigies, the Senate would ask these priests to consult the Sibylline books and give advice on how to respond. Their recommendations frequently led to religious innovation.[10] They were also charged with the admission of new oracles.

---

[7] *Tarquin the Elder*: the fifth king of Rome, an Etruscan.

[8] In Livy's day the statue was evidently no longer there. Perhaps it had not been replaced after the Forum fire in 52 BCE.

[9] For the story, see 2.9.

[10] See chapter 8.

Dionysius of Halicarnassus describes the quindecimvirs' supervision of the sacred books, their destruction in the fire of 83 BCE, and their replacement.

5.7 DIONYSIUS OF HALICARNASSUS, *ANTIQUITIES* 4.62.5-6. Since the expulsion of the kings, the state has taken upon itself the guardianship of the oracles, appointing the most distinguished men as their custodians. These men hold this position for life and are exempt from military service and all civic responsibilities. Public slaves are appointed to assist them. Unless these slaves are present, it is not lawful for the others to inspect the books. In a word, there is no possession so sacred (*hieron*) or holy (*hosion*) that the Romans guard as carefully as they do the Sibylline oracles. They consult them on the order of the Senate, when political strife grips the city or when a great calamity has befallen them in war or when some important prodigies and phenomena have appeared that are difficult to interpret,[11] as has often happened. Until the so-called Marsian War these oracles were kept underground in the temple of Jupiter Capitolinus in a stone chest, under the guardianship of the board of ten.[12]

At the end of the one hundred and seventy-third Olympiad,[13] either deliberately, or as some think, by accident, these oracles together with all the god's votive offerings were destroyed by fire. Those which we now have were gathered from many places, some from cities in Italy, others from Erythrae in Asia [Minor] where three ambassadors were sent by decree of the Senate to copy them, and others were brought from other cities and transcribed by private individuals. Some of these are found to be interpolations among the genuine Sibylline oracles, and are proved to be so by means of the so-called acrostics.[14] My source for all this is Marcus Terentius Varro in his work on religion.[15]

Cicero points out that Sibylline oracles are not a product of a frenzied mind, but rather of rational calculation. Thus, he argues for maintaining them under the firm control of the Senate and quindecimvirs.

5.8 CICERO, *ON DIVINATION* 2.110 - 12. We Romans venerate the verses of the Sibyl who is said to have uttered them in a frenzy. Recently a false rumor was put about that one of their interpreters was going to declare in the Senate that, if we were to be safe, the man whom we had as a king in fact should also be given the title of king.[16] If this is in the books, to what man and to what time does

[11] *portents and prodigies*: see Glossary.
[12] *Marsian War*: the Italian or Social War, 91-89 BCE.
   board of ten: *decemvirs*, whose number was increased to fifteen soon after the fire of 83 BCE.
[13] *Olympiad*: a period of four years used by the Greeks. The 173rd Olympiad is 83 BCE.
[14] *acrostics*: As Cicero notes in the passage below, the initial letters of each verse, when taken in order, convey a meaning.
[15] *Varro*: the learned antiquarian of the late republic. This particular work survives only in excerpts quoted by other authors.
[16] *title of king*: an allusion to a Sibylline oracle that declared that the Parthians could only be conquered by a king and that thus Julius Caesar should be given the title of king; see Suetonius, *Julius Caesar* 79.

it refer? The individual who composed this prophecy cleverly devised it in such a way that whatever happened should appear to have been foretold because all reference to persons or time had been left out. He also employed a cloak of obscurity so that the same verses might be adapted to different situations at different times. Moreover the [quality of] the poetry itself shows that this is not a work of frenzy (for it shows artistic care rather than excited emotion). This is especially apparent from the fact that it is written in acrostics, wherein the initial letters of each verse, when taken in order, convey a meaning .....

Surely this is the work of a concentrated rather than a frenzied mind. From the opening verse in the Sibylline books, each prophecy is embellished so that the initial letters of each line gives the subject of that particular prophecy. This is the work of a writer who is not frenzied, one who is painstaking, not insane. Therefore let us keep the Sibyl under lock and key so that, in keeping with the tradition of our ancestors, her books may not even be read without the order of the Senate and so have the power to suppress rather than encourage superstitious ideas (*religiones*). Let us plead with the priests to bring from those books anything rather than a king whom neither gods nor men will permit in Rome.

The *flamen Dialis* (priest of Jupiter)

> The institution of this priesthood is attributed to Numa.[17] Aulus Gellius, writing in the second century CE, describes the duties and taboos that were imposed on the holder of this office. These restrictions are an indication of the antiquity of the priesthood and would have made it virtually impossible for the holder to pursue a political or military career. Consequently the office lapsed in the late republic.

5.9 AULUS GELLIUS, *ATTIC NIGHTS* **10.15.1-25.** Many ritual duties are imposed on the *flamen Dialis*, and likewise a variety of taboos .... The following is more or less what I remember; there is a rule against the *flamen Dialis* riding a horse; likewise there is a rule against him seeing 'the levy arrayed' outside the pomerium, that is, the army equipped for battle. For this reason the *flamen Dialis* was rarely made consul, since the consuls took charge of war. Likewise it is never lawful (*fas*) for the *Dialis* to take an oath; nor is it lawful for him to wear a ring, unless it is perforated and without a stone. It is not allowed to remove any flame from the *flaminia*, the house of the *flamen Dialis*, except for a ritual purpose. If a man in chains enters his house, he must be freed and the chains taken up through the *impluvium* onto the roof and from there let down into the street outside.[18]

He has no knot in his headdress, nor in his belt, nor any part of his clothing. If anyone who is being taken off to be flogged falls as a suppliant at his feet, it is deemed unlawful for him to be beaten on that day. No one except a free man may cut the hair of the *Dialis*. It is the custom that the *Dialis* does not touch

---

[17] See 2.6.

[18] *impluvium*: the opening in the roof of the *atrium* (central area) of a Roman house.

or even name a she-goat, raw flesh, ivy or beans. He does not pass under an arbor of vines. The feet of the bed in which he sleeps must be smeared with a thin layer of clay. He must not sleep away from that bed three nights in a row; nor is it lawful (*fas*) for anyone else to sleep in that bed. At the foot of his bed there must be a box with a set of sacrificial cakes. The cuttings of the nails and hair of the *Dialis* are buried in the earth under a fruitful tree.

For the *Dialis* every day is a day of religious ceremony. He is not allowed to be in the open air without his *apex*.[19] That he should be allowed to go without it indoors was, according to Masurius Sabinus,[20] a recent decision of the *pontifices*; and it is said that some other obligations have been relaxed and he has been excused from observing them....

If his wife dies, he resigns from the flaminate.[21] The marriage of the *flamen* cannot lawfully be dissolved, except by death. He never enters a place where there is a tomb; he never touches a dead body, but is not prohibited from attending a funeral.

Vestal virgins and the worship of Vesta

The poet Ovid relates several aspects of the worship of Vesta, including the fact that she is not represented by a statue in her temple.

5.10 OVID, *FASTI* 6.249 - 98. Vesta, grant us your favor. It is in your honor that we now open our lips, if it is lawful for me come to your sacred rituals. I was deep in prayer. I felt the presence of the celestial deity, and the glad earth radiated a purple light. Not of course that I saw you (farewell to poet's lies),[22] nor was it proper that a man should look upon you. But my ignorance and errors were corrected without the help of any instructor.

It is said that Rome had celebrated the Parilia forty times when the goddess, guardian of the flame, was received in her temple.[23] It was the work of that peaceful king, the most god-fearing individual ever born in Sabine territory.[24] The buildings you now see roofed with bronze, you then would have seen roofed with thatch, and the walls woven with rough osiers. This little spot, which now supports the Hall of Vesta, was then the great palace of unshaven Numa. Yet the shape of the temple, as it still exists today, is said to have been the same then....[25]

---

[19] *apex*: the distinctive pointed headdress worn by a *flamen*.

[20] *Masurius Sabinus*: a jurist of the first century CE.

[21] His wife was also subject to various taboos.

[22] *farewell*: the Latin *valeant*, can mean either 'goodbye' or literally 'be well/ strong'. Ovid's pun thus leaves his meaning ambiguous.

[23] *Parilia*: festival celebrating the foundation of Rome, held on 21 April. On this reckoning, Numa founded the temple in 713 BCE.

[24] *peaceful king....born in Sabine territory*: Numa.

[25] Vesta's temple, unlike most others, was circular.

Why, you ask, is the goddess attended by virgin priestesses? I will discover the real reasons for this too. It is said that Juno and Ceres were born of Ops from the seed of Saturn.[26] Vesta was the third daughter. The other two married and both are said to have borne children. Of the three, one remained who refused to submit to a husband. Is it strange then that a virgin delights in a virgin priestess and admits only chaste hands to her sacred rites? Conceive of Vesta as nothing other than living flame, and you see that no substance is born of flame. Rightly, then, she is a virgin, who gives no seed nor takes any and who loves the company of virgins.

For a long time I foolishly thought that there were statues of Vesta. Later I learned that there are none under her curved dome. An undying fire is hidden in that temple; there is no effigy of Vesta, nor of the fire....

> Aulus Gellius describes the 'taking' of a Vestal Virgin from her family of birth to live in the sanctuary of the goddess.

5.11 AULUS GELLIUS, ATTIC NIGHTS 1.12.1-3, 5, 10, 13-14. A girl chosen to be a Vestal Virgin must, according to law *(fas)*, be no less that six and no more than ten years old. Both her father and mother must be alive. She must not be handicapped by a speech or hearing problem or marked by some physical defect.[27] ... Neither one nor both of her parents may have been slaves or engaged in menial occupations....

As soon as a Vestal has been chosen, escorted to the House of Vesta, and handed over to the *pontifices*, she immediately leaves the control of her father, without a ceremony of manumission or loss of civil rights, and she acquires the right to make a will....[28]

The Vestal is said to be 'taken', it seems, because the *pontifex maximus* grasps her by the hand and she is led away from from the parent under whose control she is, as if she had been 'taken' in war....

The words which the *pontifex maximus* should speak when he accepts a Vestal Virgin are these: 'I take you, Amata,[29] as one who has fulfilled all the requirements to be a priestess of Vesta and to perform the sacred rites which it is lawful for a priestess of Vesta to perform on behalf of the Roman people.'

> Dionysius of Halicarnassus describes the rules governing the Vestal Virgins and the punishments inflicted for infringement.

5.12 DIONYSIUS OF HALICARNASSUS, ANTIQUITIES 2.67. The virgins who serve the goddess were originally four in number and chosen by the kings in accordance with the rules established by Numa. Later, because of the great number of sacred rites they perform, their number was increased to six, and has so remained until our time. They live in the sanctuary of the goddess, where no one who

---

26 *Ops*: a minor goddess associated with the abundance of crops.
   Saturn: the name is connected with sowing.
27 Loss of a parent or a physical defect would constitute a *vitium*.
28 See the fifth of the Twelve Tables, cited in section 3.9.
29 *Amata*: literally means the beloved one. Gellius notes that it was the name of the first Vestal (1.12.19).

wishes can be prevented from entering during the day. It is unlawful, however, for any man to remain there by night.

These priestesses were required to remain chaste and unmarried for thirty years, offering sacrifices and performing other rites ordained by law. During the first ten years they must learn these rites, in the second ten perform them, and in the third ten teach them to others. When they have completed the thirty years, there is nothing to prevent those who wish to marry from laying aside their head-bands and the other emblems of their priesthood. Some though very few have done this, but the rest of their lives were not happy or enviable. Thus the rest, regarding their misfortunes as ominous, remain virgins in the sanctuary of the goddess until their death, and then again another is chosen by the pontifices to fill the vacancy.

The Vestal Virgins are given many high honors by the state and so do not feel the desire for marriage or children. Severe penalties are imposed on those who err. According to the law, the *pontifices* both inquire into and punish their offenses. They whip with rods those Vestals who have committed lesser offenses, but they sentence those who have lost their virginity to a most shameful and pitiable death.[30] While still living they are carried on a bier with all the formality of a funeral. Their friends and relatives join the procession, mourning them. They are taken as far as the Colline Gate and, dressed in their funeral shroud, they are placed in an underground cell prepared within the walls.[31] But they do not receive a monument or funeral rites or any other customary solemnities.

If a priestess is no longer a virgin, there are apparently many indications in the performance of her duties, the main one being the extinction of the fire. This the Romans dread above all catastrophes, regarding it as an omen that portends the destruction of the city, whatever the cause of the extinction. They bring fire back into the temple with many supplicatory rites.

Haruspices

Haruspices were diviners or seers who came originally from Etruria. Loss of Livy's account of the early third century prevents us from knowing exactly when it became the practice to consult these non-Roman seers. They were not constituted as a college until the emperor Claudius created an order of sixty-one *haruspices* in 47 CE.

Haruspices dealt with signs thought to indicate future happenings in the entrails of sacrificial animals (*exta*), lightning *(fulgura)* and prodigies *(prodigia)*. The Senate consulted them to determine which god was responsible, why the sign or prodigy was sent, how it could be expiated, and what it meant.[32] In predicting from entrails (*exta*), the haruspex would take the liver in his left

---

[30] *a most shameful and pitiable death*: see 7.15 for an example of this punishment when, after the Roman defeat at Cannae, the violation of chastity was regarded as a *prodigy* that was expiated by human sacrifice.

[31] *Colline Gate*: one of the gates of the city.

[32] Apparently in more serious cases, the matter was referred to the *quindecimviri*.

hand and 'read' it clockwise, as he stood with his right foot on the ground and his left on a stone (illustration, p. 57). In the case of lightning, he would attempt to discover in which of the sixteen divisions of the sky the lightning had appeared and what it had struck.

In 212 BCE, during the Hannibalic War, the consul Tiberius Sempronius Gracchus fails to heed the warnings of the *haruspices* and later is ambushed and killed.

5.13 LIVY 25.16.1-5. As Gracchus was sacrificing before he left Lucania, a unfavorable prodigy occurred. After the victim had been killed, two snakes came gliding from a hidden place up to the entrails and ate part of the liver.[33] When they were spotted, they suddenly disappeared from sight. On the advice of the *haruspices* the sacrifice was repeated and a closer watch kept on the entrails. The story is that the snakes glided up a second and third time, tasted the liver, and went away unharmed. Although the *haruspices* warned that this prodigy applied to the commander and so he must beware of men in hiding and of covert strategy, his imminent fate could not be averted by any foresight.

Aulus Gellius tells how a group of *haruspices* were found guilty of giving a false recommendation and put to death.

5.14 AULUS GELLIUS, *ATTIC NIGHTS* 4.5. The statue of that bravest of men, Horatius Cocles, which stood in the Comitium at Rome, was struck by lightning.[34] *Haruspices* were summoned from Etruria to expiate the thunderbolt. These men, because of their personal and national hatred of the Romans, decided to give false directions for the expiation of the matter. They wrongly advised that the statue be move to a lower position, on which the sun never shone because it was cut off on all sides by the high surrounding buildings. When they had persuaded the people that this should be done, they were betrayed and brought to trial before the people. Having confessed to their treachery, they were put to death. It became evident that the statue had to be moved to an elevated place and set up in a higher location in the area of Vulcan, just as the true instructions that were later discovered advised. Once that was done, the matter turned out well and successfully for the Romans.

Cicero uses two examples to deride the *haruspices*.[35]

5.15 CICERO, *ON DIVINATION* 2.51-3. Cato knew what he was talking about when, many years ago, he said,[36] 'I am amazed that an *haruspex* doesn't laugh when he sees another *haruspex*.' For how many of their predictions really come true? If

---

[33] Linderski, *ANRW* 2200 notes that the snakes were 'an oblative sign which functions as a premonition. Techically it was a prodigy and not an *auspicium malum* (bad auspice), for it did not refer to any concrete action of Gracchus.'

[34] *Horatius Cocles*: an early Roman hero who held the bridge against the invading Etruscans until it could be broken, thus saving the city.
Comitium: see Glossary.

[35] Compare, however, 1.15.

[36] *Cato*: Cato the Elder; see Glossary.

Etruscan bronze mirror, late fourth century BCE, representing Calchas, the Greek prophet of the *Iliad*, as an Etruscan diviner (*haruspex*) (surprisingly winged), examining a liver which he holds in his left hand, while his left foot rests on a stone. Scala/Art Resource, N.Y.

any does come true, what reason can be advanced to show that the result was not due to chance? When Hannibal was an exile at the court of King Prusias, he advised the king to go to war, but the king replied, 'I don't dare, because the entrails prevent it.' To which Hannibal replied, 'Do you put more faith in pieces of ox-meat than in a veteran commander?'

Again when Caesar was warned by a most eminent *haruspex* not to cross over to Africa before the winter solstice, didn't he make that crossing?[37] If he had not done so, all the forces of his enemies would have amassed in one place. Why need I recount instances (countless, indeed, are the ones I could give) where the prophecies of *haruspices* were either without result or turned out to be the opposite of what was foretold. Ye gods! How many times were they wrong in the recent civil war!

---

[37] During the winter of 47/6 BCE, Julius Caesar crossed to Africa and defeated the Pompeian forces at Thapsus.

RELIGIOUS CELEBRATIONS
AND THE CALENDAR

6.1 MACROBIUS, *SATURNALIA* 1.16.2-5. Numa divided the year into months and then each month into days, calling each day either 'festival,' 'working-day,' or 'half-festival.' The festivals are days dedicated to the gods; on the working days people may transact private and public business; and the half-festivals are shared between gods and humans. Thus on festival days there are sacrifices, religious banquets, games and holidays.... On the half-festival days it is lawful *(fas)* to administer justice during certain hours, but not in others. For while the victim is being slain, no legal business may be enacted, but in the interval between the slaying of the victim and the placing of the offering on the altar such business may be enacted. But when the offering is being burned it is not permissible....

The celebration of a religious festival consists of the offering of sacrifices to the gods, or a day that is marked by a ritual feast, or the holding of games in honor of the gods or the observance of holidays. There are four kinds of public holidays: 'fixed,' 'movable,' 'extraordinary,' and 'market days.' All the people participate in the fixed holidays. They are held on fixed days in appointed months which are noted in the calendar, and have fixed observances.... Movable holidays are those which are proclaimed annually by the magistrates or priests, as they see fit....

> The official state calendar was a basic institution of Roman religion and, as such, was regulated by the *pontifices*. The sequence of the various religious festivals regulated the timing of business and religious activities throughout the Roman year.
>
> Among the *pontifices'* duties was the charge of keeping the Roman year of 355 days in synchronisation with the seasonal or solar calendar. This they did by intercalation, that is, periodic insertion of an additional month.[1] During

---

[1] See 2.5 for the institution of intercalation which Livy attributes to Numa.

the political turbulence of the late 50s BCE and the Civil War that followed, however, intercalation was neglected and the Roman calendar year became badly out of synchronisation with the seasons. In 47 BCE Julius Caesar as *pontifex maximus* called on an Egyptian man of science to reform the system by introducing a solar calendar. This Julian calendar is still in use today, albeit with slight modifications introduced by Pope Gregory XIII in 1582.

One of our most important sources for the Roman calendar is Ovid's *Fasti*, although the work is incomplete, dealing only with the first six months of the year. Though obviously a literary rather than a historical work, it is nonetheless a mine of information, as we have already seen in the extracts concerning the Parentalia, Feralia and Lemuria, festivals honoring the dead.[2] Other sources include calendars inscribed on stone or painted on walls, recording month by month the days on which business could be transacted, courts could sit, and the dates of the chief religious festivals.[3]

Lupercalia

The Lupercalia was a festival celebrated on 15 February. Although the ancient sources describe the rituals in some detail, they were uncertain about its origins and significance. Plutarch describes some of the peculiar rituals of the festival, giving two explanations of its origin.

6.2 PLUTARCH, ROMULUS 21.3-8. The Lupercalia, as is suggested by the time of its celebration, would seem to be a festival of purification. For it is performed on the inauspicious days[4] of the month of February (a name that can be explained as meaning 'purificatory')[5] and in early times they used to call the actual day 'Februata'. But the name of the festival has a sense equivalent to the Greek wolf-festival (Lycaea)[6] and thus it seems to be exceedingly ancient, going back to the Arcadians under Evander.[7] In fact this is the generally accepted meaning of the name, for it can be derived from she-wolf *(lykaina)*. Moreover, we see that the *luperci*[8] begin their circuit of the city from the place where Romulus is said to have been exposed.[9]

---

[2] See 3.12 and 3.22.

[3] See *BNP* 2.61-77 for examples of calendars from different periods.

[4] *inauspicious days*: the days marked N (*nefastus*), on which no assembly could meet, nor could a court sit. The festival also coincided with the Parentalia, a festival in honor of the dead.

[5] *purificatory*: see 6.3.

[6] *Lycaea*: The Greek word for wolf, *lykos*, is related to the Latin *lupus*.

[7] *Evander*: is said to have come from Arcadia in Greece and settled on the site of the future Rome.

[8] *luperci*: the priests who participated in the ritual.

[9] The *luperci* apparently set out on the circuit of the city from the Lupercal, the cave where the wolf is said to have suckled Romulus and Remus. The exact course traversed by the *luperci* is not known, since the ancient sources are inconsistent in their descriptions.

But what actually happens in the festival makes it hard to guess its origin. For they sacrifice goats; then two boys of noble birth are brought forward. Some touch their foreheads with a bloody knife, and others immediately wipe off the blood with wool soaked in milk. After their foreheads are wiped, the boys must laugh. Next they cut the goat skins into strips and run about naked but for a belt around their waist, striking anyone in their path with the thongs. And women of childbearing age do not try to avoid the blows, believing that they promote fertility and easy childbirth. A distinctive feature of the festival is that the *luperci* also sacrifice a dog.

A certain Butas,[10] who wrote mythical explanations of Roman customs in elegiac verse, says that the followers of Romulus, once they had defeated Amulius,[11] raced joyfully to the spot where the she-wolf suckled the twins when they were babies; that the festival is conducted as an imitation of their race, and that the boys of noble family run:

> Striking all whom they meet,
>   as long ago
> Romulus and Remus from Alba ran,
>   brandishing their swords.

And he suggests that the bloody sword is applied to their foreheads as a symbol of the slaughter and danger of that time; and the cleansing with milk is a reminder of the nourishing of the twins. Gaius Acilius,[12] on the other hand, writes that before the foundation of the city the flocks of Romulus and his companions disappeared; they prayed to Faunus[13] and then ran off to find them, naked so that they should not be bothered by sweat. And this, he suggests, is why the *luperci* run around naked. As for the dog, one might say (if it really is a purificatory sacrifice) that it is sacrificed as a means of purification.... But if they perform these rites as a thank-offering to the she-wolf for saving and nourishing Romulus, it is not without reason that a dog is sacrificed, for the dog is the enemy of wolves. Unless, of course, the animal is being punished for annoying the *luperci* when they run their course.

The Lupercalia fell within the period of the Parentalia (13-22 February), the major festival of the dead in the Roman calendar.[14] Thus it is not surprising to find the antiquarian Varro, in his comments on the derivation of the name 'February,' suggesting that the Lupercalia is to be seen in the context of the underworld and the spirits of the dead.

---

[10] *Butas*: a Greek poet whose work has not survived.

[11] *Amulius*: the usurper who had deposed his brother Numitor, the grandfather of Romulus and Remus, and who exposed the twins.

[12] *Gaius Acilius*: a Roman historian of the second century BCE whose work only survives in fragments quoted by other writers.

[13] *Faunus*: an Italic deity of the countryside, often identified with the Greek god Pan.

[14] *Parentalia*: see 3.23.

6.3 Varro, *On the Latin language* **6.34.** Two months were added to these:[15] the first was called January (*Januarius*) after the god who comes first in order.[16] The second, as the same writers say, is called February (*Februarius*) after the gods of the underworld (*di inferi*) because these deities are offered sacrifice at this time of year. I prefer to think that February derives from the Day of Purification (*dies februatus*) because the people are purified (*februatur*) on that day – that is, the naked *luperci* go round the ancient Palatine city, which is surrounded by human flocks.[17]

> Mark Antony, participating as a priest (*lupercus*) at the Lupercalia in 44 BCE, offers Julius Caesar a diadem, shortly before the latter's assassination.[18]

6.4 Plutarch, *Caesar* **61.3-4.** Caesar was watching these ceremonies, seated on the Rostra on a golden throne, dressed in triumphal garb.[19] Antony was one of the runners of the sacred race and he was also consul. He rushed into the Forum, and the crowd parted to make way for him. He was carrying a diadem entwined with a wreath of laurel and offered it to Caesar. There was some applause, not very outstanding, but sparse and contrived. But when Caesar pushed the diadem away, the whole people applauded. Just a few applauded when Antony offered it a second time, but everyone applauded when Caesar refused it. So the experiment failed, and Caesar rose and ordered the wreath to be taken to the Capitoline temple.

Megalesia

> This festival began on 4 April and was celebrated in honor of the Magna Mater, the Great Mother goddess who was also known as Cybele.[20] Cicero reminds his audience about the religious origin of the Megalesian games, noting that the goddess herself was a spectator at these games.

6.5 Cicero, *On the reply of the haruspices* **24.** What am I to say about those games that our ancestors wished to be held and celebrated on the Palatine in front of her temple and in the very sight of the goddess.

> Ovid, in describing the opening procession of the Megalesia, refers to the staging of plays as part of the games.[21]

---

[15] *added to these*: the original ten months of the Roman year were March to December.

[16] *comes first in order*: Janus is invoked first, even before Jupiter, in the *devotio* of Decius Mus; see 4.18.

[17] *human flocks*: it has been plausibly suggested that, rather than referring to the mobbing of the *luperci* by human beings, this refers to flocks of ghosts who were prevalent in the city during February; see Michels (1953) 35-59.

[18] *diadem*: this was a symbol of monarchy, a concept that was totally incompatible with the traditions of the Roman republic.

[19] *Rostra*: the Speakers' Platform in the Roman Forum.

[20] On the bringing of this foreign goddess to Rome, see 8.15-8.18.

[21] In the early second century the plays of Plautus and Terence were performed at the Megalesia; see 10.4 and 10.5.

6.6 OVID, *FASTI* **4.179-190.** Let the sky revolve three times on its never-resting axis, and let Titan three times yoke and three times unyoke his horses.[22] Then immediately the Berecyntian flute will blow on its bent horn and it will be the festival of the Idaean mother.[23] Eunuchs will march and beat their hollow drums, and cymbals clashed on cymbals will ring forth.[24] The goddess herself, seated on the unmanly necks of her attendants, will be borne through the city streets amidst howls. The stage is clattering, the games are summoning. Go watch the games, citizens of Rome, and let the squabbling law-courts be free of their customary battle-strife.[25] I have many questions to ask, but I am terrified by the sound of clashing brass and the bent flute with its scary sound.

Parilia

> This festival was celebrated on 21 April in honor of Pales, god of flocks and herds, and also marked the birthday of Rome. The problem is: does this duality represent a progression from pastoral to political, or are the two aspects to be regarded as synchronous?[26]

> Varro and Plutarch report the tradition connecting the founding of Rome on the Parilia with Rome's pastoral origins:

6.7 VARRO, *ON AGRICULTURE* **2.1.9.** Who indeed denies that the Roman people are descended from shepherds? Who does not know that it was a shepherd Faustulus who reared and educated Romulus and Remus? Will not the fact that they chose the Parilia as the time to found a city indicate that these men were indeed shepherds?

6.8 PLUTARCH, *ROMULUS* **12.1.** It is generally agreed that the foundation of the city took place on 21 April. The Romans celebrate this day with a festival, which they call the birthday of their country. In the beginning, so it is said, they sacrificed no living creature – but thought they should keep the festival pure and bloodless since it commemorated the birthday of their country. However, even before the city's foundation, they had a herdsmen's festival on that day and they called it the 'Parilia.'

> Ovid describes some of the rituals at the Parilia, asserting that he himself has participated in these rites.

6.9 OVID, *FASTI* **4.721-746, 777-806.** Night has passed and Dawn is appearing. I am called on to sing of the Parilia. Nor is my calling in vain, if kindly Pales grants her favor.[27] Kindly Pales, favor me as I sing of pastoral rites, if I honor

---

[22] *Titan*: the sun

[23] *Berecyntian*: epithet regularly used of the goddess to denote her Phrygian origin. *Idaean*: from Mount Ida near Troy, where the goddess Cybele was worshipped and, according to Ovid, was brought to Rome; see 8.17.

[24] The priests of the Magna Mater were eunuchs.

[25] *free... battle strife*: this day was free for public meetings and assemblies, but closed to suits in the praetor's court.

[26] See BNP 2.117 with bibliography.

[27] *Pales* is here addressed as a goddess, although elsewhere the deity is regarded as male. Compare the ambiguity concerning the gender of Robigo, in 6.10 and 6.11.

your benefactions with my service. Be assured that I have often brought with full hands the ashes of a calf and the bean stalks, the burnt means of purification.[28] Be assured that I have leaped over the flames, arranged three in a row, and the moist laurel branch has sprinkled drops of water over me. The goddess is moved and grants her favor to my work. My ship leaves the dock, and already my sails have fair winds.

Go, people, and bring from the virgin's altar the material for purification. Vesta will give them, and by Vesta's gift you will be pure. The material will be the blood of a horse and the ashes of a calf;[29] the third thing will be the empty stalk of a hard bean. Shepherd, purify your well-fed sheep as dusk first falls. First sprinkle the ground with water and sweep it with a broom. Decorate the sheepfold with leaves and branches fastened on it. Adorn the entrance and cover it with a long garland. Make blue smoke from pure sulphur, and let the sheep bleat when she is touched by the smoking sulphur. Burn rosemary, pine and juniper, and let the laurel crackle as it singes in the middle of the hearth. Put a basket of millet with the cakes of millet; the country goddess takes particular delight in this food. Add her favorite meat and a pail of milk, and when the meat is cut up, pray to wood-dwelling Pales with an offering of warm milk...

> [There follows a long prayer, asking pardon for inadvertent past offences, and seeking future benefits.]

This is how the goddess is to be propitiated. Face the east and pronounce the above prayer four times, washing your hands in living dew. Then you should set down a wooden bowl as if it were a mixing bowl, and drink the snow-white milk and the purple new wine. Next with swift foot you should energetically leap through the burning heaps of crackling straw.

I have described the custom; it remains for me to relate its origin. The multitude of explanations makes me doubtful and holds back my project at the outset. Devouring fire purges all things and burns out the impurities of metals: therefore it purges the sheep as well as their shepherd. Or is it because two discordant deities, fire and water, are two opposing principles from which everything is composed? And so our ancestors joined these elements, thinking that it was appropriate to touch the body with fire and sprinkled water. Or is it because the origin of life is contained in these elements that the exile is deprived of them and by them the bride is made a wife.[30]

---

[28]   *burnt means of purification*: the Vestals had prepared this material by ritually burning and mixing it; see Fantham (1998) 229.

[29]   *blood of a horse*: this would have been the October horse, the trace-horse of the winning chariot in a race held on 15 October. After the race, this horse was sacrificed and its blood preserved for the Parilia.

[30]   An exile was formally debarred from fire and water, and a new bride was presented with these two elements when she entered her new home.

Some suppose (though I can hardly do so) that the allusion is to Phaethon and to Deucalion's flood.[31] Some also say that a spark suddenly leaped out when the shepherds were striking rock upon rock. The first spark perished, but the second was caught in straw. Is this the reason for the flame at the Parilia? Or does this custom derive from the piety of Aeneas to whom fire gave a safe passage even in his defeat? Or is it nearer the truth that, when Rome was founded, orders were given to transfer their household gods (Lares) to new homes and that in changing their abode, the farmers set fire to their dwellings in the fields and the huts they were about to leave, and they and their cattle too leaped through the flames? This is the practice that continues even now on your birthday, Rome.[32]

Robigalia[33]

> This festival in honor of Robigo or Robigus, the spirit of blight, mildew or rust (both masculine and feminine forms appear in our sources) was celebrated on 25 April. At the beginning of his work *On Agriculture*, the antiquarian Varro invokes the special patron deities of farmers; the fourth such pair he calls on are Robigus and Flora.[34]

6.10 VARRO, *ON AGRICULTURE* **1.1.6.** For when they are propitious, mildew will not harm the grain and the trees; thus in honor of Robigus, the state festival of the Robigalia has been instituted, and in honor of Flora, the games called Floralia.

> Ovid describes the rituals and prayers used in the apotropaic worship of Robigo.

6.11 OVID, *FASTI* **4.905-942.** On the dawn of that day [25 April], when I was returning from Nomentum to Rome, a white-robed crowd blocked the middle of the road. A *flamen* was on his way to the grove of ancient Robigo, to throw the entrails of a dog into the flames and also the entrails of a sheep. Immediately I went up to him to learn of the rite. Your *flamen*, Quirinus, uttered the following words: 'Scaly Robigo, may you spare the sprouting corn, and let the smooth top quiver on the surface of the ground. Let the crops grow, nourished by the propitious constellations of the heavens, until they are ready for the sickle. Your power is considerable: the grain on which you have made your mark the farmer sadly counts as lost. Neither winds nor rain nor glistening frost that nips and pales the grain harm it as much as when the sun warms the wet stalks.

---

[31] *Phaethon*: son of Helios, the Sun, who attempted to drive his father's chariot, was unable to control it and would have set the world on fire had not Zeus intervened with a thunderbolt and killed him.
Deucalion: a Greek mythical figure who, like Noah, built an ark in order to survive a flood. Ovid explicitly rejects Greek myths as an explanation for the rites of the Parilia.

[32] Ovid then proceeds to describe the taking of auspices by Romulus and Remus; see 2.2.

[33] As Fantham (1998) 264-265 notes, Ovid incorrectly assigns the rising of the Dog Star to late April rather than high summer.

[34] The *Floralia* was held from 28 April to 3 May.

Then, fearful goddess, is the time for your anger. Spare, I pray, and take your scabby hands from the harvest and do not harm our fields of grain. It is enough that you have the power to harm. Do not embrace the tender crops, but rather embrace hardy iron. First destroy what can destroy others. Better that you pick on swords and harmful weapons. There is no need of them: the world is at peace. Now let hoes, the hardy two-pronged mattock, and the curved plough-share, the wealth of the countryside, shine brightly. But let rust defile arms, and let anyone who tries to draw his sword from its scabbard feel it stick from long disuse. But do not defile the grain, and may the farmer always be able to pay vows to you in your absence.'[35]

These were his words. From his right hand hung a napkin with a loose nap, and he had a box of incense together with a bowl of wine. The incense and wine, and the entrails of a two-year old sheep and the foul guts of a filthy dog he placed on the hearth – we saw him do this. Then he said to me, 'You ask why an unusual victim is assigned to this rite?' For I had asked this question. 'Learn the reason,' the *flamen* said, 'It is the Dog (they call it the Icarian dog)[36] and when that constellation rises the earth is parched and dry, and the crop ripens prematurely. This dog is put on the altar in place of the Dog Star; there is no reason for killing him other than the name.'

Floralia

As the Robigalia was intended to avert destruction from the developing crops, so the Floralia was celebrated to ensure the successful setting of the grain, the fruit of plants, orchards, olives and vines. The festival extended from 28 April to 3 May, was first instituted in 238 BCE, and made annual in 177 BCE.

Ovid introduces the festival in his calendar notice for 28 April, but defers a full discussion until the month of May.

6.12 OVID, *FASTI* **4.943-947.** When the wife of Tithonus has left the brother of Phrygian Assaracus and has three times lifted her radiant light in the bright firmament, there comes a goddess decked with garlands of a thousand different kinds of flowers, and the stage enjoys the customary licence of jollity.[37] The rites of Flora also extend into the beginning of May.

Ovid calls on the goddess to describe who she is.

6.13 OVID, *FASTI* **5.183-192.** Come, Mother of flowers, that we may honor you with fun and games! Last month I postponed giving you your due. You begin in April and cross into the time of May, the one month has you as it flees, the other as it comes. Since the borders of the months are yours and yield to you,

---

[35] The more usual prayer is for the presence, not the absence, of a deity.
[36] *Icarian dog*: the dog Maera who discovered the body of his master Icarius and was subsequently transformed into a star.
wife of Tithonus: Aurora, or Dawn. Tithonus is connected with Aeneas, since he is identified as the brother of Anchises, Aeneas' father.
[37] At the Floralia there were stage performances of mimes, a bawdy kind of musical comedy.

either of the two is fitting for your praises. The games of the Circus and the victor's palm fall into this month; let my poem also run side by side with these games in the Circus. Tell me goddess, who you are....

The goddess describes some of her functions.

6.14 OVID, *FASTI* **5.261-272.** Perhaps you may think that my sole realm is dainty garlands. My divinity also touches the tilled fields. If the crops have blossomed well, the threshing floor will be rich. If the vines have blossomed well, there will be wine. If the olives have blossomed well, it will be a brilliant year, and the fruits will have a successful harvest. If once the blossom is damaged, the vetch and beans perish, likewise, foreign Nile, your lentils perish. Wines also flourish, laboriously stored in mighty cellars, and a scum covers the surface at the top of the jars. Honey is my gift. I summon to the violet, clover and grey thyme the winged creatures to produce their honey.

The goddess tells how her games came to be made annual.

6.15 OVID, *FASTI* **5.312-330.** I myself was once neglected by the Senate. What was I to do? How could I make clear my resentment? What punishment could I exact for this censure? In my sadness, I did not perform my duties. I did not protect the countryside, nor did I concern myself with fertility of the gardens. The lilies had fallen. You could see the violets were parched, and the tendrils of the crimson saffron languishing. Often the west wind said to me, 'Don't spoil your own dowry.' But my dowry was worthless to me. The olives were blossoming; violent winds blighted them. The crops were blooming; the crop was damaged by hail. The vines were promising, the sky grew black under the south wind, and a sudden shower shook down the leaves. I did not want this to happen, nor am I cruel in my anger, but I did not care to ward off any of this. The Senate met, and vowed that if the year should prove fruitful, my festival would be made annual. I consented to the vow. The consuls Laenas and Postumius celebrated the games that had been vowed to me.[38]

Ovid reflects on the jocular nature of the games and the goddess' appeal to the masses and to prostitutes.

6.16 OVID, *FASTI* **5.331-354.** I was trying to ask why these games are marked by a greater wantonness and a freer spirit of fun and games, but it occurred to me that the deity is not strait-laced, and that the goddess' gifts lend themselves to delights. The brows of drinking party-goers are wreathed with stitched garlands, and the polished table lies hidden under a shower of roses. The drunken guest dances, his hair crowned with bark from the linden tree and, uninhibited, he enjoys the pleasure of unmixed wine. Drunk, the lover sings at the hard threshold of his lovely girl-friend, his perfumed hair crowned with soft garlands. No serious business is done by the one whose brow is garlanded, no clear water is drunk by those who bind their hair with flowers....

The levity of the stage well befits Flora. She is not, believe me, to be counted among your goddesses of tragedy. The reason why a crowd of prostitutes celebrate these games is not hard to discover. She is not one of your gloomy

---

[38] Consuls in 173 BCE.

or highfalutin types. She wants to open her rites to the plebeian throngs. She warns us to enjoy the splendor of age while it still blooms. For the thorn, she reminds us, is despised when the roses have fallen.

Saturnalia

This festival in honor of Saturn began on 17 December, extending by the late republic to 23 December. Saturn is thought by some scholars to be the god of sowing or of seed-corn, others consider him to be of Etruscan origin. A third possibility is that he is a Roman-Italic god. A major problem is that he was worshipped according to the Greek rite, that is, with the head uncovered. He is also assimilated to the Greek Kronos, which might account for the Greek rite.

His temple in the Roman Forum is said to date to the early republic; it contained a statue of the god which was bound with woollen bonds that were only released on the festal day, a ritual that has led some to regard him as a god of liberation. The poet Catullus (14.15) describes the Saturnalia as the 'best of days.' Coming near the time of the winter solstice, it was a period of rest, merry-making, gift-giving and also a reversal of social roles. Even the stern and parsimonious Cato the Elder relaxed and gave his dependents an additional measure of wine.

Religious festivals were frequently an opportunity for licence as well as festivity. Nowhere is this better seen than in the Saturnalia, when the social rules and hierarchies were not only suspended but also disrupted and even inverted. Macrobius quotes Accius, an early Latin poet of the second century BCE, as saying that masters waited on their own slaves at this feast.

6.17 MACROBIUS, *SATURNALIA* 1.7.37. They celebrate the day, and almost everyone joyfully holds feasts throughout the countryside and towns, with each man waiting upon his own slaves.

Macrobius interrupts the dialogue of his *Saturnalia* (the setting of which was this particular festival) to announce the slaves' dinner party.

6.18 MACROBIUS, *SATURNALIA* 1.24.22-23. Meanwhile the head of the slave household, whose responsibility it was to offer sacrifice to the Penates, to manage the provisions and to direct the activities of the domestic servants, advised his master that the household had dined in accordance with the annual ritual custom. For at this festival houses that observe the proper religious customs first of all honor the slaves with a dinner prepared as if for the master; and only afterwards is the table again prepared for the head of the household. So, then, the man in charge of the household slaves intervened to announce the time of dinner and summon the masters to table.

Livy reports the institution of a permanent annual festival to Saturn as one of the measures taken at the beginning of 217 BCE, the year of the Roman defeat at Trasimene.[39]

---

[39]   The festival had probably been long established; the innovation was probably the public feast prepared by the senators.

6.19 Livy **22.1.19-20.** Finally, for it was now December, victims were slain at the temple of Saturn in Rome and a *lectisternium* was ordered (the couch was set out by the senators) and also a public feast. Throughout the city for a day and a night the cry 'Saturnalia' was maintained and the people were ordered to hold it a sacred day and to keep it in perpetuity.

> But not everyone wanted to join in the festivities. Much later Pliny the Younger describes how he retreats from his house at the time of the Saturnalia.[40]

6.20 Pliny, *Letters* **2.17.** When I retreat to this garden-apartment, I seem to be far from my own house, and I take particular pleasure in it at the time of the Saturnalia, when the rest of the house resounds with shouts of festivity because of the licence of that season. Thus I neither interrupt their festivities, nor they my studies.

> The poet Statius (late first century BCE) proclaims that the festival will be as long-lived as Rome.

6.21 Statius, *Silvae* **1.6.98.** Time shall not destroy that sacred day, so long as the hills of Latium endure and father Tiber, while your city and the Capitol remain.

---

[40] See 13.18 for the advice of the Stoic philosopher, Seneca the Younger, on dealing with the Saturnalia.

WAR AND RELIGION

In the Introduction, we noted the patriotic belief that Rome owed her success and greatness to acknowledging the gods and maintaining their favor (*pax deorum*). In reflecting on the Romans' piety (*eusebeia*) especially in time of war, the Greek historian Dionysius of Halicarnassus summarizes the main functions of the fetial priests.[1]

7.1 DIONYSIUS OF HALICARNASSUS, *ANTIQUITIES* 2.72.3-4. ... it may not seem surprising to those who are unacquainted with the piety practised by the Romans that all their wars had a most successful outcome. For you will see that they conducted the beginnings and basics of all of them with utmost piety. For this reason in particular, the gods were kind to them in times of danger. Because of their number it is not easy to enumerate all the duties that fall within the province of the fetials but, to give a brief summary, they are as follows. It is their task to take care that the Romans do not undertake an unjust war against any city that is in alliance with them, and if others begin to violate treaties against them to go as ambassadors and first make a verbal demand for justice; then if they do not comply with the fetials' demands, to sanction war.

Fetial procedure and the declaration of war

The ritual declaration of war by the fetial priests is attributed to King Ancus Marcius (616-578 BCE). Originally these priests performed both ritual and diplomacy prior to the beginning of actual hostilities. These protracted and elaborate rituals and diplomatic exchanges were apparently aimed at ensuring that the war not only was but should seem to be a just war (*bellum iustum*) in the eyes of the gods.

There were three stages in the procedure: seeking of reparation, calling of the gods to witness that the Roman cause was just, and the actual declaration of war. Livy's account contains several archaisms, suggesting an antiquarian's

---

[1] *fetial priests*: for the function of the fetials in making treaties, see 2.7.

reconstruction of the original procedure that had been modified long before Livy's time.

7.2 LIVY **1.32.6-14.** Since Numa had instituted religious practices in time of peace, so Ancus Marcius provided a ceremonial for war that wars might not only be waged but also declared with some form of ritual. So he adopted from the ancient people of the Aequicolae the law that the fetials now have by which a state demands redress for an act of hostility. When the legate arrives at the frontier of those from whom redress is demanded, he covers his head with a woollen cap and says: 'Hear, Jupiter, hear, boundaries of — naming whatever nation they belong to — let divine law hear! I am the official herald of the Roman people. I come in the name of justice and religion; let there be trust in my words.' Then he recites his demands. Next he takes Jupiter to witness: 'If I unjustly or impiously demand that this property and these men be surrendered to me, then never let me have enjoyment of my native land.'

He recites these words when he crosses the boundary line, again to the first person he meets, again when entering the town gate, and again when he has entered the market-place, with only a few changes in the formula and wording of the oath. If his demands are not met at the end of thirty-three days (for this is the conventional number), he declares war as follows: 'Hear, Jupiter and you Janus Quirinus, and all you heavenly gods, and you gods of the earth, and you gods of the underworld, hear! I call you to witness that this people — naming whatever people it is — is unjust and does not make just reparation. But regarding these matters we will consult the elders in our fatherland, how we may obtain our due.' Then the legate returns to Rome for the consultation.

Immediately the king consults the senators with words something like this: 'With regard to the property, disputes and causes, concerning which the *pater patratus* of the Roman people of the Quirites has made demands on the *pater patratus* of the Ancient Latins and the men of the Ancient Latins, with regard to those things that they have not delivered, nor fulfilled, nor discharged, being things that ought to have been delivered, fulfilled and discharged, speak.' Here he would turn to the man whose opinion he would first ask, 'What think you?' And he would reply, 'I deem that these things must be sought in a war that is just and our sacred duty. Thus I agree and so vote.' The others were then asked the question in order of rank. When the majority of those present voted for the same opinion, war had been agreed upon.

The usual procedure was for the *fetialis* to carry to the boundary of the other nation a spear of iron or fire-hardened cornel wood and, in the presence of not fewer than three adult males, to say: 'Inasmuch as the tribes of the Ancient Latins and the men of the Ancient Latins have committed acts and offences against the Roman people, and inasmuch as the Roman people of the Quirites has ordered that war be made on the Ancient Latins, and the Senate of the Roman people of the Quirites has approved, agreed, and voted that there be war with the Ancient Latins, I and the Roman people therefore declare and make war on the tribes of the Ancient Latins and the men of the Ancient Latins.' Having said this, he would hurl the spear across their boundary.

This is the procedure by which at that time redress was sought from the Latins and war was declared, and the custom has been accepted by later generations.[2]

> The fetial procedures as described by Livy in context of the regal period were no longer feasible when wars were waged overseas against non-Italic peoples. By the mid-republic the practical details of diplomacy had been assigned to legates or ambassadors appointed by the Senate, but the fetials were still consulted on ritual matters and continued to perform certain, albeit modified, rituals.

> Livy gives an account of the religious rituals involved in the declaration of war on Philip V of Macedon in 200 BCE.

7.3 LIVY 31.5.3-4. On the Ides of March [15 March], the day on which the new magistrates entered office at that period, the first action of the consul Publius Sulpicius was to offer a motion which the Senate passed, that the consuls should perform a sacrifice with full-grown victims to whatever gods should seem best to them with the following prayer: Whatever the Senate and Roman people shall resolve for the common good and with reference to beginning a new war, may this decision turn out well and happily for the Roman people, the allies and the Latin name.[3]

> After the war-vote had been passed by the People's Assembly, the Senate gave instructions for various religious rituals to be enacted, and consulted the fetials on the technicality of delivering the actual declaration of war.

7.4 LIVY 31.8.2-5. A three-day period of prayer (*supplicatio*) was ordered by decree of the Senate, and gods were implored at all their couches (*pulvinaria*) that this war that the people had ordered with Philip would succeed and prosper. The fetials were consulted by the consul whether they would order that the declaration of war against King Philip be delivered to him in person, or whether it was sufficient to announce it at the first fortified post in his territory. The fetials replied that he would act correctly whichever way he acted.[4] The consul was permitted by the senators to send anyone he chose, other than a senator, to declare war upon the king.

The opening and closing of the temple of Janus

> Livy attributes the institution of a temple of Janus to Numa, the legendary second king of Rome, while also alluding to its recent closing by Augustus.

7.5 LIVY 1.19.1-3. Numa built a temple of Janus at the foot of the Argiletum as an indicator of peace and war, so that when open it signified that the state

---

2   Octavian, later Augustus, revived the ritual when he declared war on Cleopatra. By then it had become the custom to hurl the spear into an area near the temple of the war goddess Bellona, which had technically been declared as enemy territory. This avoided the problem of travel to distant lands like Egypt.

3   See 4.16 and 4.17 for a further example of prayers offered prior to undertaking a new war.

4   We do not hear which method was chosen.

was at war, when closed, that all the surrounding people were pacified.[5] Twice since the reign of Numa it has been closed, once during the consulship of Titus Manlius after the First Punic War, and the second time, which the gods granted our generation to see, after the war at Actium when the commander Caesar Augustus achieved peace on land and sea.[6]

> Vergil, also writing in the early years of Augustus' reign, describes the opening of the temple of Janus.

7.6 VERGIL, *AENEID* 7.607-615. There are the twin gates of War (for this is their name), made sacred by religion and fear of savage Mars. A hundred brass bolts and the everlasting strength of iron keep them shut, nor does the guardian Janus depart from the threshold. When the Senate has decided on battle, the consul himself, conspicuous in Quirinus' cloak worn in the Gabine mode,[7] unbolts these gates, as he draws back the creaking doors and gives the call to battle. Then the rest of the youth follow, and the bronze horns blast forth in raucous assent.

Portents and prodigies in time of war

> Portents and prodigies were unusual or unnatural occurrences, either solicited or unsolicited, that were thought to have been sent by the gods as an indication of a future event. Although the two terms are often used interchangeably, the term prodigy (*prodigium*) should strictly refer to a sign that had been accepted by the state authorities as indicating that the favor of the gods (*pax deorum*) had been broken or was about to be broken.

> From the prodigy lists given by Livy, six stages of dealing with a prodigy are apparent.[8] The report of a particularly strange occurrence, for example, a monstrous birth, would be given to a magistrate, a consul or praetor, who would then refer the problem to the Senate. That body would decide whether to reject or acknowledge (*suscipere*) the prodigy. This decision would be made in consultation with priests, who themselves were often members of the Senate by virtue of being ex-magistrates. The Senate would formally entrust the task of interpreting the prodigy to *haruspices* or, apparently in more serious cases, to the keepers of the Sibylline books. The priests would present their finding to the Senate both orally and in writing, and propose measures to be taken. The Senate would then instruct the magistrates or priests to carry out the prescribed ritual of expiation.[9] This process was probably expedited or

---

5   *Argiletum*: an area north of the Roman forum.

6   The First Punic War ended in 241 BCE, and Titus Manlius was consul in 235 BCE. Octavian defeated Antony and Cleopatra at Actium, in Greece, in 31 BCE, closed the gates of the temple of Janus in 29 BCE, and took the title Augustus in 27 BCE. He again closed the gates in 25 BCE after his campaign in Spain.

7   *Quirinus*: title of the deified Romulus. Thus, as he pronounced the call for battle, the consul was wearing a garment said to have belonged to Romulus.
     Gabine mode: the robe was firmly tied round the waist; see chapter 4 n.32.

8   See Linderski (1995) 613.

9   *expiation*: an action intended to make amends or atonement for an offense against the gods.

protracted as was deemed politic, thus demonstrating the control exercised by the Senate and magistrates.

Livy's account of the war against Hannibal gives several examples of the Senate's political control over religious matters in the late third century BCE, thus implicitly corroborating Polybius' theory that *deisdaimonia* held the Roman state together.[10] It is also apparent that the reported occurrences of prodigies and their expiation are directly related to crises during that war.

The Roman defeat at Trasimene (217 BCE)

After Hannibal's crossing of the Alps and two Roman defeats late in 218 BCE, prodigies and their expiations form a prominent part of Livy's narrative for each year. Flaminius, consul for 217, left Rome to begin his campaign against Hannibal before his term of office had actually begun. Thus he did not take the auspices in Rome. When he did make his inaugural sacrifice in northern Italy, a dire omen occurred. He perished soon after in the battle at Lake Trasimene.

7.7 Livy 21.63.7-14. Flaminius, the senators said, was waging war not only with the Senate, but now also with the immortal gods. Earlier [223 BCE] he had become consul without confirmation of the auspices and, though both gods and men had tried to recall him from the very battle-line, he had not obeyed. Now, conscious of having spurned them, he had fled the Capitol and the vows that were regularly undertaken....

...he entered on his magistracy and, as he was offering up a calf, it escaped from the hands of the sacrificing officials after it had been struck, spattering many of the by-standers with blood. The consternation and confusion was greater among those who did not know the cause of the panic. Most people regarded the incident as an omen of great terror.

Livy prefaces his account of the battle of Trasimene with a particularly long list of prodigies. These are reported as having occurred not only in various parts of Italy but also in Sicily and Sardinia, Roman provinces that were threatened by the Carthaginians. Unusual occurrences in these critical areas apparently had to be dealt with to maintain Roman morale.

7.8 Livy 22.1.8-13. In Sicily some soldiers' javelins had burst into flames. The same had happened in Sardinia to a cavalry officer's staff while he was inspecting the guards around the defences of the town. The gleam of fire had been seen at many points on the seashore. Two shields had sweated blood. Some soldiers had been struck by lightning. The sun had appeared to be diminished in size. At Praeneste it had rained red-hot stones and at Arpi shields had been seen in the sky and the sun seemed to be fighting with the moon. At Capena two moons had risen in the daytime. At Caere waters had flowed mixed with blood, bloodstains had appeared in the water that trickled from the very spring of Hercules. At Antium bloody ears of grain had fallen into the basket of some

---

10 See 1.35. Further examples of the authorities' response to portents and prodigies during times of acute danger are given in chapter 8.

reapers. At Falerii the sky had seemed to be torn with a great fissure, and through the opening a bright light had shone. Lots had shrunk in size and one had fallen out without being touched on which was written, 'Mavors brandishes his spear.'[11] In Rome about the same time the statue of Mars on the Appian Way and the images of the wolves had sweated,[12] at Capua the sky had seemed to be on fire and a moon given the appearance of falling in the midst of a shower of rain. Afterwards less memorable prodigies were also given credence: certain folk had found their goats to have woolly fleeces; a hen had changed into a cock, and a cock into a hen.

The following expiations were prescribed.

7.9 LIVY 22.1.16-18. It was voted that these prodigies should be expiated in part with greater victims, in part with lesser, and that there should be a three-day *supplicatio* at all the couches of the gods. With regard to the rest, when the decemvirs had consulted the Sibylline books, action was to be taken in accordance with what the sacred verses declared was pleasing to the gods. On the advice of the decemvirs, they decreed that the first gift should be made to Jupiter, a golden thunderbolt weighing fifty pounds. Juno and Minerva should be given offerings of silver. Juno Regina on the Aventine and Juno Sospita at Lanuvium should receive a sacrifice of greater victims.[13] The matrons, each contributing as much as each could afford, should collect a sum of money and carry it as a gift to Juno Regina on the Aventine and celebrate a *lectisternium*.

Before the battle, Flaminius disregards an omen.

7.10 LIVY 22.3.11-13.[14] Reprimanding the soldiers, he ordered them to take up the standards quickly and vaulted upon his horse. Suddenly the animal stumbled and, unseating the consul, threw him over his head. All who were present were terrified by what seemed an evil omen for beginning the campaign. Then it was reported that the standard could not be pulled up, even though the standard-bearer was exerting all his strength. Rounding upon the messenger the consul cried, 'Do you also bring me a dispatch from the Senate telling me not to fight? Go, tell them to dig the standard out, if their hands are too numb with fear to pull it up!'

After news of the defeat at Trasimene and Flaminius' death, Quintus Fabius Maximus, the newly appointed dictator, addresses the Senate, blaming Flaminius' neglect of religious matters for the disaster and advising consultation of the Sibylline books. Several remedial measures are recommended.

7.11 LIVY 22.9.7-10. Beginning with religious matters, Fabius convinced the Senate that the consul Flaminius had been in error more through his neglect of the rituals and auspices than through his recklessness and ignorance. So he

---

[11] *Mavors*: an older form of Mars' name.

[12] *statue of Mars ... sweated*: an allusion to the myth of Romulus' parentage and the wolf's suckling of him and his brother Remus.

[13] *Juno Regina*: Juno the Queen.

Juno Sospita: Juno the Protectress, who had a temple at Lanuvium near Rome.

[14] See 1.16 for Cicero's report of this episode.

said that they ought to enquire of the gods themselves how the gods' anger (*ira*) could be appeased. Thus he prevailed on them to do what is rarely done except when dreadful prodigies have been announced: the board of ten (*decemvirs*) was ordered to consult the Sibylline books.[15] When these priests had inspected the fatal books, they reported to the Senate that the vow which had been made to Mars on account of this war had not been duly performed, and must be performed anew and on a larger scale. Great games must be vowed to Jupiter, and temples to Venus Erycina and Mind. Finally a *supplicatio* and *lectisternium* must be celebrated and a Sacred Spring vowed, if they should prove victorious and the state remain the same as it had been before the outbreak of hostilities.[16]

> Cicero cites a comment of Coelius, an earlier Roman historian whose work has largely been lost.

7.12 CICERO, *ON THE NATURE OF THE GODS* 2.8. Coelius writes that Flaminius was killed at Trasimene because he neglected religious matters (*religio*). Thus he inflicted a great wound on the state.

The Roman defeat at Cannae (216 BCE) leads to human sacrifice

> In the next year the auspices were unfavorable, and so the consuls Aemilius Paullus and Varro decided not to fight on that day. Later, however, Paullus, who had reported the unfavorable auspice, was killed whereas his colleague Varro, who had reluctantly obeyed the signs, survived the slaughter at Cannae.

7.13 LIVY 22.42.8-10. Varro gave the order to start. Paullus himself wished to delay and, when the sacred chickens refused to eat, gave orders that his colleague be notified.[17] Varro was just setting out with the standards from the gate and was greatly angered, but the recent disaster of Flaminius and the memorable defeat of Claudius in the First Punic War struck him with a sense of religious awe (*religio*). On that day, the gods themselves postponed but did not prevent the disaster that was threatening the Romans.

> Cicero expresses some puzzlement when considering the fates of Flaminius and Paullus.

7.14 CICERO, *ON DIVINATION* 2.71. Flaminius did not obey the auspices and so he perished along with his army. But a year later Paullus obeyed the auspices and yet didn't he nonetheless fall at Cannae along with his army?

---

[15] *decemvirs*: see Glossary under *quindecimviri*.

[16] *supplicatio* : a period of collective prayers and offerings to the gods by the whole state.
lectisternium: see Glossary.
Sacred Spring: all the animals born in a certain spring were consecrated and sacrificed to the gods; see 4.15.

[17] Auspices were sought through the feeding of chickens that were kept specially for that purpose.

> After news of the disastrous defeat at Cannae and the conviction of two Vestal Virgins for unchastity, the Romans consulted the Sibylline books and resorted to human sacrifice, which Livy deems 'a most un-Roman ritual.'

7.15 LIVY 22.57.2-6. In addition to these dreadful disasters they were also terrified by a number of prodigies, especially because in that year two Vestals, Opimia and Floronia, had been convicted of unchastity. Of these one had been buried alive, as the custom is, near the Colline Gate,[18] and the other had committed suicide. Lucius Cantilius, a scribe of one of the pontiffs,... had been guilty with Floronia, and the *pontifex maximus* had him scourged in the Comitium so severely that he died under the blows.[19] Since in the midst of so many misfortunes this act of impiety (*nefas*) was regarded as a prodigy, the decemvirs were ordered to consult the [Sibylline] books and Quintus Fabius Pictor was despatched to Delphi.[20]...

In the meantime, in accordance with the books of fate, some unusual sacrifices were made: one of them consisted in burying alive in the Forum Boarium a Gallic man and woman and a Greek man and woman,[21] in a place walled in with stone, which even before this time had been defiled with human victims, a most un-Roman ritual.

The later part of the war

> In 208/7 BCE Hannibal's brother Hasdrubal attempted to invade Italy from Spain to reinforce Hannibal, who had had no clear victory since Cannae. When this invasion was imminent, several dire prodigies were reported and the consuls had great difficulty in obtaining the *pax deorum*. Later in the year both consuls were ambushed by Hannibal and slain.

7.16 LIVY 27.23.1-4. The praetors left for their provinces, but the consuls were detained by certain religious difficulties (*religio*). A number of prodigies had been reported and they had difficulty in obtaining a favorable outcome (*litatio*). From Campania reports had come that the temples of Fortune and of Mars had been struck by lightning, also several tombs. At Cumae mice had gnawed the gold in the temple of Jupiter — thus does perverted *religio* bring the gods even into the smallest things. At Casinum a large swarm of bees had settled in the forum. At Ostia the wall and a gate had been struck by lightning. At Caere

---

[18]   See 5.12.

[19]   *Comitium*: see Glossary

[20]   *Delphi*: the location in Greece of an oracle of Pythian Apollo. Fabius Pictor was an early Roman historian.

[21]   *Forum Boarium*: the cattle market down by the Tiber.
    Gallic man and woman and a Greek man and woman: the choice of these particular victims has occasioned much scholarly discussion. Rome had been fighting the Gauls in northern Italy since the 230s but there is no record of hostility at this time with the Greeks. An earlier similar sacrifice or scapegoating is reported by Plutarch, *Life of Marcellus 3*, in 225 BCE at the approach of the Insubres, a Celtic tribe. For brief discussion of the incident see Dowden (1992) 34 and *BNP* 1.80-82.

a vulture had flown into the temple of Jupiter, and the lake at Volsinii had flowed with blood.

Because of these prodigies, one day of public prayer (*supplicatio*) was held. For several days full-grown victims were offered in sacrifice but without success and, for a long time, the favor of the gods was not obtained. The ruinous outcome of these prodigies fell upon the heads of the consuls, while the state remained unharmed.

> In 207 BCE, after several prodigies had been expiated, report of the birth of an androgyne was received. The *haruspices* declared that this constituted a prodigy and that it must be drowned at sea. During preparations for the second part of the expiation, another prodigy occurred that necessitated appeasing Juno the Queen.

7.17 LIVY 27.37.3-15. Relieved of their religious fears (*religiones*), men's minds were troubled again by a report that a child as large as a four year old had been born at Frusino. This was not so much a wonder because of its size as because, just at Sinuessa two years before, it was uncertain whether it was male or female. In fact the *haruspices* summoned from Etruria pronounced that it was a foul and loathsome prodigy: it must be removed from Roman territory, far from contact with earth, and drowned at sea. They concealed it alive in a chest, carried it out to sea, and threw it overboard.

Likewise the pontifices decreed that twenty-seven maidens should sing a hymn as they processed through the city. When they were in the temple of Jupiter the Stayer learning the hymn that had been composed by Livius the poet,[22] the temple of Juno the Queen on the Aventine was struck by lightning. The *haruspices* opined that this prodigy concerned the matrons and that the goddess must be appeased by a gift. By edict of the curule aedile, all the matrons living in the city of Rome or within ten miles were summoned to the Capitol. From their own number they themselves chose twenty to whom they should bring a contribution from their dowries. From this sum a golden bowl was made as a gift and taken to the Aventine. The matrons offered it as a sacrifice after due purification.

Immediately the decemvirs announced a day for another sacrifice to the same goddess. The order of procedure was as follows: from the temple of Apollo two white cows were led through the Porta Carmentalis into the city. Behind them were carried two cypress wood statues of Juno the Queen. Then came the twenty-seven maidens, clad in long robes, singing the hymn in honor of Juno the Queen.... Behind the line of maidens there followed the decemvirs, wearing laurel crowns and purple-bordered togas. From the gate they went along the Vicus Iugarius into the Forum. In the Forum the procession halted. Passing a rope from hand to hand the maidens advanced, tempering the sound of their voice to the beat of their steps. Then by way of the Vicus Tuscus and the Velabrum, through the Forum Boarium they proceeded to the Clivus Publicius

---

[22] *Livius the poet*: Livius Andronicus, who is said to have been the first Latin poet to translate Greek poetry into Latin.

and the temple of Juno the Queen. There the victims were sacrificed and the cypress wood statues carried into the temple.

> In 205/4 BCE, on the advice of a Sibylline oracle, the Great Mother goddess (Magna Mater) was brought to Rome in an attempt to get Hannibal out of Italy.[23] The Romans invaded Africa in 204, defeating Hannibal at the battle of Zama in 202. After making peace with Carthage, Rome declared war on Philip of Macedon who had allied himself with Hannibal after the battle of Cannae.

The beginning of the Second Macedonian War

> Livy places the prodigy list for 200 BCE in context of the declaration of war. In this list are reports of several abnormal births, including two androgynous humans. The latter recalled the incident of 207 and was similarly expiated.

7.18 LIVY 31.12.6-10. Further obscene offspring of animals were reported. Among the Sabines, a child of uncertain sex was born, while another was found whose sex, at the age of sixteen, could not be determined. At Frusino a lamb was born with the head of a pig, at Sinuessa a pig with the head of a man, on the public land in Lucania, a colt with five feet. All these foul and deformed creatures seemed to be signs that nature was producing aberrations in strange offspring. But beyond all else, the androgynes were abhorrent; so they were ordered to be carried out to sea, as had been done with a similar prodigy not long before....[24]

Nevertheless, the decemvirs were ordered to consult the [Sibylline] books concerning this portent. They, as a result of the consultation, ordered the same rites that had been performed when such a prodigy had occurred before. In addition, they ordered that a hymn be sung throughout the city by twenty-seven maidens, and an offering be made to Juno the Queen. Gaius Aurelius [the consul] attended to the performance of these rites in accordance with the response of the decemvirs.

A Roman triumph

> During the republic triumphs were granted by the Senate to generals for outstanding victories. The triumphal procession was an ancient ritual which became more spectacular as the Romans conquered much of the Mediterranean world. The victory procession began outside the *pomerium*, near the temple of Bellona (a goddess personifying battle frenzy), passed through the Circus Flaminius and Circus Maximus, round the Palatine Hill and through the Forum along the Sacred Way to the Capitoline Hill, where it terminated with a sacrifice to Jupiter Optimus Maximus in the Capitoline temple.
>
> Plutarch describes the spectacle of the triumph of Lucius Aemilius Paullus over King Perseus of Macedon in 167 BCE. Displayed in the procession were

---

[23] For details, see 8.15 and 8.16.

[24] See 7.17.

the spoils of war, captives, the victorious general and his soldiers. It was, in effect, a victory parade for the whole city to enjoy. Such spectacles doubtless aroused deep public emotion, while also enhancing the political reputation of the triumphing general.[25]

7.19 PLUTARCH, *LIFE OF AEMILIUS PAULLUS* **32-34.** The people erected platforms in the stadia for horse-races that the Romans call circuses, and around the Forum. They also took up their position in the other parts of the city that provided a good view of the procession. Then, dressed in pure white garments, they watched the spectacle. All the temples were open and filled with garlands and incense. Numerous officials and lictors restrained the disorderly streaming crowds as they rushed into the midst, keeping the streets open and clear.[26] Three days were assigned for the triumphal procession. The first was barely sufficient for the display of captured statues, paintings and colossal figures that were transported on two hundred and fifty chariots. On the next day the finest and richest of the Macedonian arms were carried in numerous carts.... After the carts bearing the armor came three thousand men carrying silver coins in seven hundred and fifty vessels, each of which contained three talents and was carried by four men.[27] Others carried silver bowls, drinking horns, dishes and cups, all arranged for display, remarkable for their size and in the depth of their engraving.

On the third day, immediately at dawn, trumpeters marched out, playing not a march or processional tune, but the kind of sound that the Romans use to rouse themselves for battle. Following these came one hundred and ten stall-fed oxen with gilded horns, adorned with ribbons and wreaths. Leading the animals to sacrifice were young men wearing aprons with fine purple borders, and boys bearing silver and gold libation cups....

After these [the procession of Perseus' family and Perseus himself] wreaths of gold were carried, four hundred in all, which the cities had sent by embassy to Aemilius as prizes for his victory. Then came Aemilius himself, mounted on a magnificently adorned chariot, a man worthy to behold even without the trappings of power. He was dressed in a purple robe interwoven with gold, holding in his right hand a branch of laurel. The entire army also carried laurel, following the general's chariot in their companies and divisions. Some sang the traditional songs interspersed with ribaldry, others victory hymns and the praises of Aemilius who was gazed upon and admired by all...

---

[25] For a further description of a triumph, see 11.3 with illustration.

[26] *lictors*: attendants who accompanied the magistrates, carrying the *fasces*, the symbols of the magistrates' power (*imperium*).

[27] *talent*: a Greek unit of coinage, of considerable value.

ACCEPTING NEW GODS, CULTS AND RITUALS

> Throughout their history the Romans were willing to adopt new gods and religious practices, provided that such innovations were authorised by the state authorities.

8.1 CICERO, *LAWS* **2.19.** No individual shall take gods for himself, either new or alien ones, unless they have been recognised by the state. Privately they shall worship those gods whose proper worship they have received from their ancestors.

> While Cicero's statement indicates the openness of a polytheistic religion to change, it is important to note the proviso elucidated by the Greek historian Dionysius of Halicarnassus: those foreign cults that were *officially* adopted were *adapted* to traditional religion by the removal of undesirable features.[1] Thus it is misleading to speak in terms of the Romans' toleration of non-Roman religions, as will be seen in the measures enacted to suppress the cult of Bacchus or Dionysus in 186 BCE.[2] Rather we should think in terms of patrol and control by the state.

8.2 DIONYSIUS OF HALICARNASSUS, *ANTIQUITIES* **2.19.3.** Notwithstanding the influx into Rome of innumerable foreigners who are under great obligation to worship their ancestral gods in accordance with the customs of their own countries, the city has never officially emulated any of these foreign practices, as have many cities in the past. But even though Rome has introduced certain rites on the recommendation of oracles, she celebrates them in accordance with her own traditions, discarding all mumbo-jumbo.

---

[1] One of the key words in Dionysius' statement is *officially*, as Wiseman (1984) 117-8 emphasized. What also needs to be emphasized, however, is the translation of the Greek, *eis zelon eleluthe*, as 'emulated' or 'imitated' rather than 'adopted.'

[2] See 9.2-9.7.

The third century Christian writer Minucius Felix opines that Roman receptivity to foreign cults contributed to their success in gaining an empire.

8.3 MINUCIUS FELIX, *OCTAVIUS* **6.** Throughout the entire empire, in provinces and towns, we see that each local group of people has its own religious rituals and worships local gods. The Eleusinians worship Ceres, the Phrygians the Great Mother, the Epidaurians Aesculapius, the Chaldaeans Baal, the Syrians Astarte, the Taurians Diana and the Gauls Mercury. The Romans, however, worship all the gods in the world. Their power and authority have encompassed the whole world, and they have extended their empire beyond the paths of the sun and the confines of the ocean itself. All the while they practice their god-fearing valor (*virtus religiosa*) in the field and strengthen their city with awesome religious rites, chaste virgins and many a priestly dignity and title.

When they have captured a town, even in the fierceness of victory, the Romans respect the deities of the conquered people. They invite to Rome gods from all over the world and make them their own, raising altars even to unknown gods and to the shades of the dead.[3] And thus, while the Romans were adopting the religious rites of all nations, they also earned for themselves dominion.

As Polybius observed, fear of the supernatural (*deisidaimonia*) kept the Roman state together. The ideology seems to have been: the more gods we worship and the larger the scale of that worship, the greater will be the chance of securing the gods' favor (*pax deorum*) and thus success.

The following excerpts show that religious innovations frequently coincided with a particular crisis, such as plague or a disaster in war. Although this could suggest that the existing deities were proving inadequate, the actual infiltration of a cult leaves little, if any, trace in the archaeological or literary record. What the sources attest is the presence but not necessarily the original arrival of a deity. Thus it is equally possible that the state authorities were sanctioning a cult that was already prevalent by officially accepting and modifying it to conform with Roman traditions.

Once a cult had gained a hold on the populace, it was the easier and wiser course for the authorities to accept and adapt it, rather than attempt to eradicate it completely. For the most part, this policy worked until the Romans were confronted with monotheistic religions.

The literary sources indicate that the agent of change was frequently the Sibylline books which prescribed expiations involving innovation.[4] It is, however, important to note that these books were consulted on the advice of the Senate by the *quindecimviri de sacris faciundis,* the state board of priests in charge of rituals, who alone had access to them. During the republic, these prophetic books were thus under strict state control. Augustus transferred them to the temple of Apollo on the Palatine.

---

[3]   See 8.6 on the summoning of Juno from Veii.

[4]   *Sibylline books*: see 5.7 and 5.8.

Eight temples are reported to have been constructed after consultation of these books: the temple of Ceres, Liber and Libera dedicated in 493 BCE,[5] Aesculapius in 291, Hercules the Guardian probably in the third century, Flora in 241 or 238, Mens (Mind) and Venus of Eryx in 215,[6] Cybele who was brought to Rome in 204 and adopted as the Great Mother (Magna Mater), and Venus Verticordia (Turner of Hearts) in 114 BCE. Three of these deities, Aesculapius, Venus of Eryx and Cybele were identifiably non-Roman gods, of whom the last two were given temples within the *pomerium*, an evident innovation made at two critical junctures in the Hannibalic war.

An early arrival: the cult of Apollo

In 433/2 BCE, in a time of plague, the Romans vowed a temple to Apollo for the people's health. This temple was dedicated two years later (Livy 4.29.7) and was situated outside the *pomerium*, apparently because Apollo was a non-Roman deity. There was probably an earlier shrine on the site of this temple that is later referred to as that of Apollo Medicus (the Healer) (Livy 3.63.5 and 40.51.6). Since there were temples of Apollo at Veii and Cumae, the cult could have entered Rome from Etruria or southern Italy, gradually infiltrating to the point at which a public shrine was established. In this, as in most instances, the original arrival of a god cannot be discerned.

8.4 LIVY 4.25.3-4. That year a plague offered a respite from other problems. A temple was vowed to Apollo on behalf of the health of the people. The *duumvirs* did many things on the advice of the books to appease the anger of the gods and avert the plague from the people.[7] Nevertheless the losses were severe, both in the city and the countryside, men and beasts being afflicted without distinction.

The first *lectisternium*[8]

In 399 BCE, again in a time of plague, the Romans introduced the *lectisternium*, originally a Greek practice, on the advice of the Sibylline books.

8.5 LIVY 5.13.4-7. Plague was rife, affecting all living creatures. Since no cause or end to this incurable disease was found, the Senate decided to consult the Sibylline books. The *duumvirs* celebrated over a period of eight days the first *lectisternium* ever held in Rome in order to win the favor of Apollo, Latona,[9] Diana, Hercules, Mercury and Neptune, spreading couches for them that were

---

[5]   Ceres, Liber and Libera were apparently original Italic fertility deities of crops and the vine. Later this triad was assimilated with the Greek Demeter, Dionysus and Kore (the Maid, Persephone); see Orlin (1997) 100-101.

[6]   *Eryx*: a town in Sicily.

[7]   *duumvirs*: a board of two priests who dealt with the performance of sacred rites (*sacris faciundis*); see Glossary.

[8]   *lectisternium*: literally a strewing or draping of couches on which the gods' statues were displayed outside the temples, as if at a banquet.

[9]   *Latona*: mother of Apollo and Diana.

as richly furnished as was possible at that time. The ritual was also celebrated in private houses.

The *evocatio* of Juno of Veii[10]

In 396 BCE, when the Romans were about to take the city of Veii, an important, wealthy Etruscan city to the north of Rome, they performed the ritual of *evocatio*, inviting their their enemies' god to come over to their side. Camillus, the Roman dictator,[11] addresses the Veientine goddess Juno, offering her a temple in Rome in return for her desertion of Veii. By *evocatio* the Romans deprived the enemy of divine protection, while also adopting the gods of the vanquished into their own pantheon.

8.6 LIVY 5.21.1-7. A huge crowd set out and filled the camp. After taking the auspices, the dictator went out and ordered the soldiers to take up their arms. 'It is under your leadership,' he said, 'Pythian Apollo, and inspired by your divine will, that I am advancing to destroy the city of Veii. To you I vow a tenth part of the spoils. To you, Queen Juno, who now dwell in Veii, I pray that you will accompany us in our victory to our city, soon to be your city, where a temple worthy of your greatness will receive you.'

After these prayers, he attacked the city with vast numbers from every side, in order to distract attention from the danger that threatened the inhabitants from the tunnel.[12] The people of Veii were unaware that they had been betrayed by their own seers and by foreign oracles. They also were unaware that already some of the gods had been invited to share in the plunder, while others had been summoned to leave their city and were turning their eyes to the temples of the enemy for their new homes.

After the fall of the city, the goddess is taken to Rome and installed on the Aventine, an area outside the *pomerium*, as was appropriate for a goddess of non-Roman origin. With apparent skepticism, Livy reports various stories about her removal.

8.7 LIVY 5.22.3-8. When the wealth that belonged to men had been removed from Veii, they began to remove gifts to the gods and the gods themselves, but more in the manner of worshippers than plunderers. Young men were selected from the entire army. After ritually cleansing their bodies, they put on white robes and were entrusted with the task of carrying Queen Juno to Rome. With reverence they entered her temple, at first they scrupled (*religiose*) to lay hands on the image because it was one that, according to Etruscan practice, only a priest of a certain family was accustomed to touch.

When one of the youths, whether divinely inspired or in youthful jest, asked, 'Juno, do you want to go to Rome?', the rest all cried out that the goddess had nodded her assent. There is an additional story that her voice was heard to say

---

[10] *evocatio*: a summoning forth or calling out.

[11] *dictator*: an official who was specially appointed as commander-in-chief, though only for a period of six months. His power overrode that of the two consuls.

[12] *tunnel*: the Romans were digging a tunnel under the walls of the city.

that she was willing. In any event, we are told that she was moved from her abode with contrivances of little power and was light and easy to transport, as if she followed of her own accord. She was brought undamaged to the Aventine, her eternal home to which the vows (*vota*) of the Roman dictator had summoned her. There Camillus later dedicated to her the temple that he had vowed. Such was the fall of Veii, the wealthiest city of the Etruscans....

> Macrobius (c. 400 CE) reports the ancient formula for *evocatio* recited by a Roman commander in charge of a siege. Apparent at the end of this formula is the *do ut des* principle.

8.8 MACROBIUS, *SATURNALIA* **3.9.7-8.** Whether you are a god or goddess who hold under your protection the people and city of Carthage, and you also, greatest god, who have taken this city and people into your protection, I pray, venerate and ask your indulgence that you abandon the people and city of Carthage, desert their structures, temples, sanctuaries, their city, and depart from them. I pray you to afflict that people and citizenry with fear, terror, and oblivion, to abandon them and come to me and my people. I pray that our places, temples, sanctuaries and city may be more acceptable and more honorable to you, and that you may be propitious to me, the people of Rome and my soldiers so that we may know and perceive it. If you will do this, I vow that I will build temples to you and celebrate games in your honor.

The importation of Aesculapius

> Because of a plague, the Romans consulted the Sibylline books which advised bringing Aesculapius, the Greek god of healing, from Epidauros in Greece. Envoys were eventually sent to Greece. The god is said to have approached them in the form of a snake and, when nearing Rome, indicated the Tiber island as the location for his temple (292 BCE). Again a foreign deity was installed outside the *pomerium*.

8.9 LIVY **10.47.6-7.** Although the year had been successful in many respects, it was hardly a consolation for one misfortune, a plague that devastated both the city and countryside. It was now a calamity more like a portent, and the [Sibylline) books were consulted to discover what end or remedy the gods might offer for the misfortune. The advice discovered in the books was that Aesculapius should be summoned to Rome from Epidaurus; but nothing was done about it in that year because the consuls were engaged with the war, except that a one-day *supplicatio* to Aesculapius was held.[13]

8.10 ANON. *ON FAMOUS MEN* **22.2-3.** Because of plague and on the advice of the oracle, the Romans sent ten ambassadors under the leadership of Quintus Ogulnius to summon Aesclapius from Epidaurus.[14] When the Roman envoys arrived there and were marvelling at the huge statue of the god, a serpent glided from the temple, an object of veneration, not of horror. To the amazement of all, making its way through the midst of the city to the Roman ship, it curled

---

[13] *supplicatio*: see Glossary.
[14] *Ogulnius*: also the sponsor of the Ogulnian Law giving plebeians access to priesthoods.

itself up in the tent of Ogulnius. The envoys sailed to Antium, carrying the god.[15] Here, through the calm sea, the serpent made for a nearby temple of Aesculapius and, after a few days, returned to the ship. When the ship was sailing up the Tiber, the serpent leaped down from the ship onto the nearby island, where a temple was established. The pestilence subsided with amazing speed.

The importation of Venus Erycina to the Capitoline hill

During the Hannibalic War, several expiations were recommended by the Sibylline books after the Roman defeat at the battle of Trasimene and the death of Flaminius. One was the building of a shrine to Venus Erycina. The epithet derives from Eryx, a town in northwest Sicily where the principal deity, Astarte, was the Carthaginian equivalent of Venus. This area had been an important stronghold of the Carthaginians during the First Punic War (264-241 BCE) and had only been conquered by the Romans with great difficulty. In 217, the fear was that this part of Sicily might defect from Rome. This importation would seem to be another instance of *evocatio*, even though not explicitly mentioned as such in the scanty sources. Since her temple was located on the Capitoline hill (Livy 23.21.10), Venus Erycina is the first known example of a foreign deity to be brought inside the *pomerium*.

8.11 LIVY 22.9.9-10. The books were duly inspected and the board made its report: first, the offering made to Mars, in view of the present war, had been incorrectly performed, and must be perfomed afresh and on a greater scale; secondly, Great Games should be vowed to Jupiter and a shrine to Venus Erycina and to Mens (Mind);[16] thirdly, public prayers should be held and a *lectisternium*.[17]

An outbreak of non-Roman *religio* in Rome[18]

In 213 BCE the continuing war resulted in religious hysteria in Rome and the abandonment of Roman ritual. The Senate ordered the praetor to collect all written prophecies and rituals, and to forbid sacrifice in 'a new or foreign rite.'

---

[15] *Antium*: a coastal town in Italy, about forty miles south of Rome.

[16] *Mind*: the vowing of a temple to the abstract deity Mind seems to reflect the need for a new strategy after the disastrous loss at Trasimene, that of delay advocated by Quintus Fabius Maximus who became dictator after the death of Flaminius (for the preceding part of this excerpt which also involves Fabius Maximus, see 7.11.

[17] This *lectisternium* marks the first appearance in a Roman religious festival of twelve gods who have their counterparts in the twelve Greek Olympian gods: six couches were displayed: one for Jupiter and Juno, a second for Neptune and Minerva, a third for Mars and Venus, a fourth for Apollo and Diana, a fifth for Vulcan and Vesta, a sixth for Mercury and Ceres (Livy 22.10.9).

[18] *religio*: note the recurrence of this word in this and the ensuing excerpts from Livy. It can mean 'superstition' or 'religiosity,' with the general implication that awe and fear of the supernatural are involved, for good or ill.

The 'foreign superstition' was evidently orgiastic and was perhaps an outbreak of Bacchic worship or that of the Magna Mater, or even of both cults.

8.12 LIVY 25.1.6-12. The longer the war dragged on and success and failure kept changing both the situation and men's attitude, so superstition (*religio*) of a mostly foreign nature (*externa*) invaded the state.[19] The result was that either the gods or men suddenly seemed to have changed. Roman rituals were now being abandoned not only in secret and within the confines of men's houses, but also in public places, in the Forum and on the Capitol. There was a mob of women who were not following the ancestral mode of worship either in their sacrifices or in their prayers to the gods. Phony priests and fortune-tellers (*sacrificuli et vates*) had taken hold of men's minds....[20]

At first good men's indignation was expressed in private; then the matter came to the notice of the Senate as a matter of official complaint. The aediles and the three city commissioners were seriously reprimanded by the Senate because they were not stopping it.[21] After they had tried to remove that crowd from the forum and scatter the paraphernalia required for the sacrifices, they had narrowly escaped violence. Now that the trouble seemed too strong to be quelled by the lesser magistrates, the Senate assigned to Marcus Aemilius, the urban praetor,[22] the task of freeing the people from such superstitions (*religiones*). In an assembly, he read the decree of the Senate and also issued an edict that whoever had books of prophecies or prayers or a ritual for sacrifice should bring all these books and writings to him before 1 April, and that no one should sacrifice in a public or consecrated place in a new or foreign rite.

The institution of games to Apollo

In the following year (212 BCE), Livy reports the results of the praetor's edict. Two oracles were published and, in response to the second, games to Apollo were authorized after consultation of the Sibylline books.

8.13 LIVY 25.12.8-15. Then the second prophecy was read out loud...: 'If you wish, Romans, to drive out the ulcerating sore of nations that has come from afar,[23] I propose that a festival of games be vowed to Apollo that will be graciously observed in Apollo's honor each year. When the people shall have given a part out of the public treasury, private citizens shall contribute on their own behalf and on that of their families. The praetor who is the chief judge for the

---

[19] *superstition ... invaded the state*: compare this phrase with Livy's introduction to the bringing of the Magna Mater, see 8.15.

[20] *phony priests and fortune-tellers*: Livy uses the same terms in context of the outbreak of Bacchic worship in 186 BCE to indicate that these practices were not a part of the official state religion; see 9.2.

[21] *three city commissioners*: minor officials charged with protecting the city from crime.

[22] *urban praetor*: an elected official who frequently had charge of the city in the absence of the consuls.

[23] *sore of nations that has come from afar*: an allusion to Hannibal. Compare this prophecy with that given in 205 which resulted in the bringing of the Magna Mater (Great Mother) goddess to Rome, see 8.15.

people and the commons will be in charge of the conduct of that festival. The decemvirs shall offer the victims according to the Greek rite.[24] If you do this properly, you will always be glad and your state will change for the better. For the god who peacefully nurtures your meadows will destroy your foes.'

They spent one day interpreting this prophecy. On the next day the Senate passed a decree that the decemvirs should consult the [Sibylline] books in regard to making a festival and sacrifices in honor of Apollo. When the results of this consultation were reported to the Senate, the senators voted that a festival should be vowed and celebrated in honor of Apollo and that, after the festival had been held, the sum of twelve thousand asses should be given to the praetor for the celebration, and two full-grown victims.

A second decree was passed that the decemvirs should make the sacrifice according to the Greek rite and with the following victims: to Apollo an ox with gilded horns, and two white she-goats with gilded horns, and to Latona a cow with gilded horns.[25] When the praetor was about to open the festival in the Circus Maximus, he proclaimed an edict that during the festival people should make a contribution to Apollo according to their means. Such is the origin of the festival of Apollo, vowed and celebrated for victory, not for health, as most people think.[26] The people wore garlands as they watched the games, the matrons offered prayers, everybody feasted in the atrium with open doors, and the day was celebrated with every kind of ceremony.

The Apolline Games are made an annual event

> A few years later Hannibal was still in Italy and his brother Hasdrubal was en route from Spain to invade from the north in an attempt to bring him reinforcements. In 208, because of plague, the Senate ordered that the festival of Apollo be made an annual celebration.

8.14 LIVY 27.23.5-7. The festival of Apollo was instituted in the consulship of Quintus Fulvius and Appius Claudius by Sulla the urban praetor (212 BCE). Thereafter all the urban praetors celebrated it, vowing it for a single year but not holding it on a fixed date. This year a serious plague descended on the city and the surrounding countryside, causing a lingering sickness that was not often fatal. Because of the plague, prayers were offered at the cross-roads throughout the city. Publius Licinius Varus the praetor was ordered to propose to the people a bill that these games be vowed in perpetuity for a fixed date.

---

[24] *according to the Greek rite*: note the apparent concession, since in the previous year there had been such concern about non-Roman ritual practices. Worship of Apollo according to the Greek rite was apparently offered as a substitute for the more exotic practices that the Senate clearly wished to control, if not eliminate.

[25] *Latona*: mother of Apollo; see 8.5 on the *lectisternium* of 399, where Latona is one of the honored deities.

[26] *victory*: Livy's emphasis on victory rather than health foreshadows the next two excerpts in which the games are made an annual fixture and the Magna Mater is imported to Rome to get Hannibal out of Italy.

The bringing of the Magna Mater to the Palatine hill

In 207 Hasdrubal was defeated and killed at the battle of Metaurus before he could reach Hannibal. But the latter still remained in southern Italy. In 205, the Romans were considering an invasion of Africa in the hope that this would cause Hannibal to withdraw from Italy. In the midst of this debate, the Romans consulted the Sibylline books which advised them to bring to Rome the Magna Mater (Great Mother), who is also known as the Mother of the Gods, the Idaean Mother, and Cybele or Cybebe.

This goddess was worshipped extensively in the area later known as Asia Minor (modern Turkey) and throughout the Greek world. One of her most important sanctuaries was at Pessinus in Phrygia, her priests were eunuchs, known as Galli, and her cult was orgiastic. In Livy's account of her arrival in Rome from Asia Minor, however, there is no sign of the orgiastic nature of her worship.[27] This foreign goddess was given a Romanised name, Magna Mater, her reception was celebrated with a *lectisternium*, an earlier imported Greek ritual, and new games that were given a Greek title, the Megalesia, all in an apparent attempt to present her as a Greek rather than an Asiatic deity.

There are several variants in the sources, including three different versions of her provenance. The antiquarian Varro, writing in the late republic, derives her from Pergamum (*On the Latin Language* 6.15), Livy reports that she was brought from Pessinus, and Ovid unequivocally states that the goddess was to be found on Mount Ida, near Troy. Livy reports that a 'sacred stone' was brought from Pessinus, whereas Ovid seems to imply an anthropomorphic statue.[28]

The historical context of the Roman decision to receive the goddess officially in Rome is narrated by Livy.

8.15 LIVY 29.10.4-11.8. At this time sudden superstition (*religio*) invaded the state.[29] The Sibylline books had been consulted because it had rained stones that year more often than usual, and in the books a prophecy was found that, if ever a foreign enemy should invade Italy, [30] he could be defeated and driven out if the Idaean Mother of the Gods[31] were brought from Pessinus to

---

[27]   See 8.18 and 8.19 for descriptions of these orgiastic aspects.

[28]   Most modern sources, including *BNP* 2.44, combine the ancient testimony, asserting that the stone brought to Rome in 204 was black, although it is not until the Christian authors, Arnobius (*Against nations* 7.49) and Prudentius (*Crowns of the martyrs* 10.156), that the stone is referred to as being black. For Ovid's reference to 'her image,' see 8.18 with n. 50.

[29]   Livy's introduction to this episode is almost identical to the account of foreign *religio* in 213 BCE.

[30]   *if ever a foreign enemy should invade Italy*: a more explicit allusion to Hannibal than that in 213 BCE, see 8.13.

[31]   *Idaean Mother of the Gods*: the official title of the Magna Mater in later republican times was *Mater Deorum Mater Idaea* (Mother of the Gods, Idaean Mother). The epithet Idaean refers to Mount Ida near Troy, and thus has connections with Aeneas, see Wiseman (1984) 117-123.

Rome.[32] The effect upon the Senate of the discovery of this prophecy was all the greater because the envoys who had taken the offering to Delphi declared that they had had a favorable response when they sacrificed to Pythian Apollo, also that they had been granted a response by the oracle to the effect that a much greater victory was awaiting the Roman people than the one of the spoils from which they were bringing their offering.[33]...

The envoys on their way to Asia went up to Delphi, where they consulted the oracle, inquiring what hope it foresaw for them and the Roman people of bringing their mission to a successful conclusion. The answer, so it is said, was that they would get what they wanted through the help of King Attalus,[34] and that when they had brought the Goddess to Rome it would be necessary for them to make sure that she was hospitably welcomed by the best man in the City. The envoys then visited Attalus in Pergamum. He received them courteously, escorted them to Pessinus in Phrygia, gave them the sacred stone that the inhabitants said was the Mother of the Gods, and told them to take it back to Rome.[35] Falto was sent in advance by the other envoys to announce that the Goddess was on the way and to tell the people that the best man in the state must be sought to welcome her with due ritual and hospitality.[36]

> In the following year, after reporting the prodigies and their expiation, Livy returns to the theme of the bringing of the Magna Mater. With elaborate ceremony the goddess was received from the 'best man' by the matrons, brought to Rome and installed in the temple of Victory on the Palatine hill, the second known instance of a foreign deity being brought within the *pomerium*. The Romans invaded Africa, and Hannibal was recalled from Italy and finally defeated at the battle of Zama in 202 BCE. The installation of the goddess on the Palatine had apparently fulfilled both parts of the oracle.

8.16 LIVY 29.14.5-14. There followed discussion of the reception of the Idaean Mother after the recent news that she was already in Terracina,[37] in addition to the fact that Marcus Valerius, one of the ambassadors, had arrived in advance, announcing that she would soon be in Italy.... Publius Scipio... was the young

---

[32] *Pessinus*: site of a temple of Cybele in Phygia. That the Idaean goddess was to be brought from Pessinus presents an long-recognized anomaly, since Pessinus is in Phrygia, more than 240 miles to the east of Mount Ida near Troy.

[33] *offering to Delphi*: Earlier in the year, the Romans had sent ambassadors to Delphi with a gift from the spoils of their victory over Hasdrubal at the Metaurus (Livy 28. 45.12).

[34] *King Attalus*: king of Pergamum, an ally of the Romans in the First Macedonian War (215-205 BCE).

[35] *the sacred stone...*: Livy's scepticism is apparent in his comment 'the inhabitants said ...' Compare Ovid's reference to 'her image,' in 8.18 with n. 50.

[36] *hospitality*: the Latin *hospitium* implies reciprocity of guest and host, thus underscoring the foreignness of the newly imported goddess.

[37] *Terracina*: a town on the west coast of Italy, some 70 miles south of Rome.

man, not yet of an age to be quaestor, whom they judged to be the best of good men among the citizen body.[38]...

Publius Cornelius was ordered to go with all the matrons to meet the goddess at Ostia.[39] He was to receive her from the ship, carry her to land and hand her over to the matrons for them to carry. After the ship had reached the mouth of the river Tiber, he sailed out into the salt water, just as he had been ordered, and received the goddess from her priests and carried her to land. The leading matrons of the state, among whom the name of Claudia Quinta is outstanding, received her. Claudia's reputation, previously dubious according to tradition, has made her chastity more famous because of her scrupulous performance of her religious duties.

The women passed the goddess from hand to hand,[40] from one to another in turn, as the whole citizen body poured out to meet her. Incense burners had been placed in front of the doors along the route and, as they burned the incense, people prayed that she might enter Rome willingly and propitiously. On 12 April, they carried the goddess to the temple of Victory which is on the Palatine,[41] and it was a festal day. The people flocked to the Palatine bringing gifts for the goddess. There was a *lectisternium* and also games that were called the Megalesia.[42]

> Ovid's account of the bringing of the Magna Mater to Rome is markedly different from that of Livy. In the historian's version the Sibylline oracle offered the hope of defeating Hannibal and getting him out of Italy. Ovid, however, makes no reference to the Hannibalic War, nor to Pessinus as her origin. Rather he locates her in the area of Troy and focuses on the tradition of Rome's Trojan origins as portrayed in Vergil's *Aeneid*. Ovid presents the episode as a dialogue between himself and the Muse Erato to whom he attributes the answers to his questions, thus distancing himself from the fabulous aspects of his narrative.

8.17 OVID, *FASTI* 4.247-273. 'Instruct me too, guide of my work,[43] from where was she sought and from where did she come? Or was she always in our city?'

'The Mother always loved Dindymus, Cybele, Ida and the kingdom of Troy.[44] When Aeneas carried Troy to the Italian land, the goddess almost followed

---

[38] *Publius Scipio*: Publius Cornelius Scipio Nasica, consul in 191 BCE, was the cousin of Publius Scipio Africanus, consul in 205, who invaded Africa in 204 and defeated Hannibal at Zama in 202.

[39] *Ostia*: a town at the mouth of the Tiber.

[40] *the goddess*: presumably the sacred stone acquired in Pessinus.

[41] *temple of Victory which is on the Palatine*: this location was not only within the *pomerium* but also close to the site on which Romulus had founded Rome. The goddess' own temple, adjacent to that of Victory, was dedicated in 191 BCE (Livy 36.36.3).

[42] *Megalesia*: the name is derived from *Megale Meter*, the Greek for 'Great Mother.' On the Megalesian games, see 6.5 and 6.6.

[43] *guide of my work*: Ovid is here addressing the Muse Erato.

[44] *Dindymus, Cybele, Ida*: mountains in the area near Troy that were sacred to Cybele.

the ships that carried the sacred objects,[45] but she felt that the fates did not yet demand the presence of her divinity in Latium.[46] So she remained in her accustomed place.

Afterwards, when mighty Rome had already seen five centuries and had raised her head above the conquered world,[47] the priest consulted the fateful words of Euboean prophecy.[48] They say that this is what he found: "The Mother is absent. Roman, I order you to seek the Mother. When she comes, she must be received by chaste hands." The obscure oracle puzzled the senators with its ambiguity: who was the absent Parent, and where she was to be sought? Apollo was consulted and he replied: "Summon the Mother of the Gods, she is to be found on Mount Ida."

Nobles were sent. At that time Attalus was the ruler of Phrygia. He refused the request of the men from the western land. Let me tell you a miracle. The earth trembled with a long rumbling and the goddess spoke in her shrine: "It was my own wish that I be sought. Let there be no delay. Send me: I'm willing. Rome is a worthy place to which every god should go." Trembling at the sound of these words, Attalus said: "Go forth. You will still belong to us. Rome traces her origin to Phrygian ancestors."

> Ovid gives the itinerary of the voyage to Rome. At Ostia the ship is met by crowds of people from Rome, but becomes grounded in the shallows of the river and cannot be moved. Claudia Quinta performs a miracle. Ovid's detailed account is in sharp contrast to the terseness of the Livian version.

8.18 OVID, *FASTI* **4.304-47.** Astounded at the portent, the men stood and trembled. Claudia Quinta traced her descent from Clausus of old,[49] and her beauty was not unequal to her noble birth. She was chaste, though not reputed so. An unfair rumor had wronged her, and she had been accused on a false charge ....

---

[45]   *sacred objects*: an allusion to Aeneas' bringing Troy's gods to Rome, see Vergil, *Aeneid* 1.68 and 2.296-7.

[46]   *fates...*: an allusion to a prominent theme in Vergil's *Aeneid*.

[47]   *five centuries and had raised her head above the conquered world*: although five centuries (*saecula*) are not to be taken literally, the reference to Rome raising her head above the conquered world hardly fits with Livy's dating of the bringing of the Magna Mater to the last years of the Second Punic War when Hannibal was still in Italy. The Livian date is corroborated by Cicero, *On old age* 45. Ovid is evidently indulging in poetic exaggeration.

[48]   *fateful words of Euboean prophecy*: an allusion to the Sibylline books. Euboea, an island off the north east mainland of Greece, sent out a colony to Cumae in Italy where there was a temple to Apollo which also housed the Sibyl from whom the Elder Tarquin is said to have bought the Sibylline books.

[49]   *Clausus of old*: the Sabine Attus Clausus who is said to have come to Rome in the late sixth century BCE. He was the founder of the famous Claudian family into which the empress Livia had been married before her marriage to Augustus. Her son, the future emperor Tiberius, was thus a member of the Claudian family. Hence, Ovid's emphasis on Claudia's family origin.

When she had stepped forth from the line of chaste matrons and taken the pure river water in her hands, three times she sprinkled her head, three times she raised her hands to the heavens .... On bended knee she fixed her gaze on the image of the goddess [50] and with dishevelled hair uttered these words: 'Fruitful Mother of the gods, be kind and accept the prayers of your suppliant on one condition. I am said not to be chaste. If you condemn me, I will confess my guilt. Convicted by the judgment of a goddess, I will pay the penalty by my death. But if there is no basis for the charge, by your action you shall give proof of my innocence. Chaste as you are, yield to my chaste hands.'

She spoke and, with a slight effort, drew the rope. The goddess was moved, followed Claudia's lead and, by following, restored her reputation. ...

A white-haired priest in a purple robe washed the Mistress and her sacred objects in the waters of the Almo.[51] Her attendants howled, the frenzied flute blew, and unmanly hands beat the drums of bull's hide.[52] With joyful face and attended by a throng, Claudia walked in front, her chastity at last believed, though barely, because of the goddess' testimony. The goddess herself, seated in a wagon, was borne into the city by the Capena Gate; fresh flowers were scattered upon the yoked oxen. Nasica received her.[53]

> The poet Lucretius, writing in the late republic, describes a procession in the goddess' honor, explaining her different attributes and interpreting her as an allegory of Earth. [54]

8.19 LUCRETIUS, *ON THE NATURE OF THINGS* 2.600-628. The earth also has the capacity to produce shining crops and fruitful orchards for the races of men, and to supply rivers, leaves and fruitful pastures for the breed of wild beasts that roam the mountains. That is why the earth has uniquely been called the Great Mother of the Gods, the Mother of Beasts and Creator of our human body.

She it is who the ancient and learned poets of the Greeks celebrated in song, as seated in a chariot driving her twin-yoked lions.... They yoked her to wild beasts, because children, however fierce, must be conquered and tamed by the devotion owed to their parents. They surrounded her head with a turreted crown because the earth, being fortified in special places, supports cities. Thus adorned with this emblem, the image of the divine Mother is carried through the mighty lands with awesome effect.

---

[50] *image of the goddess*: the Latin *imago* would seem to imply an anthropomorphic statue.

[51] *Almo*: a tributary of the Tiber.

[52] *her attendants* ...: allusions to the cries of her eunuch priests and the music that were typical of the goddess' orgiastic worship. These several lines suggest an annual ritual purification of the goddess' statue which was not an official part of her cult until the reign of Claudius.

[53] *Nasica received her*: Publius Cornelius Scipio Nasica; see n. 38. The Latin *Nasica accepit* forms a terse and abrupt conclusion to this account of the advent of the Magna Mater, apparently in deliberate contrast to the detail given by Livy.

[54] See also Ovid's description of the procession in 6.6.

She it is whom the different nations call the Idaean Mother by the ancient custom of their ritual. As her retinue, they give her an escort of Phrygians because they claim that it was in that area that crops were first created to spread throughout the world.[55] They assign eunuchs (*galli*) as her priests, because they wish to demonstrate that those who have violated the divinity of the Mother and proved themselves ungrateful to their parents must also be considered unworthy to bring living offspring into the shores of light.

Taut drums resound in their hands and all around there is a clash of hollow cymbals. Horns blast with their raucous tone and the hollow flute goads the mind with its Phrygian strain. They carry before them emblems of the violent frenzy. These have the power to terrify the ungrateful hearts and impious minds of the mob with fear of the the goddess' divinity.

So when she is first carried through the cities and silently bestows on mortals a wordless well-being (*salus*), they strew all her path with bronze and silver, enriching her with much largesse. They shower her with rose blossoms which overshadow the Mother and her retinue.

> The above testimony of Ovid and Lucretius indicates that by the late republic the Magna Mater had assumed many aspects of the original cult of Cybele. Statuettes of the goddess' consort Attis[56] discovered in the foundations of the temple of the Magna Mater on the Palatine (191-114 BCE) show that the cult of Attis must have arrived some time during the second century BCE, perhaps even as early at the Magna Mater herself, though it was evidently not officially adopted in 205/4 at the time of the state's adoption of the Magna Mater and the initiation of the Megalesia. The authorities had apparently tried to control the cult at the time of its official adoption by adapting it to Roman customs, but they had not been able to prevent the infiltration of the exotic aspects of the cult of Cybele, Attis and her eunuch priests.

> Dionysius of Halicarnassus cites the cult of the Magna Mater as an example of the control exercised by the state over the admission of foreign cults, noting that no Roman was allowed to be a priest of Cybele, nor were Romans allowed to participate in her procession wearing non-Roman dress.

8.20 **DIONYSIUS OF HALICARNASSUS, *ANTIQUITIES* 2.19.3-5.** But even though Rome has introduced certain rites on the recommendation of oracles, she celebrates them in accordance with her own traditions, discarding all mumbo-jumbo. The rites of the Idaean goddess are an example of this. For the praetors perform sacrifices and celebrate games in her honor every year according to the laws of Rome. Her priest and priestess are Phrygian; and it is they who carry her image through the city, begging alms, as is their custom, wearing medallions on their chests and beating tambourines, while flute-players play hymns in honor of the Mother.

---

[55] *crops*: the Latin *fruges*, fruits of the earth, yields an etymological word-play with the epithet *Phrygius*, Phrygian.

[56] *Attis*: for the story of the castration of Attis, inspired by a frenzy induced by Cybele, see Catullus 63 and Ovid, *Fasti* 4.223-244. On the statuettes, see *BNP* 1.97-8, 2.47-8.

It is contrary to the law and decree of the Senate that any native-born Roman walk in procession through the city wearing multi-colored clothes, begging alms, being escorted by flute players, or celebrate the goddess' orgies in the Phrygian manner. So careful are the Romans with regard to religious practices that are not indigenous. So great is their abomination of empty display that lacks decorum.

In the reign of Claudius (41-54 CE) restrictions on Roman participation were removed and the *quindecimviri* now took part in her procession. A new festival was instituted, the Hilaria, lasting from 15 to 27 March. On the final day of this festival, the cult statue of Cybele was ritually bathed in the river Almo, a ceremony mentioned earlier by Ovid in his description of the goddess' cult (see 8.18). Also incorporated into the goddess' worship was the *taurobolium*, an initiation ceremony in which the sacrificant was drenched with the blood of a bull. The date of the origin of this ceremony, however, is unknown, the ancient literary source being the Christian writer Prudentius who gives the supposed words of a Christian martyr contrasting his own martyr's blood with that of the pagan sacrifice.[57]

---

[57]   For details, see Turcan (1996) 49-50, *BNP* 2.160-2 and *OCD* 3 s.v. Cybele.

CONTROL OF NON-ROMAN CULTS

9.1 JUVENAL, *SATIRES* 3.60-63. Citizens, I cannot bear a Greekized Rome. And yet what portion of our dregs comes from Greece? The Syrian Orontes has long since flowed into the Tiber, bringing with it its language and its customs....

As the above passage from the early second century CE satirist Juvenal shows, not everyone was favorably disposed to the assimilation of other cultures. In this chapter we see two examples of control from two different periods that illustrate the authorities' aversion to non-Roman cultic practices, the worship of Bacchus, also known as Dionysus, and that of the Egyptian goddess Isis. Both these cults were 'mystery religions,' involving an initiation ceremony, a ritual that set the initiate apart from the rest of society, and offering an intense, often ecstatic, communion with the deity.[1] These cults, with their appeal to the individual as member of a cultic group rather than the civic community, were likely to incur the suspicions of the state authorities.

Less than twenty years after the importation of the Magna Mater to the Palatine hill, a senatorial decree imposed severe restrictions on Bacchic worship. This incident is attested in two sources: the historian Livy and an inscription giving the Senate's decree. The opposition to the cult of Isis in the first centuries BCE and CE is less fully documented. Nonetheless, many of the apprehensions apparent in the reactions of the Roman authorities to both cults re-emerge in later encounters with Judaism and Christianity: a fear that meetings and organizations outside the control of the traditional political elite were politically subversive.

---

[1] 'Every initiation means a change in status that is irreversible; whoever has himself initiated on the basis of his individual decision separates himself from others and integrates himself into a new group. In his own eyes the *mystes* (initiate) is distinguished by a special relation to the divine, by a form of piety.' Burkert (1985) 301.

The suppression of Bacchic worship

Evidence of social disruption in the aftermath of the Hannibalic War indicates an environment that would have offered ample scope for the spread of a cult that had a more personal appeal than that of the traditional gods of Roman state religion. An increase in the popularity of the worship of Bacchus is attested for the early second century BCE.[2] The cult had probably been present in Rome since the beginning of the republic when a temple was established to Ceres, Liber and Libera, Italic deities that were later assimilated with the Greek Demeter, Dionysus and Kore (the Maid, Persephone).[3] Livy's account of the suppression of Bacchic worship in 186 BCE indicates that new manifestations of the cult had entered Rome from Etruria and Campania.[4] In response to these developments the Senate passed a decree that imposed strict controls on Bacchic worship throughout Italy, while not banning it completely.[5]

A bronze tablet inscribed in archaic Latin includes a letter addressed by the Roman consuls to Rome's Italian allies incorporating the Senate's actual decree. The contemporary evidence of this inscription not only confirms the historicity of the episode but also offsets the dramatic embellishments of Livy's account. From these two sources it is evident that the Senate did not intend to eliminate the cult, but rather to impose stipulations that were designed to curb the excesses threatening traditional Roman religion and Roman mores (*mos maiorum*). Apparent in both sources is the Roman authorities' fear of political subversion: they dealt with the problem as a 'conspiracy.'[6]

Livy describes the outbreak of the problem.

9.2 LIVY 39.8.1-9.2. The following year (186 BCE) diverted the consuls from the army and administration of wars and provinces to the suppression of an internal conspiracy (*intestina coniuratio*).... Both consuls were assigned the investigation (*quaestio*) of secret conspiracies. A low-born Greek came first to Etruria,...

---

[2]   Bacchic worship may have been part of the foreign religion (*religio externa*) that invaded the state in 213; see 8.12.

[3]   Liber: an original Italic god of fertility, especially wine, later identified with Dionysus, see chapter 8 n. 5. The temple to Ceres, Liber and Libera was located on the Aventine hill, outside the *pomerium*, where the poorer classes lived.

[4]   *Campania*: a fertile plain in the hinterland of the Bay of Naples. During the Hannibalic War, several cities of Campania, including the principal city Capua, had defected to Hannibal. When the Romans recaptured Capua after a long seige, they executed the leaders and deprived the city of its civic status. The popularizing of the Bacchic cult in this particular area would thus have been a concern to the Roman authorities.

[5]   See Warrior (1998) 100-105.

[6]   *conspiracy*: the Latin *coniuratio* literally means a swearing-together or oath-taking for a common purpose. The noun or a cognate occurs nine times in Livy's account. The verb, *coniurare*, is part of a key phrase in the decree: 'No one shall participate in an oath, a vow, a pledge, or promises, or exchange a pledge of loyalty...' This series of legalistic terms underscores the Senate's perception of a political threat.

a phony priest and fortune-teller.[7] Nor was he one who taints men's minds with error by publicizing his *religio* and proclaiming his profession and his teaching. He was a practitioner of secret rites held at night.[8]

There were initiation rites that at first were entrusted to a few, then they began to be spread among men and women.[9] To the religious element (*religio*) were added the delights of wine and feasting so that the minds of a larger number might be enticed. When wine had inflamed their minds, and night together with the mingling of males with females, youth with age, had extinguished every distinction of modesty, all kinds of corruption first began to be practised, since each individual had ready access to the pleasure to which his lustful nature was more inclined.[10] There was not one type of vice alone: promiscuous debauchery of freeborn males and women, false witnesses, forged seals and wills, manufactured evidence, all originated from the same workshop.[11] Likewise there were poisonings and domestic murders of such a kind that often bodies were not even found for burial. Many deeds were ventured by guile, more by violence. The violence was concealed because amidst the debauchery and murders no cries of protest could be heard above the howling and the din of drums and cymbals.

This destructive evil spread from Etruria to Rome like the contagion of a plague. At first the size of the city, which was quite large and thus able to tolerate such evils, kept it hidden. Finally information reached the consul Postumius in the following way....

> There follows a complicated story in which Hispala, a freedwoman who herself had been initiated into the Bacchic rituals, revealed to the consul details of recent religious innovations, the initiation of men, night rituals and a sharp increase in the number of days for initiations.

9.3 LIVY 39.13.8-14. Hispala explained the origin of the rites. At first, she said, it was a ritual for women; it was not customary to admit any man. Three days

---

[7] *phony priest and fortune-teller*: the same derogatory terms were used in context of the outbreak of foreign *religio* in 213, see 8.12.

[8] *secret rites held at night*: nocturnal rituals were contrary to Roman practice. Cicero (*Laws* 2.36) proposed for his ideal state that initiation into the rites of Ceres be held not by night but by day. Night was thought to offer cover for all kinds of licentious behavior. Any unauthorised assembly constituted a threat to the state, hence the charge of *coniuratio*. Assemblies had to be convened by magistrates, as was the assembly (*contio*) that was addressed by the consul Postumius, see 9.4. Similar accusations were later made against the Christians because of their secret meetings which were often held at night.

[9] *initiation rites*: several mystery religions in the ancient Mediterranean world required novices to undergo secret rituals which often re-enacted myths connected with a particular deity.

[10] Drunkenness, promiscuous sex, poisoning and murders are typical allegations in cases of religious and political persecution.

[11] *false witnesses* ..: these allegations are peculiarly Roman, as opposed to the charges of intoxication and promiscuity that are also made by Pentheus in Euripides' *Bacchae* 220-225.

a year had been appointed on which initiations in the Bacchic rites were held by day. Married women were usually appointed in turn as priests. Paculla Annia, a Campanian priestess, had changed all this, supposedly on the advice of the gods. For she had been the first to initiate men, her sons Minius and Herennius Cerrinius.[12] She had conducted the rites by night rather than by day, and established five days of initiation per month instead of three per year.

From the time that the rites involved the promiscuous mingling of men with women and the liberation of the darkness, no kind of crime, no kind of wickedness had been been left untried. There was more debauchery among men with each other than with women. Anyone who was less tolerant of disgrace and rather slow to commit crime was sacrificed as a victim. To regard nothing as wrong (*nefas*) was the acme of *religio* among them. Men prophesied with fanatical convulsions of their bodies, as if their minds were possessed. Married women, wearing Bacchic dress, their hair loose, and carrying blazing torches, rushed to the Tiber.[13] They plunged the torches into the water, bringing them out again with the flame still burning because they contained live sulphur mixed with calcium. Men were said to have been carried off by the gods; they were bound to a machine and whisked out of sight into hidden caves. These were the ones who had either refused to join in conspiracy (*coniurare*) or participate in crimes or endure debauchery. It was, she said, a huge crowd, almost a second citizenry.[14] Among them were certain nobles, both men and women. Within the last two years it had been ordained that no one over the age of twenty should be initiated.[15] People of under this age were sought because they were susceptible to vice and debauchery....

> The consul brings the matter before the Senate which orders a special investigation (*quaestio extra ordinem*) throughout Italy.[16]

9.4 Livy 39.14.3-10. When both witnesses [Hispala and her lover Aebutius] were in his charge, Postumius brought the matter before the Senate, setting forth everything in detail, first what had been reported and then what he himself had discovered. Great panic seized the senators, both on the public account for fear that these conspiracies (*coniurationes*) and nocturnal meetings might produce

---

[12] The names Paculla, Cerrinius and Minius are attested in Campania; see Walsh (1994) 122. Minius is later named as one of the leaders of the *coniuratio* (Livy 39.17.7) and, with his brother, was imprisoned under strict guard in Ardea, some twenty-five miles from Rome (Livy 39.19.2).

[13] Such behavior and dress would have been highly inappropriate for Roman matrons.

[14] *a second citizenry*: this and the subsequent sentences encapsulate the threat to the state. Since the center of Bacchic worship was on the Aventine, the reference to *alter populus* was probably intended to recall the secessions of the plebs in the fifth century BCE.

[15] Reference to initiates under the age of twenty implies doubts about the suitability of such initiates for military service.

[16] *special investigation*: the consuls had summary power in this investigation, as the death penalty and power to imprison indicate.

some hidden treachery or danger, and each privately on his own account, for fear that a relative might be involved in the crime.

The Senate decreed that the consul be thanked because he had pursued the matter with extreme diligence and without causing a public disturbance. Then they assigned to the consuls a special investigation of the Bacchanals and their nocturnal rites .... The priests of these rites were to be sought out, be they men or women, not only in Rome but throughout all the villages and communities so that they come under the charge of the consuls.[17] Proclamation was to be made in Rome and edicts sent to all of Italy that no one who had been initiated into the Bacchic rites was to consent to gather or assemble for these rites or perform any such ritual.[18] Above all, it was decreed that an investigation (*quaestio*) should be conducted into those people who had come together or conspired to commit debauchery or crime. Such was the decree of the Senate.

The consuls ordered the curule aediles to seek out the priests of this rite, arrest them and keep them in open custody until the investigation.[19] The aediles were to see that the rites were not celebrated in secret. The three city commissioners were entrusted with the task of posting guards throughout the city, ensuring that no meetings took place by night and guarding against arson.[20]

> Livy reports that the consuls summoned an open meeting of the people (*contio*). In a dramatic speech the consul Postumius contrasts the ancestral Roman gods with those deities who, 'by means of goads implanted by the Furies, spur minds enslaved by debased and alien rites to perform every kind of crime and lustful deed' (39.15.2-3). The threat to the state becomes explicit as the consul declares: 'Daily the evil swells and creeps in. It is already too great to be purely a private matter. Its objective involves the state' (39.16.3). The consul then addresses the crux of the problem: the threat to traditional Roman religion and the *mos maiorum*.

9.5 LIVY 39.16.6-12. Nothing is more deceptive in appearance than depraved religion (*prava religio*). When the authority of the gods is offered as a cloak for crime, a fear steals into the mind that in punishing human misdeeds we may violate something of divine law that is involved in them. Countless edicts of the pontifices, decrees of the Senate, and finally responses of the *haruspices* free you from this religious scruple (*religio*).

How often in the time of our fathers and grandfathers has the task been assigned to the magistrates of forbidding the celebration of foreign rituals (*sacra externa*), of excluding phony priests and fortune-tellers from the Forum, the Circus and

---

[17] *charge of the consuls*: at this time, inhabitants of such communities in Italy came under the jurisdiction of their local magistrates. This empowering of the consuls represents the Senate's attempt to reassert political control over the Italian communities.

[18] *no one should consent to gather...*: Livy's language corresponds closely with that of the inscription, see 9.7.

[19] *curule aediles*: minor magistrates.

[20] *the three city commissioners*: minor officials charged with protecting the city from crime. They had also been involved in the outbreak of foreign *religio* in 213; see 8.12.

the City, of seeking out and burning books of prophecies, and of abolishing every form of sacrifice except the Roman. Men most learned in all law, divine and human, used to judge that there was nothing so prone to the destruction of religion (*religio*) as sacrifices offered with foreign rather than our ancestral ritual.

I have thought that these warnings should be given to you so that no superstitious fears (*superstitio*) disturb your minds when you see us destroying the Bacchic shrines and breaking up wicked assemblies. This we will do if the gods are favorable and willing. They, because they were indignant that their own divinity was being polluted by crime and lust, brought these actions from darkness into light. Nor did they wish these deeds to be revealed that they go unpunished but that they might be avenged and suppressed. The Senate has entrusted the special investigation (*quaestio*) of this matter to me and my colleague.

> After the consul's speech, the Senate's decrees were read and a reward announced for informers. Those named by informers were to respond by a certain date and were forbidden to sell or buy anything for the purpose of flight. Failure to appear meant condemnation; aiding of fugitives was forbidden. News of the Senate's decree spread panic throughout Rome and Italy. Many were caught trying to escape. The involvement of both sexes is emphasized: more than seven thousand men and women were said to have been implicated in the conspiracy. Livy records the names of the leaders of the conspiracy, including Minius Cerrinius. Only those who had committed debauchery or murder, or who had given false testimony, forged seals, substituted wills, or committed other frauds were put to death. Those who had merely been initiated were imprisoned. Executions exceeded imprisonments.[21]

> Bacchic shrines in Rome and Italy were destroyed, except those that antedated this new form of Bacchism, and official permission had to be sought for establishing new shrines. The number of participants was limited to five, a restriction that would not only have eliminated the danger of public hysteria but also destroyed one of the basic appeals of the ritual, that of mass participation in a ceremony that involved exotic music and dancing.

9.6 LIVY 39.18.7-9. Then the consuls were given the task of destroying all the Bacchic shrines, first in Rome and then throughout Italy, except where an ancient altar or image had been consecrated.[22] For the future it was decreed that there should be no Bacchic shrines in Rome or in Italy. If any person considered such worship to be traditional or necessary and that it could not be abandoned without incurring a religious obligation (*religio*) and expiation, he had to make a declaration before the urban praetor who would consult the Senate.[23] If he were granted permission at a meeting of the Senate at which no

---

[21] Livy 39.17.1-18.6. Prescription of the death penalty indicates treasonous activity and the gravity of the perceived threat.

[22] This exemption would apply to such shrines as that of Liber on the Aventine; see n. 3.

[23] *urban praetor*: an elected official who frequently had charge of the city in the absence of the consuls. The stipulation of travel to Rome would have been prohibitive for the majority of people who lived more than a day's distance from Rome.

Bronze copy of Roman Senate's decree suppressing the worship of Bacchus in 186 BCE that was set up in Bruttiium in southwest Italy. Courtesy Kunsthistorisches Museum, Vienna.

fewer than one hundred members were present, he should offer the sacrifice provided that no more than five people took part in the rites.[24] Also there was to be no common fund and no official in charge of the ceremonies or priest.[25]

> The senatorial decree was passed in 186 BCE. The copy that was set up in Bruttium in southwest Italy was later discovered by archaeologists. (see illustration above).

9.7 *ILS* **18; 511,** *CIL* **1.2.581.** The consuls Quintus Marcius, son of Lucius, and Spurius Postumius, son of Lucius, consulted the Senate on 7 October in the temple of Bellona. Present at the writing were Marcus Claudius, son of Marcius, and Lucius Valerius, son of Publius, and Quintus Minucius, son of Gaius.

Concerning the Bacchic shrines they have resolved that the following is to be

---

[24] Obtaining such a dispensation would have been difficult, since senators could easily refuse to complete the quorum of one hundred.

[25] The ban on having a fund and an official priest reflects the Senate's fear of any kind of organization that was outside their control.

announced to those who are allies:[26]

None of them shall have a Bacchic shrine. If there are any persons who say that it is necessary for them to have a Bacchic shrine, they should come to the urban praetor in Rome. The Senate, when it has heard their case, will make a decision, provided that there are no less than one hundred senators present when the matter is under discussion. No man, be he a Roman citizen, of Latin status,[27] or an ally, shall be present among female Bacchic worshippers, unless he has appeared before the urban praetor, and he has ordered it in accordance with the will of the Senate, provided that there are no less than one hundred senators present when the matter is under discussion. Decided.

No man is to be a priest. No man or woman is to be an official. Nor is any of them to have a common fund. Nor shall anyone make a man or a woman an official or a pro-official.[28] Nor shall anyone hereafter participate in an oath, a vow, a pledge, or promises. Nor shall anyone exchange a pledge of loyalty.[29] No one shall conduct the rites in secret, either publicly or privately, or outside the city, unless he has appeared before the urban praetor, and he has ordered it in accordance with the will of the Senate, provided that there are no less than one hundred senators present when the matter is under discussion. Decided.

No one shall perform rites in the presence of more than five persons altogether, both male and female. Nor shall more than two men and three women be present, unless this is in accordance with the will of the urban praetor, as written above.

You are to announce these measures at a public meeting on three successive market days. And, so that you may know the decision of the Senate, that decision is as follows: If there are any persons who have acted contrary to what is written above, the Senate has resolved that they must be tried for a capital offense.[30] The Senate has also resolved that it is just that you inscribe this on a bronze plaque and order it to be set up where it can most easily be read. Within ten days of receiving this letter, you shall also ensure the destruction of any existing shrines of Bacchus, other than what is sacred,[31] as prescribed above.

Social disruption continued in southern Italy for a few years after the Senate's action. In 185 there was a serious slave uprising in Apulia in southeastern Italy.

---

[26] *those who are allies*: Italian communities who were in alliance with Rome but retained their local autonomy.

[27] *Latin status*: a status originally granted to allies within Latium, the area close to Rome, that gave greater privileges than the status as ally granted to communities at a greater distance from Rome.

[28] The term 'official' (*magistratus*) has political connotations that underscores the Senate's perception of 'conspiracy.' Note also the anticipation implicit in the measure against those who have the intent of appointing an official.

[29] The legal precision of these various terms covers all aspects of 'conspiracy.'

[30] In imposing the death penalty, the Senate was infringing upon the autonomy of the local magistrates.

[31] *other than what is sacred*: an allusion to the exception made for the ancient altars or consecrated statues mentioned in Livy 39.18.7 in 9.6.

A praetor conducted an investigation into a conspiracy of shepherds whose brigandage was menacing roads and public pastures (Livy 39.29.8-9). This praetor also completed the Bacchic investigation (Livy 39.41.6 and 40.19.9). In 184 and 181 investigations of alleged poisonings were ordered (Livy 39.38.3 and 40.37.4-9). Also in 181, the praetor Lucius Duronius was ordered to investigate Bacchanalia in Apulia where there was an apparent resurgence of the earlier troubles (Livy 40.19.9-10).

All these events had profound religious, political, social and cultural implications. In treating these outbreaks as a political *coniuratio* and instituting a *quaestio extra ordinem*, the Senate was infringing upon the jurisdiction of the local magistrates in the Italian communities and, in effect, declaring a state of emergency throughout Italy. Outbreaks of new forms of Bacchic worship had thus offered an opportunity for the Senate to reassert the political control it had exercised over Italy during the war against Hannibal. Since we hear no more of social disorder in this area until the slave revolt of Spartacus (73-71 BCE), these repressive measures were apparently successful in controlling, if not suppressing, the more extreme forms of Bacchic worship.

The cult of Isis

In the popular religion of the Hellenistic period, the Egyptian goddess Isis was a multi-faceted deity, being worshipped as the 'mistress of the house of life,' the protector of women and marriage, goddess of maternity and the new-born, guarantor of the fertility of fields and the abundance of harvest, and protector of people both by land and sea. Her mysteries date back to the early third century BCE when the Ptolemies adopted the Egyptian practice of brother-sister marriage, identifying themselves with Isis and Osiris.[32] The Ptolemies also introduced the worship of Serapis who was frequently worshipped along with Isis.[33] These two cults became widespread throughout the eastern Mediterranean, particularly in trading areas, and were apparently brought to Campania by Italian merchants in the early first century.

As with the cults of Cybele and of Bacchus, that of Isis seems to have entered Rome during a period of social and political upheaval. Inevitably there was official opposition to a cult that had its own priests, offering through initiation a more personal appeal than the official state cults. Opposition to the cult manifested itself during the politically turbulent years of the so-called First Triumvirate. Orders were given to demolish shrines of Isis in Rome in 59, 58, 53, 50 and 48 BCE, a period when restrictions were also imposed upon political clubs (*collegia*).

Valerius Maximus, writing in the early first century CE, tells of the destruction of shrines in 50 BCE.

9.8 VALERIUS MAXIMUS, *FAMOUS WORDS AND DEEDS* **1.3.4.** When the Senate had decreed that the shrines of Isis and Serapis should be destroyed and none of the

---

[32] *Osiris*: Egyptian consort of Isis, whose Greek counterpart was Dionysus.

[33] *Serapis*: his cult was connected with the dead and thus the underworld.

workmen dared touch them, the consul Aemilius Paullus took off his official robe. Picking up an axe, he struck the doors of the temple.

> The construction of a temple to Isis and Serapis was authorised by the Second Triumvirate: Antony, Lepidus, and Octavian. The temple, however, was not built because of Antony's departure for Egypt and his alliance with Cleopatra. After the suicides of Antony and Cleopatra, who had identified themselves as Osiris and Isis, Augustus' opposition to the cult of Isis was only to be expected. Private Isiac worship, however, evidently continued, as is indicated by references to female devotees of Isis in the poems of Ovid, Propertius and Tibullus. In 19 CE the emperor Tiberius banned Egyptian cults in Rome, razing a shrine of Isis and forcing the priests to burn their holy vestments and religious paraphernalia. But in 43 CE the emperor Claudius, a grandson of Antony, officially established the temple of Isis on the Campus Martius.[34]

> Though at first the cult appealed primarily to non-Romans, during the empire it came to have a more universal appeal to men and women of all social classes. As Takacs has noted: 'Since the worship of the Egyptian goddess had neither the frenzied character of the Great Mother cult... nor the emotional outbursts of the Bacchanalia, Isiac worship did not promote behavior that could be considered asocial by Roman standards.... This highly structured cult could attract some of those who questioned the success of Roman cults and, by extension, that of the state. By providing them 'cultic' stability, it kept them from falling outside state accepted norms.' [35]

> In Apuleius' novel *Metamorphoses*, more generally known as *The Golden Ass*, the protagonist Lucius was turned into an ass and later restored to human form. He was then initiated as a priest of Isis, whereupon he invoked Isis in her various aspects.

9.9 APULEIUS, *METAMORPHOSES* 11.25. Holy and eternal protector[36] of the human race, you who are ever beneficent in nourishing mortals, offering the sweet affection of a mother to the afflictions of the distressed. Neither day nor the restful night nor even the smallest moment passes without your beneficence: you protect people by land and sea and, scattering the storms of life, you stretch out your saving right hand. With this hand you unravel the threads of the Fates even when they are inextricably entangled. You calm the storms of Fortune and restrain the dangerous movements of the stars. The gods above respect you, those below respect you. You rotate the earth, light the sun, rule the universe and tread Tartarus beneath your heel.[37]

For you the stars move, the seasons return, the divine powers rejoice, and the elements are your slaves. At your command, the winds blow, the clouds give nourishment, seeds sprout, and seedlings grow. The birds travelling the sky

---

[34] This became the major temple and was within the *pomerium* after its extension by Claudius.

[35] Takacs (1995) 30-31.

[36] The Latin title *sospitatrix* means protector and thus 'savior.'

[37] *Tartarus*: the underworld, abode of the dead.

are in awe of your majesty, so too the wild beasts wandering the mountains, the snakes that glide on the ground, and the monsters that swim in the deep.

Earlier in the work, Apuleius describes a procession of Isis.

9.10 APULEIUS, *METAMORPHOSES* 11.9-11. And now the special procession of the Savior goddess was moving forward. Women radiant in white garments, rejoicing in their varied finery and garlanded with spring flowers, scattered the flowers held in their arms on the ground along the path where the sacred procession was passing....

Then came a large throng of both men and women with lamps, torches, candles, and other kinds of artificial light, propitiating the goddess who is the source of the heavenly stars. Then came charming music, pipes and flutes creating the sweetest melodies. There followed a beautiful choir of the most select boys, in special snow-white vestments, repeating a lovely song that a skillful poet, inspired by the Muses, had set to music....

A large number of people were shouting out, 'Keep the way clear for the sacred procession.' Then the throngs of those initiated into the divine mysteries flowed by, both men and women, of every age and social class, dazzling in their linen vestments of pure white. The women's hair was anointed and covered with a transparent veil. The men's heads were completely shaven and their bald pates shone brightly, earthly stars of the great religion. In unison, with their *sistra* of bronze and silver and even gold, they made a shrill tinkling noise.[38]

Next came the foremost high priests of the sacred rites, clad in white linen garments wrapped tightly around the chest and reaching down to their feet, as they carried the distinguished emblems of the mightiest gods. The first priest held forth a lamp shining with a bright light .... The second priest wore a similar vestment but in both hands he carried an altar, that is, 'a source of help,' an appropriate name derived from the helping providence of the supreme goddess.[39] A third priest came, holding up a palm-branch with leaves of fine gold and a *caduceus* like that of Mercury.[40] A fourth displayed an emblem of justice, a deformed left hand, its palm outstretched.[41]... He also carried a small gold vessel rounded like a breast from which he poured libations of milk. A fifth carried a gold winnowing basket woven from golden twigs, and a sixth carried a two-handled wine jug.[42]

Immediately after these came gods who deigned to walk with human feet.[43] Here was Anubis, awesome messenger of the gods, both those above the earth and those below, his face now black, now gold, raising high his dog's neck. In his left hand he held a *caduceus*, and in his right he brandished a green palm-

[38] *sistra* (sing. *sistrum*): rattles that were a peculiar feature of the worship of Isis.

[39] For Isis as helper, protector, see n.36.

[40] *Mercury*: a Roman god, who acted as messenger and so carried a special staff, the *caduceus*.

[41] The precise significance of this is obscure.

[42] *winnowing basket*: a basket or sieve used for separating grain from chaff.

[43] *human feet*: people dressed as gods, representing the various deities.

branch.[44] Closely on his footsteps followed a cow lifted in an upright posture, representing the fecundity of the goddess who is the parent of us all. One of the priesthood carried it on his shoulders with proud and rhythmic steps. Another carried a box holding the secret things that concealed within it the mysteries of the glorious religion. Still another held in his blessed arms the revered image of the highest deity. It was not shaped like a farm animal, or a bird, or a wild animal, or even a human, inspiring reverence by a clever discovery and its very strangeness, an ineffable symbol of a deeper sanctity that must be cloaked in silence....

> At this point in the narrative Lucius eats a rose carried by one of the priests and is miraculously restored to his human form. The priest proclaims that the transformation was the work of Isis, the kindly and compassionate goddess. Lucius joins the procession, and is later initiated into her rites.

9.11 APULEIUS, *METAMORPHOSES* **11.22-24.** The courteous aged priest took my right hand and led me to the very doors of the spacious temple. After the ritual of the opening of the temple had been celebrated and the morning sacrifice performed, he brought out from the hidden part of the temple certain books written in unknown characters. Some of them conveyed, through the shapes of all kinds of animals, abridged expressions of liturgical language; others were protected from being read by curious profane readers since the tops of the letters were knotted and curled into the shape of a wheel and intertwined like the tendrils of a vine. From these writings, the priest indicated to me the preparations necessary for my initiation....

Since the occasion now demanded it, as the priest said, he led me with an escort of initiates to the nearby baths and submitted me to the customary ablution. Then, praying for the forgiveness of the gods, he cleansed me with a sprinkling of the purest water. When he had taken me back to the temple in the afternoon, he placed me right in front of the feet of the goddess, giving me certain secret instructions which are too sacred to be revealed. One command, however, he pronounced clearly for all to serve as a witness, ordering me to curb my desire for food for ten consecutive days, abstaining from animal flesh and wine.

I duly maintained this fast with reverent restraint. Finally that day arrived which had been set for my pledge to the goddess. The setting sun brought on the evening star when, behold, throngs of initiates poured in from all directions, honoring me with various gifts, in accordance with their ancient rite. Then, when all the uninitiated had been removed afar, the priest dressed me in a new linen garment, took my hand, and led me into the inmost part of the sanctuary.

Zealous reader, perhaps you are anxious to ask what was said and what was done there. I would tell if it were lawful to say, and you would learn all, if it were lawful for you to hear. But both ears and tongue would then incur equal guilt, the latter from their impious chatter, the former from their rash curiosity.

---

[44] *Anubis*: an Egyptian god who was portrayed with the head of a dog or jackal. He, like Mercury, was a messenger; hence the *caduceus*, see n. 40.

I will not torture you with further anguish since your suspense is probably of a religious nature. Listen then, but believe, for what I say is true.

I approached the boundary of death and, after treading on the threshold of Proserpina,[45] I was carried through all the elements and then returned. In the middle of the night, I saw the sun flashing with brilliant light. I came face to face with the gods who dwell above the earth and those who dwell below, and I worshipped them being close at hand. See, I have told you things which, though you have heard them, you must fail to understand. Therefore, I shall recount only what can be communicated to the understanding of the uninitiated without incurring guilt.

When morning came and the solemn rites had been completed, I came forth wearing twelve shawls as a sign of my consecration, a garb that was indeed most sacred. I'm under no obligation not to mention it because many people who were present on that occasion saw it. I was ordered to stand on a wooden dais that stood in the middle of the temple, in front of the goddess' statue. I attracted attention because of my tunic which, although it was only of linen, was elaborately embroidered.... In my right hand I carried a torch blazing with flames and my head was garlanded with a lovely crown of shining palm with leaves jutting out like rays. When I had been adorned like the sun and set up in the guise of a statue, suddenly the curtains were opened and people wandered in to gaze at me.

Then I celebrated the festal day of my birth and initiation, a delicious feast and a merry party. And the third day, too, was celebrated with a similar ceremonial ritual. There was a sacred meal and my initiation was duly consummated.[46]

Minucius Felix, a Christian writer of the third century CE, comments on various aspects of the cult of Isis.

9.12 MINUCIUS FELIX, *OCTAVIUS* 23.1. Consider the sacred rites of the mystery religions. You will find sorrowful deaths, fates, funerals, grief, and lamentation for the pitiful gods. Isis, along with the Dog-headed Anubis and her bald priests, mourns for her dead son, grieving and searching for him. Her pitiful worshippers beat their breasts and share the sorrows of the unhappy mother. When the boy is found, Isis rejoices, the priests exult, and Anubis exults in his discovery. Year after year, without fail, they lose what they will find, and they find what they have lost. Isn't that ridiculous, either to mourn for the object you worship, or worship the object you mourn for? Yet these Egyptian rites are now Roman.

The cult of Mithras

Another mystery religion which gained currency throughout the Roman world from about 100 CE is the cult of Mithras, which apparently derives

---

[45] *Proserpina*: goddess of the underworld, wife of Pluto. The initiation probably represents a spiritual death and rebirth.

[46] Communal meals were a part of Isiac worship. He remains a few days longer but before departing makes a prayer to the goddess; see 9.9.

from Mithra, an Indo-Iranian divinity who was a god of compact (the literal meaning of his name), cattle-herding and the dawn light. Roman Mithras was a sun god, invoked as the invincible sun god Mithras, bull-killer and cattle-thief. The god is represented as a distinctive figure wearing a Phrygian cap and Persian trousers. The sanctuaries (Mithraea) were the antithesis of the typical temple, being of modest size and resembling caves that were decorated to represent the cosmos. Regularly depicted in these sanctuaries was Mithras slaying a bull.

The precise origins and diffusion of the cult are difficult to discern because of the paucity of evidence. There are very few literary references, the evidence being mostly archaeological: meeting places of the cultists, the largest number of which have been found in Rome itself, inscriptions and sculptural representations that are often difficult to interpret. The question is whether the cult developed from Zoroastrianism or whether it was a western creation with Persian elements. One suggestion is that the cult was acquired from the Hellenized near east and came to Rome as a result of Roman campaigns in Anatolia and Armenia during the reign of Nero. It was open only to men, was especially popular with the military, and does not seem to have appealed to the upper classes. Initiates met in small groups, meeting for a ritual meal. When the group expanded beyond a certain size, a new group would be organized to preserve the intimacy of the individual community. Comparison is often made with the organization and ritual of Masonic Lodges.

There were seven grades of initiation, each of which was under the protection of one of the planets: Raven (Mercury), Bridegroom (Venus), Soldier (Mars), Lion (Jupiter), Persian (Moon), Courier of the Sun (Sun), Father (Saturn). This hierarchy is illustrated in a mosaic on the floor of a sanctuary at Ostia, a dedication by one Felicissimus.[47]

The Christian writer known as Pseudo-Augustine mocks the Mithraic initiation ceremonies.

9.13 PSEUDO-AUGUSTINE, *QUESTIONS ON THE OLD AND NEW TESTAMENTS* 114. Moreover, what about the ludicrous performance that they experience blindfold in the Cave? They are blindfolded in case their eyes shudder at being so disgustingly degraded. Some, like a bird, flap their wings, imitating the cry of a raven. Some roar like lions. Some have their hands bound by chicken-gut and are cast over pits full of water, while someone who calls himself the 'liberator' comes up with a sword and breaks this gut.

Tertullian describes the ritual for initiation into the grade of soldier.

9.14 TERTULLIAN, *THE CROWN OF MARTYRDOM* 15.3-4. The initiation takes place in a Cave, a veritable camp of darkness… a garland [*corona*, garland or crown] is offered to the novice on a sword, a kind of mockery of martyrdom. It is then fitted on his head, but he is instructed to put his hand in the way and cast it from his head, transferring it, if possible, to his shoulder, saying that Mithras

---

[47] For illustrations of the mosaic and Mithras the bull-slayer, see *BNP* 2. 88-91 and 306-7.

is his garland. And from then on he never wears a garland and this is the mark of his initiation, whenever he is put to the test at the oath-taking, and is immediately recognized as a soldier of Mithras, if he casts aside the garland, if he says that the garland lies in his god.

> Several Mithraic texts have been found painted onto the walls of the Mithraeum below the church of Santa Prisca in Rome. Beneath a fresco depicting the seven grades of initiation is the following:

9.15 VERMASEREN AND VAN ESSEN (**1965**) **168-9.** Hail to the Sun-runners under the protection of Sun. [Hail to the Persians under the protection of Moon]. [Hail to Lions] under the protection of Jupiter. Hail to the fierce? Soldiers [under the protection of Mars]. Hail to the Male brides under the protection of Venus.

> The following couplet may be part of Mithraic liturgy and illustrates the connection of the Lions with fire, purification and mediation.

9.16 VERMASEREN AND VAN ESSEN (**1965**) **224.** Accept, Father, accept in holiness the incense-burning Lions, through whom we offer incense, through whom we ourselves are consumed.

GAMES (*LUDI*), RELIGION AND POLITICS

10.1 POLYBIUS 6.56.11. Since every mass of people is fickle and full of lawless desires, irrational passion, and violent anger, it is essential that they be controlled by invisible terrors and suchlike pageantry.

> *Ludi*, games or shows, were held on public festival days (*dies festi*), originally to gain the gods' favor (*pax deorum*) for the state. The gods' statues were paraded through the city before the actual *ludi* began. Thus both gods and humans participated in the festival. As Cicero notes, the Megalesian games were celebrated and held in the very sight of the Magna Mater in front of her temple.[1] In addition to honoring the gods, such festivals offered relaxation, merriment and entertainment in a holiday, carnival-type atmosphere that would 'energise a community and restore mutual confidence.'[2]
>
> The earliest festival of this type was held in honor of Jupiter Optimus Maximus (Best and Greatest), probably originating as a celebration by a victorious general in fulfilment of a vow (votive games). By 366 BCE such celebrations had become the Roman or Great Games (*ludi Romani* or *ludi magni*), an annual festival held on 13 September. By the late republic this festival extended from 5 to 19 September, was organized by public officials, celebrated at public expense, and consisted of athletic sports, chariot racing (*ludi circenses*) and various kinds of dramatic performances or stage shows (*ludi scaenici*).
>
> At the beginning of the Hannibalic War, there were but two sets of annual games, the Roman Games and the Plebeian Games (*ludi plebeii*). During that war, as we have seen, games were instituted in honor of Apollo (*ludi Apollinares*) and the Magna Mater (the Megalesia or *ludi Megalenses*) as part of several attempts to secure the favor of the gods at critical junctures of the war.[3] In 202 we hear of annual games in honor of Ceres (Cerialia), followed by the

---

[1]   Cicero, *On the reply of the haruspices* 24.

[2]   Dowden (1992) 35.

[3]   See 8.12–8.16.

Floralia in honor of Flora in 173. Dramatic performances were a part of many *ludi*. Mimes, for example, were performed at the Floralia.[4]

In the early second century BCE the plays of Plautus and Terence were performed at the various festivals, Plautus' *Stichus* at the Plebeian Games of 200 and *Pseudolus* at the Megalesia in 191. Terence's *Mother-in-Law* was given its first, and unsuccessful, production at the Megalesia of 165.[5] As is apparent from this example, however, Roman drama was less popular than displays of gladiators, entertainments that originally were financed not by the state but by individuals acting in a private capacity. The meager extant sources indicate that by the early second century private enterprise was operating within the religious framework of these festivals. Such private productions were termed *munera* (singular *munus*, the original meaning of which is 'offering' or 'duty') and should be distinguished from the state, or public, games.

Animals were displayed at the various *ludi*. Staged hunts (*venationes*) of foxes, hares and wild goats at the Cerialia and Floralia are the earliest known examples. More exotic creatures, such as elephants, were soon displayed in addition to indigenous animals like bears, bulls, stags and boars. Livy (39.22.2) notes that the first time in Rome that there was a contest of athletes and a lion and leopard hunt was in 186 BCE at the votive games given by the victorious general Marcus Fulvius Nobilior.

Several references to repetition (*instauratio*) of the Roman and Plebeian Games attest their overall popularity. By the late republic seventeen days of April were devoted to games: seven to the Megalesia, eight to the Cerialia and two to the Floralia. Not only did the duration and number of games increase, so too did the expenditure on such shows, with the result that Livy writes that the extravagance was such that the wealth of kings could hardly support such insanity (*insania*).[6]

In charge of the production of the public games were the aediles or urban praetor, men at the beginning of their political careers. By the late republic, these magistrates were using the games as an opportunity for self-advertisement, vying with their predecessors to produce the biggest and best entertainment. Originally the concept had been the greater the expenditure, the more the gods would be pleased and so ensure the *pax deorum*. But consideration of the gods became subordinate to the political ambitions of men who hoped to impress the electorate and so advance their careers. The gods were still included in the games, but the public officials who staged them claimed a large share of the gratitude. The victory games given by Pompey, Caesar and Octavian (later Augustus) exemplify this tendency.

During the empire, the games were controlled by the emperors. Sacrifice and worship of the gods at the various festivals continued but became increasingly marginalised, as the emperors used such occasions for displays of their own

---

[4]   See 6.12.
[5]   See 10.5.
[6]   Livy 7.2.13, see 10.4.

munificence in order to keep the people happy with bread and circuses, as the satirist Juvenal remarks.[7] Frequently present at the ever more popular gladiatorial combats and beast hunts were the emperor and his family, the former generally sponsoring the spectacle.

The video, *The True Story of the Roman Arena* (1993), uses literary and iconographical evidence to show how the Romans became obsessed with spectacular entertainments, especially gladiatorial combats. Although it does not examine the religious aspects of the games, this video emphasises their fascination, noting that the acceptance of Christianity as an official state religion did nothing to diminish the Romans' addiction to these bloody spectacles.

The procession

Dionysius of Halicarnassus describes the procession that preceded the actual games.

10.2 DIONYSIUS OF HALICARNASSUS 7.72.1-13. Before the games started, the chief magistrates organized a procession in honor of the gods which started from the Capitoline, going through the Forum to the Circus Maximus. At the head of the procession came the Romans' sons who were on the verge of manhood and were of an age to take part in the procession. Those whose fathers had the financial qualification to be knights rode on horseback, while the others who were bound to serve in the infantry were on foot. The former went in squadrons and troops, the latter in divisions and companies, as if they were going to training school.[8] The purpose of this was so that strangers might see the number and size of the city's youth that was approaching manhood. The charioteers followed after these, driving four horses or two, while others rode unyoked horses. After them came the contestants in both the light and heavy events.[9]...

The contestants were followed by numerous groups of dancers arranged in three divisions, the first consisting of men, the second of youths and the third of boys. They were accompanied by flute-players who played old-fashioned short flutes, as is done even to this day, and by lyre players who plucked ivory seven-stringed lyres and instruments called 'barbita.'[10] ... The dancers were dressed in red tunics with bronze belts; they had swords at their sides and carried spears that were shorter than the normal length. The men also wore bronze helmets decorated with striking crests and plumes. Each group was led by one man who gave the figures of the dance to the rest, taking the lead in demonstrating the quick military steps, usually in a rhythm of four beats ....

---

[7] See 10.13.

[8] *training school*: evidently this part of the procession was in the form of a military parade, demonstrating that rank in the Roman army was in accordance with wealth.

[9] *light and heavy events*: the latter would include boxing and wrestling, the former races.

[10] *barbita*: the barbiton was a stringed instrument similar to a lyre.

After the armed dancers other dancers paraded, impersonating satyrs and performing the Greek dance called 'sikinnis.' Those impersonating the Sileni wore shaggy tunics that some call 'chortaioi,' and were covered in flowers of every kind. Those who appeared as satyrs wore belts and goat skins, and on their heads manes that stood up, and other such things.[11] They mocked and mimicked the serious dancing that had preceded them, turning it into a comic performance. The entry of triumphal processions also shows that mocking and satyric jesting is an ancient native Roman custom. For the soldiers escorting a victory procession are given the license to mock and satirise the most distinguished men, including even the generals....[12]

After these dancers a crowd of lyre players and large number of flute players paraded. Then came the men who carried the censers in which incense and perfumes were burned along the whole route. Next came the men bearing the gold and silver vessels on display, both those that were sacred to the gods and those that belonged to the state. Last of all in the procession came the statues of the gods, carried on men's shoulders, having much the same appearance as those made by the Greeks, the same dress, same symbols and same gifts which tradition says each of them invented and bestowed on mankind. These were the images not only of Jupiter, Juno, Minerva, Neptune, and the rest whom the Greeks reckon among the twelve gods, but also those still more ancient who mythology tells were their parents: Saturn, Ops, Themis, Latona ....

After the procession was over, the consuls and priests whose function it was sacrificed oxen.

> The poet Ovid has gone to the Circus Maximus more to be with his girlfriend than to watch the games. While waiting for the chariot races, Ovid describes the procession of the gods' statues and comments on the benefactions of the different divinities. Appropriately, the deities to whom he prays are Victory and Venus, the goddess of love.

10.3 OVID, *LOVE AFFAIRS* 3.2.1-6, 43-59. I'm not sitting here because of my enthusiasm for high-bred horses, but I pray that your favorite may win. I came here, in fact, to talk to you and sit beside you so that you would be aware of my love for you. You look at the races, and I'll look at you. Let each of us look at what we love most, and let us both give our eyes a feast.

But look, the procession's coming. Quiet everyone! Pay attention! It's time for applause. The golden procession is coming. First in the parade is Victory, her wings outstretched. Be on my side, goddess, and make my love prove victorious. You people who trust too much in the waves, can applaud Neptune. I have no interest in the sea. I'm a land-lubber. Soldier, you can applaud your god Mars. I hate warfare. Peace is my delight, and the love that is found in the midst of

---

[11] Dionysius is here making a distinction between two mythical Greek creatures: satyrs, who were usually represented as a composite of a young man and a goat, and Sileni, older figures with horse ears. Both creatures are associated with Dionysiac worship.

[12] Descriptions of Roman triumphs corroborate such ribaldry, for example, the triumph of Lucius *Aemilius Paullus* after the battle of Pydna (Plutarch, Aemilius Paullus 34); see section 7.19.

peace. Let Phoebus help the augurs, and Phoebe the hunters.[13] Minerva, turn the hands of the craftsmen to applauding you. Country-dwellers, arise in honor of Ceres and Bacchus. Let the boxer propitiate Pollux, the horseman Castor. It's you that we applaud, sweet Venus, you and your Cupids with their bow. Nod in support of my undertaking, goddess, put the right idea into my girlfriend's mind. May she be enduring of my love.

Look, she nodded and, by her movement, gave a favorable sign.[14] I ask you to promise what the goddess has already promised.

Dramatic performances

Plays (*ludi scaenici*) were performed at the various festivals, including the Megalesia.[15] Livy reports the tradition that stage entertainments were instituted in 364 BCE, after a *lectisternium* had failed to stop an outbreak of plague.

10.4 LIVY 7.2.1-13. The plague lasted during both this and following year.... In the latter year [364 BCE] nothing worthy of note occurred, except that they held a *lectisternium*, the third in the history of the republic, in order to implore the peace of the gods (*pax deorum*). When neither human wisdom nor the help of the gods alleviated the virulence of the disease, men's minds succumbed to superstitious fears (*superstitio*). Among other attempts to appease the anger of the gods, *ludi scaenici* are said to have also been instituted. This was an innovation for a war-like people, whose only public spectacle up to that time had been the circus.[16] But it began in a small way, as most things do, and even so was imported from abroad. Without any singing, without imitating the action of singers, players who had been brought in from Etruria danced to the strains of the flute, performing not ungraceful movements in the Tuscan manner.

The young Romans began to imitate them, exchanging jokes at the same time in unpolished verses, with gestures to fit the words. The practice was adopted and became established by frequent repetition. The native actors were called *histriones*, from *ister* the Tuscan word for player. They no longer alternately tossed off rude improvised lines as before, but performed medleys (*saturae*) that were full of musical measures. Singing was written to go with the flute and was accompanied by appropriate movements. ....

Among the small beginnings of other things, it has seemed necessary also to set out the early origin of drama to show the healthy beginning of something that has now reached a point where the wealth of kings could hardly support such insanity.[17]

---

13 *Phoebus... Phoebe*: Apollo and Diana.

14 Ovid imagines that the statue of the goddess has nodded her assent to his prayer.

15 See 6.5.

16 *circus*: the Circus Maximus, a race track between the Palatine hill and the river Tiber.

17 The Latin yields a contrast between healthy (*sanus*) and the insanity (*insania*) apparent in the games of Livy's own day.

In the prologue to the play *Mother-in-Law*, the playwright Terence (c. 195-159 BCE) describes the problems encountered in performing a play. The producer of the play speaks the prologue, telling how two previous performances could not be completed because the audience went into an uproar, distracted by rival kinds of entertainment, including rumor of a gladiatorial show.

10.5 TERENCE, *MOTHER-IN-LAW* 28-48. For my sake, give a fair hearing to my request. I'm again introducing Terence's play *Mother-in-Law* for which I haven't been able to get a quiet audience. Bad luck has dogged it. Your understanding, however, and your support of my efforts, will put an end to this bad luck. The first time I started to present this play, some famous boxers and then a tightrope walker caused a problem.[18] People formed claques; the uproar and shrieking of women forced us off the stage before the play was over. So, in order to give this new play another chance, I started to use an old trick: I staged it anew. And I held the audience for the first act. But then a rumor spread that some gladiators were going to perform.[19] The people flocked in, pushing, shouting, fighting for a place. In the meantime, I couldn't hold my own ground.

Today there is no disturbance. Everything is calm and quiet. I have been granted the time to stage this play, and you have been given the chance to honor the dramatic performances (*ludi scaenici*). Don't let it be your doing that music and drama falls into the hands the few.[20] Let your support be a support for me, as you favor and assist me...

Gladiators at funeral games

The precise origin of gladiators is unknown. Tradition ascribes them to Etruria, but scholars have also suggested Campanian or Oscan-Samnite origins. Gladiatorial combat is first attested in Rome for 264 BCE, when three pairs of gladiators fought in the Forum Boarium (the cattle market near the river Tiber) as part of funeral games (*ludi funebres*) in honor of a deceased noble, Junius Brutus Pera (Livy *Periocha* 16). In 216 BCE, twenty-two pairs of gladiators were exhibited at the funeral of Marcus Aemilius Lepidus, twenty-five pairs at a funeral in 200 BCE, and sixty pairs in 183 BCE.

Livy's description of the funeral of Flamininus, victor over Philip V of Macedon, indicates the popular appeal of such displays (*munera*) which could also include dramatic performances (*ludi scaenici*), as in the case of Lucius Aemilius Paullus.[21] These *munera* had the advantage of not having to be produced at the time of the original funeral, but could be held at a later date.

10.6 LIVY 41.28.11. Many gladiatorial games were given that year [174 BCE], some of them on a small scale. Above the rest was the show given by Titus Flamininus to commemorate the death of his father. It lasted four days, and

---

18   The first unsuccessful performance of this play was at the Megalesia of 165 BCE.
19   This unsuccessful attempt was at the funeral games for Lucius Aemilius Paullus in 160 BCE.
20   Roman comedies included both music and singing.
21   The second unsuccessful attempt to produce Terence's *Mother-in-Law* was at the funeral of Lucius Aemilius Paullus; see n. 19.

was accompanied by a public distribution of meat, a banquet, and dramatic performances. The climax of the show which was large for its time was that seventy-four gladiators fought over a three-day period.

Increasing politicisation of the games

Julius Caesar's extravagance during his aedileship in 65 BCE indicates how the religious origin of the games had become overshadowed by political considerations as aediles sought to win the support of the people in preparation for their next bid for public office. Note also that a gladiatorial *munus* is a part of the *ludi* produced by Caesar.

10.7 SUETONIUS, *LIFE OF JULIUS CAESAR* **10.** As aedile, Caesar adorned not only the Comitium, the Forum and its basilicas, but also the Capitolium with temporary colonnades to display the abundant material he was going to use. He produced wild animal hunts (*venationes*) and games, some with his colleague Marcus Bibulus, others on his own....

He also gave a gladiatorial show, albeit with somewhat fewer pairs of gladiators than he had intended. For he had so terrified his political enemies with the size of the group he had hired from all over the place that a bill was passed restricting the number of gladiators which anyone was allowed to keep in Rome.[22]

In addition to productions at the traditional public festivals, games were sponsored by prominent figures to commemorate their success. Such productions were an apparent continuation of games offered in fulfillment of a vow (*ludi votivi*), and thus retained a religious component. In 55 BCE, Pompey held games to celebrate the dedication of Rome's first permanent stone theater, a building into which was incorporated a temple to Venus of Victory (Venus Victrix). The temple was built into the seating area in such a way that the goddess overlooked the stage, like the rest of the spectators.[23] Cicero speaks in anticipation of the magnificence of these games.

10.8 CICERO, *AGAINST PISO* **65.** We are approaching the celebration of the most elaborate and magnificent games in the history of man. Unequalled in the past, I can't imagine how they will ever be matched in the future.

At these games, in addition to the customary dramatic performances, music, athletic and gladiatorial contests, Pompey displayed various exotic wild beasts that came from different parts of the empire: lions, leopards, panthers, elephants and such novelties as baboons, a lynx, and an Indian rhinoceros. In a letter to a friend Cicero reveals his private feelings about Pompey's extravaganza. As with the previous passage, emphasis is on the spectacle.

10.9 CICERO, *LETTERS TO FRIENDS* **7.1.** If you ask me, the games were absolutely the most magnificent, though not to your taste; this I infer from my own reactions....

---

[22] The slave revolt of Spartacus (73-71 BCE) had been brutally suppressed only a few years earlier.

[23] Compare Cicero's remark that the Megalesia was performed in the very sight of the Magna Mater in front of her temple (*On the response of the haruspices* 24).

You know what the rest of the games were like. They didn't even have the attraction of ordinary games. The fun was killed by the sight of such magnificence, a magnificence that I am sure you won't regret missing....I don't think you missed anything as far as the Greek and Oscan plays were concerned.... And why should I think that you were sorry to miss the athletes when you were so contemptuous of the gladiators. Pompey himself admits that he wasted both effort and oil on them....

All that remains are the wild-beast hunts (*venationes*), two a day for five days.[24] Magnificent, there's no denying it. But what pleasure can a man of culture get from seeing a feeble human being torn in pieces by a mighty beast, or a fine animal impaled by a hunting spear? And even if this is something that must be seen, you have seen it many a time. I, who did see it, saw nothing new.

> Julius Caesar and Augustus outdid their predecessors in their expenditure on spectacles to entertain and so maintain the support of the masses. After his triple triumph in 46 BCE, Caesar held games to mark the dedication of a new forum, the Forum Julium, and a temple to Venus Genetrix (Mother) as founder of the Julian family. Thus he maintained the connection of gods with games, while also emulating Pompey's temple to Venus Victrix and promoting his family's divine ancestry.

10.10 DIO 43.22.2-23.4. After completing this new forum and the temple to Venus as founder of his family, he dedicated them at this time and celebrated with many contests of all kinds. He built a hunting theater of wood, which was called an amphitheater because it had seats all around and no stage. In honor of this and of his daughter he put on wild beast hunts and gladiatorial combats....[25] Finally he produced a naval battle, not on the sea, nor on a lake, but on land. For he excavated an area of the Campus Martius, flooded it and introduced ships.[26]

> The biographer Suetonius comments on the precedent set by the gladiatorial show that Caesar gave in memory of his daughter.

10.11 SUETONIUS, *LIFE OF JULIUS CAESAR* 26. Caesar announced a gladiatorial show (*munus*) in memory of his daughter, something without precedent. To create the maximum expectation, he had the banquet prepared by his own household as well as letting contracts to outside caterers. He ordered that well-known gladiators who fought without winning the favor of the spectators should be rescued by force and kept alive. He had new gladiators trained.

> In the following excerpt from his own account of his reign, Augustus describes the various entertainments he provided for the people either in his own name or in that of members of his family or other magistrates. By this time the distinction between *ludi* and *munera* was all but obscured.

---

[24] These games were held in the Circus, not the new theater.
[25] These were funeral games in honor of his daughter who had died several years earlier. Compare the gladiatorial combats held at funerals.
[26] This was Rome's first *naumachia*, a mock naval battle, which became a popular form of entertainment in the empire.

10.12 AUGUSTUS, *ACHIEVEMENTS* **22.** I gave three sets of gladiatorial games in my own name and five in that of my sons or grandsons. At these games some ten thousand men took part in combat. Twice in my own name and a third time in that of my grandson I put on for the people a display (*spectaculum*) by athletes who had been brought from all areas. I produced games (*ludi*) in my own name four times and twenty-three times in place of other magistrates. On behalf of the college of *quindecimviri*, as its president, with Marcus Agrippa[27] as my colleague, I produced the Secular Games[28] in the consulship of Gaius Furnius and Gaius Silanus [17 BCE]. In my thirteenth consulship I was the first to produce the games of Mars, which have been given in each succeeding year by the consuls in accordance with a decree of the Senate and by law. I gave beast hunts of African beasts in my own name or in that of my sons and grandsons in the Circus or Forum or amphitheater on twenty-six occasions on which about 3,500 beasts were destroyed.

> In a famous passage the satirist Juvenal, writing in the early second century CE, contrasts the power of the people in the republic with their current lack of political freedom. All they now want is to be fed and entertained.

10.13 JUVENAL, *SATIRE* **10.78-81.** The people that once bestowed commands, consulships, legions and everything else now restrains itself, anxiously desiring but two things: bread and games (*panem et circenses*).

> Juvenal comments on the power of the Circus over the people, as he describes the chariot races at the Megalesian games.

10.14 JUVENAL, *SATIRE* **11.193-201.** There sits the praetor, as if in a triumph, the prey of horseflesh. And, if I may say so without offence to the huge and excessive mob, today the Circus holds all of Rome as its captive. A roar strikes my ear, making me realise that the Green[29] has won. If it had lost, Rome would be as mournful and dumbfounded as when the consuls were defeated in the dust of Cannae.[30]

Mass slaughter at the games: Reactions of a Stoic

> Seneca the Younger (d. 65 CE), an adherent of Stoicism who was the tutor and later advisor of the emperor Nero, writes of his revulsion at the spectacle of common criminals who were put in the arena to kill one another and so provide entertainment for the public.[31]

---

[27] *Marcus Agrippa*: a naval commander to whom Augustus owed his success over Antony and Cleopatra at Actium in 31 BCE and who later became Augustus' son-in-law.

[28] *Secular Games*: these games were to commemorate the passing of a *saeculum*, a period variously reckoned as 100 or 110 years; see 11.12.

[29] *Green*: there were four factions in the Circus, supporting the four racing colors: White, Red, Green and Blue, Green being the color usually favored by the emperor.

[30] *Cannae*: a disastrous Roman defeat during the Hannibalic War.

[31] See 15.4 where Tacitus describes the public execution of Christians after the fire of Rome in 64 CE.

10.15 Seneca the Younger, *Letters* 7.2-5. There is nothing more damaging to good character than attendance at some spectacle. For it is through this thrill that vices more easily creep into your soul. What do you imagine I mean? When I return home, I'm more greedy, more ambitious, more addicted to sensuousness; I am more cruel and inhumane — all because I have been among human beings! Recently by chance I stopped by a midday spectacle expecting amusement, wit, and some relaxation, giving men's eyes a rest from the slaughter of human beings. But it was just the opposite. Whatever fighting had taken place earlier was compassionate in comparison. Now all niceties were put aside and it was pure murder. The combatants have no protection. Their entire bodies are exposed to each other's blows, and no one ever strikes in vain. Most people prefer this to the regular pairs of gladiators or the matches 'by request.' And why not? There is no helmet or shield to deflect the weapon. Why bother with defensive armor or skill? All these simply delay death.

In the morning men are thrown to the lions and the bears; at noon they are thrown to the spectators. The spectators demand that the victorious killers be thrown to those who will kill them, keeping the victor for another butchering. The outcome for every combatant is death. The means are swords and fire.[32] This is what goes on while the arena is supposedly empty....

Come now. Don't you understand that bad examples recoil on the agent?

The dedication of the Colosseum

> The poet Martial wrote a book of epigrams, *On Spectacles*, commemorating the dedication of the Colosseum, or Flavian Amphitheater, in 80 BCE. In honor of this event the emperor Titus gave games over a period of a hundred days. Martial declares that this new building surpasses such traditional wonders of the world as the Egyptian pyramids, the gardens of Babylon, the temple of Diana (Artemis) at Ephesus, the altar of Apollo on Delos and the Mausoleum at Halicarnassus.

10.16 Martial, *On spectacles* 1. Let barbarous Memphis[33] be silent about the wonders of the pyramids; nor let Assyrian labor boast about Babylon; nor let the soft Ionians be praised for the temple of Trivia.[34] Let the altar with its mass of horns keep quiet about Delos; nor let the Carians exalt the Mausoleum[35] to to the skies with immoderate praise, as it hangs in the empty air. Every work yields to the amphitheater of Caesar.[36] Before all the others shall Fame speak of this work alone.

---

[32] If the combatants refused to fight or fled from the arena, the officials had them burned.
[33] *Memphis*: a town in Egypt.
[34] *Trivia*: Diana
[35] *Mausoleum*: tomb of Mausolus of Halicarnassus, one of the wonders of the ancient world.
[36] *amphitheater of Caesar*: the Colosseum was begun by the emperor Vespasian and completed and dedicated by his son Titus.

Martial recognises the presence of the emperor at the games and flatters him by suggesting that even the elephant recognises his divinity.

10.17 MARTIAL, *ON SPECTACLES* **20.** As a dutiful suppliant, the elephant adores you, Caesar, though just now the bull found him so formidable. He does this unbidden, no teacher has schooled him. Believe me, even he recognizes our god.[37]

Games in the late empire

The gladiatorial games retained their fascination well into the late empire. Augustine, writing in the late fourth and early fifth century, tells how his friend Alypius became addicted to gladiatorial combats.

10.18 AUGUSTINE, *CONFESSIONS* **6.8.** Although Alypius was opposed to such spectacles and detested them, some friends and fellow students whom he met by chance as they were coming back from lunch took him to the amphitheater in a friendly show of force. He protested vehemently and resisted, saying, 'Though you drag my body into that place, can you focus my mind and eyes on those spectacles? I'll be present in body, but absent. In this way, I will thus prevail over you and the spectacles....'

When they arrived at the amphitheater and took seats where they could, the whole place was seething with the most savage blood-lust. Alypius closed his eyes and forbade his mind to contemplate such evils. Would that he had shut his ears as well! For, when one of the combatants fell, a huge shout from the entire crowd hit him hard, and he was overwhelmed by curiosity. He opened his eyes, thinking that he was prepared to scorn and prevail over whatever he might see..... As soon as he saw the blood, he drank in its savagery. He did not turn away, but rather fixed his gaze on the sight, and drank in the madness without realising it. He was enthralled by the barbarity of the combat and became drunk with the thrill of blood. No longer was he the man he had been when he arrived, but was one of the crowd that he had joined, a true companion of those men who had taken him there.

What more can I say? He watched, he shouted, he was ablaze, and he took away from the spectacle an insanity that goaded him to return.

---

[37] *god*: on the deification of the emperor, see chapter 11.

BECOMING A GOD

One of the most fascinating features of Roman religion is the deification of a human being, either after his death or during his lifetime. No simple origin or pattern for the deification of prominent Romans can be discerned. The extant sources indicate that the deification of Julius Caesar and subsequent imperial cult have their origins in Rome's contacts with the eastern Mediterranean world, but also in Roman tradition itself. As we have seen, the wearing of funeral masks and impersonation of deceased ancestors implied that the dead lived on, thus marking an important step towards deification.[1] As Beard, North and Price have remarked, 'Every narrative of Roman apotheosis tells, at the same time, a story of uncertainty, challenge, debate and mixed motives.'[2]

Many peoples of the near east were accustomed to regard their rulers as gods, a well-known example being the Egyptian Pharoahs. When Alexander the Great (356-323 BCE) overthrew the Persian Empire, the conquered peoples expected him to accept the divine honors that they traditionally accorded their rulers. Stories circulated that Zeus in the form of a snake had entered the bed of Alexander's mother Olympias and that the oracle of Zeus Ammon in Egypt greeted him as the son of Zeus.[3] Such stories were, of course, politically advantageous.

The biographer Plutarch, writing several centuries after Alexander's death, remarks:

11.1 PLUTARCH, *LIFE OF ALEXANDER* **28.1-6.** Alexander generally conducted himself haughtily towards the barbarians, like a man fully persuaded of his divine birth and parentage, but with the Greeks it was within limits and somewhat rare that he assumed his own divinity .... It is clear that Alexander himself was not conceited or puffed up by the belief in his divinity, but used it for the subjugation of others.

---

[1] See 3.26 on the funeral of a Roman noble.

[2] BNP 1.148.

[3] Plutarch, *Life of Alexander* 2-3 and 27.

The desire to worship an individual as if he were a god was not confined to the politics of kings and military conquerors. A passage from *Acts of the Apostles* (mid-first century CE) relates how, when the apostle Paul had healed a man who had been lame from birth, the people of Lystra in southwest Asia Minor (modern Turkey) thought that he and his disciple Barnabas were gods who had come down from heaven. The official priest of Zeus was with difficulty prevented from offering the customary blood sacrifice in their honor.

11.2 *ACTS OF THE APOSTLES* **14.10-18.** The man leaped up and began to walk. There was a crowd watching what Paul did, and these people called out in the local language: 'The gods have come down to us in the likeness of humans.' So they called Barnabas Zeus and Paul Hermes since he was the chief speaker.[4]

And the priest of Zeus, whose temple was outside the city, brought bulls and garlands to the gates, wanting to hold a sacrifice with the crowd. But when Barnabas and Paul heard this, they tore their clothes, and rushed out into the crowd, saying: 'Why are you doing this? We are human beings too, of a nature like your own, preaching that you should turn away from these empty ways to the living god....' But even with these words, they had difficulty in stopping the crowds from performing the sacrifice to them.

God-like status for a day: the Roman triumph[5]

Nowhere is the elevation of a prominent Roman individual to the level of the gods more evident than in the Roman triumph, when the triumphing general 'impersonated' Jupiter, albeit only for one day.[6] Pliny (*Natural History* 33.111) notes that on festal days the face of the statue of Jupiter himself was painted with red lead and likewise the body of the triumphing general.

11.3 ZONARAS, *EPITOME* **7.21.** Dressed in triumphal garb, with bracelets on his arms and a crown of laurel on his head, and holding a branch in his right hand, he summoned the people. Then he praised the soldiers who had served under him, both collectively and in some cases individually, and gave them gifts of money and honored them also with military decorations.... Much of the booty was also distributed to the soldiers who had served in the campaign. However, some triumphing generals also gave it to the entire populace, defraying the expenses of the triumph and making the booty public property. If any was left over, they spent it on temples, porticoes, and other public works. When these ceremonies had been completed, the general mounted his chariot. This chariot, however, was not like a racing chariot or a war chariot; it was constructed to resemble a round tower. The general did not stand alone in the chariot, but, if he had children or relatives,

---

[4]   Hermes (Roman Mercury) was the messenger of the gods; Zeus (Roman Jupiter) the king of the gods. Asia Minor, though at this time part of the Roman empire, remained hellenized; hence the equation with Greek rather than Roman gods.

[5]   See 7.19, for an account of the triumph of Lucius Aemilius Paullus.

[6]   Cf. the nobles' impersonation of their ancestors by the wearing of masks at funerals; see 3.26 with n.33.

A Roman triumph: drawing of scene on a silver cup found at Boscoreale near Pompeii, showing the future emperor Tiberius mounted in a chariot with a slave holding a crown over Tiberius' head.

he took the girls and male infants in the chariot with him and put his older male relatives on the chariot horses. If there were a large number of relatives, they rode in the procession on horses, as out-riders for the general. None of the other people in the triumph was mounted; all marched along wearing laurel wreaths. However, a public slave rode in the chariot with the general, holding above his head a crown with precious gems set in gold. The slave kept saying to him, 'Look behind!' – a clear warning to consider the future and events yet to come, and not to become haughty and arrogant because of present events. ...

Thus arrayed, they entered the city. At the head of the procession were the spoils and trophies.... When the men ahead of him had reached the end of the procession, the general was finally escorted into the Roman Forum. He ordered some of the captives to be taken to the prison and executed. He then drove up to the Capitol, where he performed certain religious rites and made offerings. He then dined in the porticoes nearby. Toward evening he was escorted to his home to the accompaniment of flutes and Pan's pipes.

The 'divine connections' of Scipio Africanus

Two stories told about Scipio Africanus, the victor over Hannibal in 201 BCE, reflect a combination of Greek and native Roman influences. The legend of Scipio's miraculous conception gave him an affinity with Alexander the Great whose history would have been well-known to Romans in the late third and early second century.[7] Scipio also is said to have cultivated a special relationship with Jupiter Capitolinus.

11.4 Aulus Gellius, *Attic nights* 6.1.1-6. The Greek historians recorded that the mother of the elder Scipio Africanus[8] had the same experience as Olympias, wife of King Philip and mother of Alexander the Great.[9] For Gaius Oppius and Julius Hyginus[10] and other writers on Africanus' life and achievements relate

---

[7]   See 11.1 with comments.

[8]   *elder Scipio Africanus*: the victor over Hannibal, as opposed to Scipio Aemilianus, victor in the Third Punic War and destroyer of Carthage, who is also known as Africanus.

[9]   Philip II of Macedon ruled 359-336 BCE.

[10]   *Gaius Oppius and Julius Hyginus*: historians whose work no longer survives.

that his mother had long been believed sterile and that her husband had also given up hope of children. Then, when her husband was absent and she was sleeping on her own, a huge snake was suddenly seen lying by her side, in her room and in her bed. When those who saw the snake shouted out in terror, it glided away and could not be found. Scipio himself consulted the *haruspices* and they, after sacrificing, replied that children would be born. Not long after the snake had been seen in her bed, the woman began to show and experience the signs of pregnancy. In the tenth month, she gave birth to Publius Africanus, the man who defeated Hannibal and the Carthaginians in the Second Punic War.

But it is much more because of his achievements than because of this portent that Scipio is also [sc. as well as Alexander] thought to be a man of godlike excellence (*virtus divina*). It also is worth noting that the authorities mentioned above record that this same Africanus used to go up on to the Capitol in the latter part of the night and order the shrine of Jupiter to be opened for him. He would remain there for a long time, as though he was consulting with Jupiter about matters of state. The custodians of the temple were often amazed that Scipio was the only man at whom the temple dogs never barked or rushed, though they always were enraged at anybody else.

The Roman victor Flamininus is honored as 'Savior' by the Greeks[11]

> In 200 BCE, less than two years after the war against Hannibal, the Romans invaded the eastern Mediterranean, an area where the peoples were accustomed to revering their conquerors as gods. Flamininus, victorious over Philip V of Macedon in 196, was granted rituals in the Greek city of Chalcis that were still performed in Plutarch's own time three hundred years later.

11.5 PLUTARCH, *LIFE OF FLAMININUS* 16.3-4. Even in our own day a priest of Titus [Flamininus] is elected and appointed and after sacrifice and libations in his honor, they sing a set hymn. Because of its length I shall not quote it in its entirety, but only the closing words of the song: 'we revere the trust (*pistis*) of the Romans, cherished by our solemn vows. Sing, maidens, to Zeus the Great, to Roma,[12] to Titus and the trust of the Romans. Hail Paean Apollo.[13] Hail Titus our savior.'

The deification of Romulus

> Livy, writing in the early years of Augustus' regime, reports the story of Romulus' mysterious death and his subsequent deification, a tradition that

---

[11] *Savior*: this title refers to protection, well-being and safety in this life, not to any hope of redemption or an afterlife.

[12] *Roma*: the cult of the goddess Roma began in Smyrna (modern Izmir in Turkey) in 195 BCE at the request of this city, which was seeking a way of advertising her ties with Rome. This cult was not adopted in Rome itself until the reign of Hadrian.

[13] *Paean Apollo*: Apollo is here addressed as healer and thus savior.

goes back at least as far as the poet Ennius (239-169 BCE). Livy's account has unmistakable allusions to the assassination of Julius Caesar and the subsequent proclamation of his deification by Octavian, his great-nephew who ultimately became Augustus. Close reading of Livy's account, especially the cumulative effect of such comments as 'I believe,' 'it is said,' 'as the story goes,' and 'it is amazing...' implies his skepticism about these stories.

11.6 LIVY 1.16. After these immortal deeds, Romulus was holding an assembly of the people on the Campus Martius to review the army when suddenly a storm arose with loud claps of thunder, enveloping him in a cloud so dense that it hid him from the view of the people. Thereafter Romulus was no longer on earth. The Roman people finally recovered from their panic when a bright and sunny day returned after the storm. When they saw that the king's seat was empty, although they readily believed the assertion of the senators who had been standing nearby that he had been snatched up on high by the storm, they nevertheless remained sorrowful and silent for some time, stricken with fear as if they had been orphaned. Then, on the initiative of a few men, they all decided that Romulus should be hailed as a god, son of a god, king and father of the city of Rome.[14] With prayers they begged his favor (*pax*), beseeching him to be willing and propitious toward the Roman people and to protect their descendants forever.

There were some even then, I believe, who privately claimed that the king had been torn in pieces by the hands of the senators. This rumor also spread, though in obscure terms. Men's admiration and their current panic, however, gave currency to the other version. And it is said that it gained additional credence because of the device of one man. For, when the state was troubled by the loss of the king and in a hostile mood towards the Senate, Proculus Julius,[15] a man of authority as the story goes (he was after all vouching for a matter of importance), addressed the people. 'My fellow citizens,' he said, 'Today at dawn Romulus, the father of this city, suddenly descended from the sky and appeared before me. Overcome with fear and awe, I stood there, begging him with prayers that it might be lawful (*fas*) for me to gaze on him. And he said, "Depart, and proclaim to the Romans that it is the gods' will that my Rome be the capital of the world. So let them cultivate the art of war, let them know and teach their descendants that no human strength has the power to resist the arms of Rome." With these words,' Proculus concluded, 'Romulus departed on high.'

It is amazing what credence was given to this man's story, and how the grief felt by the people and the army for the loss of Romulus was alleviated by belief in his immortality.

---

14 *as a god*: the deified Romulus was given the name Quirinus.
15 *Proculus Julius*: here allusion to the Julian family, Caesar and his adopted son Octavian, becomes explicit. Compare the accounts of Octavian's actions after Caesar's death (see 11.7-11.9) with those here attributed to Proculus Julius. The name Proculus Julius, only attested in this story, can hardly be coincidental.

The deification of Julius Caesar

At the time of his assassination on the Ides of March 44 BCE, Julius Caesar was *pontifex maximus*, augur, consul for the fifth time, and dictator for life (*dictator perpetuus*), an accumulation of offices that illustrates the close connection between politics and religion. The claim that the Julian family was descended from Venus had been memorialised in the newly-built temple of Venus Genetrix (Venus the Mother) and on coins. Caesar had celebrated four triumphs, over Gaul, Egypt, Pontus and Africa, and had also been granted the privilege of wearing the costume of a triumphing general on all public occasions. This honor had earlier been granted to Lucius Aemilius Paullus, the victor over Perseus of Macedon, and to Pompey after his victories in the east, thus extending the association of the human and the divine beyond the day of the actual triumph.

That there were at least plans to deify Julius Caesar during his lifetime is suggested by Cicero in a speech delivered in late 44 BCE, where he makes bitter reference to the 'deified Julius' (*divus Julius*) being granted a priest (*flamen*) and other honors pertaining to divine status (*Philippic* 2.110).

The biographer Suetonius reports Caesar's death and subsequent deification.

11.7 SUETONIUS, *LIFE OF JULIUS* 88. He died in the fifty-sixth year of his life and was received into the number of the gods, not only by the words of those who decreed it but also by the conviction of the common people. For at the games which Caesar's heir Augustus established in honor of his deification and celebrated for the first time, a comet blazed for seven days in a row.... It was believed that it was the soul of Caesar who had been received into heaven. For this reason a star is added to his statue on his forehead.

Pliny the Elder has preserved a statement from Augustus' own Memoirs, written some twenty years after the event, concerning the appearance of a comet at games held soon after Julius Caesar's death.[16]

11.8 PLINY, *NATURAL HISTORY* 2.93-4. On the very days of my games [in honor of Venus Genetrix] a comet was visible for seven days in the northern region of the sky.... The common people believed that this star signified that the soul of Caesar had been received among the spirits (*numina*) of the immortal gods. Therefore, the emblem of a star was added to the head of a statue of Caesar that I dedicated soon afterwards in the Forum.

The historian Dio reports the same event.

11.9 DIO 45.7.1. However, when a certain star appeared in the north towards evening throughout all these days, some called it a comet, claiming that it portended the usual things. The majority, however, did not believe this, but attributed it to Julius Caesar, saying that he had been made immortal and was

---

[16] Ramsay and Licht (1997) 48-57 present a convincing case that the comet heralding the apotheosis of Julius Caesar appeared during funeral games celebrated in honor of Caesar by Octavian at the festival of Venus Genetrix in late July 44 BCE.

numbered among the stars. Octavian derived confidence from this and set up in the temple of Venus a bronze statue of Caesar with a star above his head.

> In 42 BCE the triumvirs Antony, Marcus Aemilius Lepidus and Octavian began the construction of a temple to the deified Julius in the Roman Forum. This temple was dedicated by Octavian soon after his victorious return from Egypt in 29 BCE.

11.10 Dio 47.18.4-19.2. They [the triumvirs] laid the foundations of a shrine to Julius Caesar as a hero in the forum on the spot where he had been cremated, and had an image of him together with one of Venus carried in the procession at the Circus games....[17] And they forced everyone to celebrate his birthday by wearing laurel and by merry-making.... Moreover, they forbade any likeness of him to be carried at the funerals of his relatives, just as if he truly was a god.... And they ruled that no one who took refuge in his shrine to secure immunity should be dragged away from there – a distinction that had never been granted to any of the gods except those worshipped in the time of Romulus.

The aftermath of Caesar's deification: from Octavian, son of a god, to the deified Augustus[18]

> Sometime after mid-November 44 BCE, Cicero noted that Octavian had taken an oath in a speech to the people, swearing in the name of 'his hopes of attaining his father's honors' as he stretched out his hand towards Caesar's statue (Letters to Atticus 16.15.3). Subsequent events illustrate that Octavian's ambition was not confined to emulation of Caesar's political honors. Since Caesar was now officially a god, Octavian, his adopted son and heir, became the son of a god (*divi filius*) and styled himself as such on coins. Soon after Caesar's assassination, Sextus Pompey, son of Pompey the Great, issued coins depicting his father as Neptune. He held triumphal spectacles and mock naval battles, representing himself as adopted son of Neptune. During his struggle with Sextus Pompey, Octavian took up the theme, representing himself as the god Neptune, a nice variant on the concept of *evocatio*. Thus, the conflict between Caesar and Pompey was replayed, with their heirs presenting themselves as the adopted sons of gods.[19]
>
> After the defeat of Sextus Pompey and the enforced retirement of Lepidus, a clash between Antony and Octavian became increasingly inevitable. At first Antony had represented himself in the guise of Hercules. But after the battle of Philippi and his first visit to Asia Minor, he chose to style himself as Dionysus, issuing coins depicting himself with a crown of ivy. After 37 BCE, when he was openly living with Cleopatra who had borne his children, he played Osiris to her Isis. Octavian responded by developing an association

---

[17] *hero*: the Greek equivalent of *divus*, showing the distinction between *deus* and *divus*; see n. 18.

[18] Price (1984) 220: 'the category of *divus* (deified, divine) emerged to distinguish the emperor from gods (*deus*) and mortals.'

[19] For details, see Zanker (1988) 53-57 and *BNP* 2.223-5.

with Apollo, vowing a temple to that god on the Palatine hill that he ultimately dedicated in 28 BCE.

Octavian acquired three major priesthoods before he had reached the age of thirty, becoming pontifex in 48, augur in 41/0, and one of the board of fifteen (*quindecimviri sacris faciundis*) c. 37 BCE. He waited, however, for Lepidus' death in 12 BCE, before assuming the office of *pontifex maximus* that Lepidus had seized after Caesar's death. Nonetheless, Augustus' accumulation of religious offices added to his political *auctoritas*, as also did his promotion of the cult of the deified Julius and the building of the temple of Apollo.

After the defeat of Antony and Cleopatra and his return to Rome, Octavian took the name Augustus. The historian Florus, writing in the late second century CE, remarks 'as if the name alone had already conferred divinity on him' (Florus 2.34.66). On the assumption of this title, Augustus himself wrote:

11.11 *ACHIEVEMENTS OF THE DEIFIED AUGUSTUS* **34.** In my sixth and seventh consulships [28 and 27 BCE], after I had put an end to the civil wars, when I had attained supreme power by universal consent, I transferred the state from my own power to the control of the Roman Senate and people. For this service of mine I was named Augustus by decree of the Senate, and the doorposts of my house were publicly wreathed with laurel, a civic crown was fixed over my door, and a golden shield was set up in the Julian senate house which, as attested by the inscription, was given me by the Senate and Roman people on account of my courage, clemency, justice and piety.[20]

> Ten years after he assumed this title, Augustus held a religious festival that is known as the Secular Games. There was a tradition in Rome that games should be held to commemorate the end of a *saeculum*, a period or either 100 or 110 years that supposedly represented the longest period of human life. Augustus fixed the end of the current *saeculum* in 17 BCE, and the poet Horace composed the *carmen saeculare* (Secular Hymn) for the occasion. An inscription survives giving details of the rituals enacted at this festival which included formal sacrifices to a multiplicity of gods, dramatic performances (*ludi scaenici*), banquets, choral singing and circus games.[21]
>
> In his *Achievements*, Augustus briefly refers to the Secular Games, noting that he celebrated them as head of the college of quindecimvirs.

11.12 *ACHIEVEMENTS OF THE DEIFIED AUGUSTUS* **22.** On behalf of the college of *quindecimviri*, as its president (*magister*), with Marcus Agrippa as my colleague,[22] I produced the Secular Games.

---

[20] *civic crown*: a wreath made of oak, a tree sacred to Jupiter.

[21] For excerpts from this inscription, see *BNP* 2.140-44.

[22] Marcus Agrippa had been Augustus' naval commander in the campaigns against Sextus Pompey and against Antony and Cleopatra. In 21 BCE, he had married Augustus' daughter Julia, and became the father of two sons whom Augustus adopted as his heirs.

At the end of his life Augustus listed the religious offices he held.

11.13 *ACHIEVEMENTS OF THE DEIFIED AUGUSTUS* **7.** I was *pontifex maximus*, augur, belonged to the colleges of fifteen (*quindecimviri*) and of the seven in charge of feasts (*septemviri epulonum*), was an Arval Brother, *sodalis Titius*, and a *fetialis*.[23]

> Suetonius, writing of Augustus' assumption of the office of *pontifex maximus*, notes that he took control of the Sibylline books, purging and transferring them from the temple of Jupiter on the Capitoline to the temple of Apollo that he had constructed on the Palatine.[24]

11.14 SUETONIUS, *LIFE OF AUGUSTUS* **31.** After he had finally assumed the office of *pontifex maximus* ... he collected whatever prophetic writings of Greek or Latin origin were in circulation anonymously or under the names of unreliable authors and burned more than 2,000 of them, retaining only the Sibylline books and making a review even of these. He deposited them in two gilded cases under the pedestal of the Palatine Apollo....

> Ovid writes of Augustus' assumption of the office of *pontifex maximus*, alluding to his kinship with Vesta.[25]

11.15 OVID, *FASTI* **3.419-28.** To [Augustus] Caesar's countless titles—which did he prefer to earn?—was added the pontifical office. The divinity (*numina*) of eternal Caesar presides over the eternal fire [of Vesta]. You see the pledges of empire close by. Gods of ancient Troy, worthy prize for him who carried them, whose burden kept Aeneas safe from the enemy, a priest born of Aeneas' line tends your kindred divinities.[26] Vesta, guard his kindred head.[27] Tended by his sacred hand, live well you fires. Live undying, both flame and leader, I pray.

> When he finally assumed that office, Augustus imported the cult of Vesta into his own home on the Palatine, making a part of his house public property (Dio 54.27.3). Ovid honors this new Vesta of the Palatine at the end of the fourth book of the *Fasti*, hailing Augustus as one of three gods within his Palatine house.[28]

11.16 OVID, *FASTI* **4.949-54.** O Vesta, win the day! Vesta has been received in the home of her kinsman. This is what the Senate has justly decreed. Phoebus

---

[23]   The college of Arval Brothers was revived by Augustus; for the Arval hymn, see 4.3. The office of *sodalis Titius* is obscure. On the fetial priests, see Glossary.

[24]   Some scholars would date the transfer to the dedication of the temple in 28 BCE.

[25]   *kinship with Vesta*: Augustus claimed descent from Venus through his adoptive father Julius Caesar, and thus through Venus from Jupiter. Vesta (Greek Hestia) was the daughter of Saturn, hence sister of Jupiter.

[26]   *gods of ancient Troy ... kindred divinities*: the Vestal fire and Penates that Aeneas is said to have brought from Troy; see Vergil, *Aeneid* 2. 293-7.

[27]   *kindred head*: an allusion to the Julian connection with Troy, through the parents of Aeneas, Venus and Anchises, the latter being a prince of Troy.

[28] The original temple of Vesta remained in the Forum. Augustus established another shrine in his own house so that he would not have to live in the official house of the *pontifex maximus* in order to perform his new duties.

[Apollo] holds a part, a second part has been given over to Vesta, what remains, he himself [Augustus] holds as the third party. Long live the laurels of the Palatine! Long live the house wreathed with oak boughs! A single house holds three eternal gods.

> Ovid bids Vesta admit the gods that Aeneas brought from Troy, while also alluding to Augustus' position as pontifex maximus, his political position and his divinity.

11.17 OVID, FASTI 1.528-30. Vesta, admit the Trojan gods. The time will come when the same individual will protect you and the world, and when the sacred rites will be conducted by one who is himself a god.

> Augustus was not formally deified until after his death, although he received cult honors during his lifetime in areas outside of Rome, and his Genius and Lar were worshipped in the city itself.[29] Following the precedent set by the triumvirs in the deification of Julius Caesar, deification required a decree of the Senate after submission of the proposal usually by the successor of the deceased emperor. Tacitus tersely notes Augustus' deification.

11.18 TACITUS, ANNALS 1.10. But when his burial had been completed according to custom, a temple and deification were decreed in his honor.

> The historian Dio, writing in the early third century CE, remarks on the beginnings of imperial cult.

11.19 DIO 51.20.6-8. Augustus meanwhile, among other business, allowed precincts in Ephesus and Nicaea to Roma and to his father, Caesar, naming him the Hero Julius. These were the leading cities of Asia [Minor] and Bithynia at this time. He ordered the Romans living among them to honor these divinities. But he permitted foreigners (whom he styled Greeks) to consecrate precincts to himself, the Asians in Pergamon and Bithynians at Nicomedia. That is where this started and has been continued under other emperors, not only among Greek nations, but among all others subject to Roman rule. In Rome itself and the rest of Italy, no one, no matter how worthy of renown, has dared to do this. However, when they die, even in Rome those that ruled with integrity are granted various divine honors and *heroa* [hero's shrines] are built to them.

Deification of later emperors

> In contrast to Augustus, who had allowed the people in the provinces to establish a cult in his honor that was often combined with that of the goddess Roma, Tiberius declared himself opposed to such practices.[30]

11.20 SUETONIUS, LIFE OF TIBERIUS 26. Tiberius forbade temples or priesthoods to be established in his name. He then forbade statues and busts to be set up without his permission, permitting them on one condition alone, that they

---

29 *Genius*: a special guardian spirit, almost a divine double, of an individual, usually male, often the *pater familias* himself.

30 Of the emperors in the first century CE, Tiberius, Caligula, Nero, and Domitian were not deified.

not be placed among images of the gods but only among the adornments of temples. He vetoed a proposal that oaths be sworn to ratify his actions, as well as a proposal that the name Tiberius be given to the month of September and that of Livia to October.[31]

Claudius was the first emperor since Augustus officially to be granted divine honors.

11.21 SUETONIUS, *LIFE OF CLAUDIUS* **46.** Claudius was buried with the solemn pomp appropriate to an emperor, and was enrolled among the gods. The main omens of his death included the rise of a long-haired star, known as a comet, lightning striking his father's tomb, and a high death rate among magistrates of all ranks.

11.22 SUETONIUS, *LIFE OF NERO* **9.** Nero started off with a show of filial dutifulness, giving Claudius a lavish funeral. He delivered the funeral oration in person and deified him.[32]

The Pumpkinification of Claudius, a satire written probably by Seneca the Younger, Nero's former tutor and subsequent advisor, illustrates not only the political nature of deification but also the skepticism with which many must have regarded the Senate's decision to deify him.

This skit on the question of Claudius' admission to Olympus parodies the procedure of the Senate, the gods and Claudius himself. The gods are divided on the issue which is finally decided by the deified Augustus who rejects Claudius' claim after listing his crimes. Although this satirical treatment of the gods might seem sacrilegeous or blasphemous to the modern mind, such a presumption underscores the complexity of the concept of divus.

11.23 SENECA? *PUMPKINIFICATION OF CLAUDIUS* **9.** Jupiter finally realised that the senators were not allowed to express opinions or take part in debate so long as non-members were loitering in the senate house. 'Gentlemen,' he said, 'I gave you permission to ask questions, but all you have done is to talk absolute rubbish. I require you to obey the rules of the Senate. What will this man (whoever he is) think of us?' So Claudius was sent out, and Father Janus was the first to be asked to give his opinion. He was the consul designate, scheduled to hold the office for the afternoon of the following first of July,[33] and a shrewd fellow who always looks 'backwards and forwards at the same time.'[34]

---

[31] *Livia*: the mother of Tiberius and widow of Augustus, who was later deified by her grandson, the emperor Claudius. Months had earlier been named after Julius Caesar (July) and Augustus (August).

[32] Subsequently, however, Nero neglected and then abolished the cult which was soon restored by Vespasian.

[33] *consul designate...*: the consul designate had the right to speak first in a senatorial debate. Here Seneca is also criticizing the short-term appointments to the consulship which contrasted with the year-long elected terms of the republic.

[34] *backwards and forwards...*: a quotation in Greek from Homer, describing one who can see both the past and the future. The allusion is particularly apt, since the Roman god Janus was represented with two faces, each facing in opposite directions.

He spoke eloquently at some length because he lives in the Forum,[35] but the stenographer couldn't keep up with him. Therefore I'm missing this out, so as not to misquote what he said. He had a lot to say about the greatness of the gods, declaring that the honor should not be handed out to every Tom, Dick and Harry. 'At one time,' he said, 'it was a great thing to be made a god, but now you have made the distinction a farce. So that my remarks don't seem to be directed at a particular individual, rather than the issue, I propose that from this day onwards no one shall be made a god from those who eat the fruits of the earth or whom the fruitful earth nourishes.[36] Anyone who, contrary to this decree of the Senate, is named or depicted as a god shall be handed over to the evil spirits and given a thorough beating amidst the new gladiators at the next public spectacle.'

> Vespasian, who became emperor after Nero's death in the so-called year of the four emperors, had a sense of humor that suggests a cynicism about his deification.

11.24 SUETONIUS, *LIFE OF VESPASIAN* **23.** Not even the fear of imminent death stopped him from joking.... At the approach of death, he said: 'O dear! I think I'm becoming a god.'

> Dio describes the stage managing of a funeral in honor of the emperor Pertinax who had died several months earlier in 193 CE. This passage shows how Septimius Severus, who had become emperor after a military coup, was using the traditional funeral and symbolic deification of Pertinax to legitimise his claim to the throne.[37]

11.25 DIO **75.4.2-5.5.** Despite the lapse of time since his death, his funeral was celebrated as follows. A wooden platform was constructed in the Roman Forum near the Rostra. On it a shrine of gold and ivory was set up.... Inside there was a bier of the same materials.... and on the bier was a wax effigy of Pertinax laid out in the dress of triumphing general....

When the whole procession [of images of the famous Romans of old] had passed by, Severus went up on the Rostra himself and read out a eulogy of Pertinax.... [the bier was then taken to the Campus Martius]. There a pyre had been built in the form of a three-storey tower.... The funerary offerings were thrown inside this pyre and the bier placed onto it. Severus and members of his family then kissed the effigy of Pertinax....

Finally the consuls set fire to the structure and, when this was done, an eagle flew up from the pyre. In this way Pertinax was made immortal.

---

[35] The temple of Janus was close to the Forum, the traditional place for the delivery of speeches (hence forensic oratory).

[36] Seneca is again quoting Homer.

[37] See 3.26 for Polybius' description of the traditional funeral of a Roman noble.

Magic, the Occult and Astrology

12.1 PLINY THE ELDER, *NATURAL HISTORY* 30.12. It is certain that magic has left traces also among the Italic peoples, in our Twelve Tables, for example, and in other sources.... It was only in the 657th year of the city when Gnaeus Cornelius Lentulus and Publius Licinius Crassus were consuls [97 BCE] that a senatorial decree was passed banning human sacrifice, which shows that these monstrous rites were still performed down to that time.[1]

12.2 PLINY THE ELDER, *NATURAL HISTORY* 28.19. There is no one who does not fear being spell-bound by malevolent prayers.[2]

> Two excerpts from the eighth of the Laws of the Twelve Tables indicate concern about the effects of spells and incantations that we would call 'black magic.' The casting of spells on the crops of a neighbor was expressly forbidden and the death penalty was prescribed for spells cast upon another human being.[3]

12.3 ROL 3.474-475. If any person has sung or composed against another person a song (*carmen*) such as was causing slander or insult to another.... he shall be clubbed to death.

No one shall take away the harvest of a neighbor by reciting spells.[4]

> Pliny the Elder, writing in the mid-first century CE, reports how a freedman who was more successful in farming than his neighbors was prosecuted for sorcery, evidently under the Law of the Twelve Tables.

---

[1] For an example of human sacrifice during the Hannibalic War, **see 7.15.**

[2] *spell-bound*: the Latin word is *defigi*, the technical term for invoking curses by means of tablets (*defixiones*).

[3] The vocabulary of these laws is particularly significant. The Latin *carmen* means a song, poem, or ritual formula which was usually 'sung.' Compare the word 'chant' and its derivative 'enchant,' from the Latin *cantus*, a song, especially an oracular song or incantation. Another reference to this prohibition uses the phrase *malum cantum incantare,* to intone an evil incantation.

[4] *reciting spells*: the verb *excantare* literally means to enchant away.

12.4 PLINY THE ELDER, *NATURAL HISTORY* 18.41-43. A freedman, Gaius Furius Cresimus, reaped from a small field a harvest much more abundant than his neighbors did from their vast properties. So he was much envied and suspected of having attracted the harvests of others by evil spells (*veneficiis*). And so the curule aedile, Spurius Albinus, appointed a day for his trial.[5]

Fearing that he would be convicted when it came to a vote, Furius transported all his farming equpment to the Forum and brought in his entire household (*familia*) who, according to Piso,[6] were well cared for and well dressed, together with well-made tools, heavy pickaxes, weighty plowshares and well-fed oxen.

Then he said, 'These are my evil spells (*veneficia*), citizens. But I cannot show or bring to the Forum my late hours, my sleeplessness, and my sweat.' So he was unanimously acquitted.

> We have already seen that a law of the Twelve Tables addressed the problem of spells and incantations, prescribing the penalty of death. The Cornelian law of 81 BCE addressed the problem of sudden deaths that might be attributable to poison or other clandestine means, specifying witchcraft or sorcery (*veneficium*) as a capital crime. The word *veneficium* literally means the making (*fic-*) of *venenum,* a word that can mean poison but is more precisely rendered as 'potion.' In a commentary on the Cornelian law, the third century CE jurist Paul writes:

12.5 PAUL, *OPINIONS* 5.23.14-19 (*FIRA* II 409-10). But if a woman or a man dies from a potion, those who are responsible for administering it receive the supreme penalty. Those who have performed or commissioned impious or nocturnal rites for the purpose of casting a spell, bewitching, or binding someone, are either crucified or thrown to the beasts.[7] Those who sacrifice a human being, take auspices with human blood, or pollute a shrine or temple are thrown to the beasts or, if they are of superior rank, executed.

It is decreed that those who are knowledgable in the art of magic are to receive the supreme penalty, that is, to be thrown to the beasts or crucified. But the magicians themselves are to be burnt alive. No one may possess books on the art of magic. Those found in possession of such books will have their property confiscated and their books burnt in public; they are deported to an island or, if of inferior rank, executed. Not only the practice of this art, but also the knowledge of it, is prohibited.

If someone dies from a potion that was administered for their health or as a cure, the person who administered it is, if of superior rank, banished to an island or, if of inferior rank, executed.

---

[5] *Spurius Albinus*: a man of this name was one of the consuls in 186 BCE, the year of the Senate's decree on Bacchanalia. Hence it is suggested that this incident dates to a few years earlier, when Albinus was a junior magistrate.

[6] *Piso*: L. Calpurnius Piso Frugi, an early Roman historian who was consul in 133 BCE.

[7] These and the ensuing distinctions of punishment were applicable during the empire rather than the republic.

Magical cures

Cato the Elder records some incantations for healing a dislocation.

12.6 CATO, *ON AGRICULTURE* 160. A dislocation can be healed with this incantation (*cantio*). Take a green reed, about four or five feet long, split it down the middle, and let two men hold it against their hips. Begin to chant: *motas vaeta daries dardares astataries dissunapiter.*[8] Continue until the two halves of the reed come together. Wave a piece of iron over the reed.

When the halves have come together and are touching one another, take the reed in your hand and cut it on the right and on the left. Bind it over the dislocation or fracture, which will then heal. Nevertheless, perform the following incantation for the dislocation every day. *huat haut huat ista pista sista dannabo dannaustra.* Or use this incantation for the dislocation: *huat haut haut istasis tarsis ardannabou dannaustra.*

Pliny the Elder describes a number of cures for various physical ailments. Note that Pliny carefully disassociates himself from the sources advocating these various remedies.

12.7 PLINY THE ELDER, *NATURAL HISTORY* 28.45. We are told that the hand of a person snatched away by a premature death cures with its touch a scrofulous tumor, diseased parotid glands and throat infections. But some say that the back of any dead person's left hand will do this, provided that the patient is of the same sex. It is said that if a person puts his hands behind his back, bites off a piece of wood that has been struck by lightning, and applies it to an aching tooth, it will serve as a remedy. Some prescribe that the tooth be fumigated with a human tooth from a person of the same sex and that a canine tooth taken from an unburied corpse be used as an amulet.[9]

The power of ritual

In context of the Feralia, a February festival honoring the dead,[10] Ovid describes a ritual that was supposed to seal the lips of one's detractors by sewing up the mouth of a dead fish.

12.8 OVID, *FASTI* 2. 571-582. Look, an aged hag, seated among young girls, performs rites in honor of the Silent One, though she herself is not silent. With three fingers she puts three pieces of incense under the threshold where the mouse has made for itself a secret path.[11] Then she binds enchanted threads with dark lead and turns seven black beans in her mouth.[12] She roasts in the fire the

---

[8] *motas vaeta....*: this and the series *huat haut huat* are nonsense syllables, magical formulae (*carmina*) that were evidently thought to have the power to heal.

[9] *amulet*: an object that is worn on the person to prevent harm, an apotropaic device.

[10] *Feralia*: see 3.23 and 3.24.

[11] *threshold ... mouse*: the mouse is a liminal creature often referred to in folklore.

[12] *threads .. dark lead ... black beans*: threads, perhaps taken from the target's clothing, were used to bind a figurine to a lead tablet. Both black and lead are commonly associated with chthonic rites, lead being the common material of curse tablets. On beans, see n. 17.

head of a small fish that she has sewn up, bound with pitch and pierced with a bronze needle. She also sprinkles it with wine. She and her companions drink the wine that is left, though she herself drinks the larger share. Then departing she says, 'We have bound fast hostile tongues and mouths.' Drunk, the old woman makes her exit.[13]

> In describing the Lemuria, a May festival in honor of the dead, Ovid records a domestic ritual intended to rid the house of ghosts.[14] He also reports some prohibitions that prevailed during the festival.

12.9 OVID, FASTI 5. 429-444. When midnight has come, giving silence for sleep, and dogs and all the various birds are quiet, he who is mindful of the ancient rite and fears the gods gets up. No bindings constrict his feet.[15] He makes a sign with his thumb in the middle of his closed fingers, lest in his silence an insubstantial ghost should run into him.[16] After washing his hands clean in spring water, he turns, and first he receives black beans and throws them away with face averted;[17] but as he throws them, he says: 'These I throw and, with these beans, I redeem me and mine.' This he says nine times, without looking back. The ghost is thought to gather the beans, and to follow behind without being seen. Again he touches water, and clashes Temesan bronze, and asks the ghost to depart from his house. When he has said nine times, 'Ghosts of my fathers, go forth!' he looks back and thinks that he has duly performed the sacred rites.

Binding spells (*defixiones, devotiones*)

> The Latin word *defixiones* derives from the verb *defigere*, to tie fast, bind, and thus immobilize, and *devotiones*, from *devovere*, to vow or dedicate. Both literary texts and archaeological finds attest to the practice of such spells, the latter evidence being lead tablets inscribed with curses, often pierced by one or more nails, and placed in graves in order to make contact with the powers of the underworld. Lead, because of its color, has appropriate chthonic associations. These curse tablets are particularly significant because, unlike most literary evidence, they reflect the religious beliefs of the ordinary people. This is 'unofficial religion,' separate and distinct from that of the state, embodying a ritual undertaken by an individual on his own behalf, usually for a negative purpose, perhaps in conjunction with an unofficial priest such as a magus.[18]

---

[13] Ovid's comments on the consumption of wine reflect his skepticism about these rituals which were probably practised in his own day.

[14] *Lemuria*: see 3.25.

[15] *no bindings...*: that is, he is bare-footed, thus making direct contact with the ground.

[16] *he makes a sign*: a magic, apotropaic signal.

[17] *black beans*: another magic device, black being appropriate to the powers of the underworld.

[18] *magus* (Greek *magos*): magician, the word is of Persian origin and is used to described a priest of an unofficial cult, a charlatan or quack.

An unnamed individual dedicates a woman, Ticene, to the powers of the underworld, invoking them to immobilize the various parts of her body. The tablet is written in Latin with several misspellings.

12.10 *CIL* 10.8249. Spirits of the underworld, if you have any power, I consecrate and hand over to you Ticene, the daughter of Carisius. Whatever she does, may it all turn out badly. Spirits of the netherworld, I consecrate to you her limbs, her complexion, her figure, her head, her hair, her shadow, her brain, her forehead, her eyebrows, her mouth, her nose, her chin, her cheeks, her lips, her breath, her neck, her liver, her shoulders, her heart, her lungs, her intestines, her stomach, her arms, her fingers, her hands, her navel, her entrails, her thighs, her knees, her calves, her heels, her soles, her toes. Spirits of the netherworld, if I see her wasting away, I swear that I will be delighted to offer a sacrifice to you every year.

A jealous lover entrusts a woman, Rhodine, to Dis Pater, the god of the underworld, so that she may lose the favor of one Marcus Licinius. Four others, two men and two women, are also included in the curse. This lead tablet was found in a cemetery outside Rome and dates to the late first century BCE.

12.11 *ILS* 8749, *CIL* 1.2.1012. Just as the dead man who is buried here can neither speak nor talk, so may Rhodine die as far as Marcus Licinius Faustus is concerned and not be able to speak nor talk. As the dead man is received neither by gods nor humans, so may Rhodine be received by Marcus Licinius and have as much strength as the dead man who is buried here. Dis Pater, I entrust Rhodine to you, that she be always hateful to Marcus Licinius Faustus. Also Marcus Hedius Amphio. Also Gaius Popillius Apollonius. Also Vennonia Hermiona. Also Sergia Glycinna.

Both victims or targets of this lead tablet of unknown date that is inscribed on both sides are identified by reference to their mother. Note the comprehensive list of body parts, some of which are mentioned twice. The objective of the first curse is to ruin not only Malcius' health but also his business profits.

12.12 Gager (1992) 172.80 modified by Versnel (1998). [Side A] Malcius [son or slave] of Nicona: eyes, hands, fingers, arms, nails, hair, head, feet, thigh, belly, buttocks, navel, chest, nipples, neck, mouth, cheeks, teeth, lips, chin, eyes, forehead, eyebrows, shoulder-blades, shoulder, sinews, bones, merilas,[19] belly, penis, shin: in these tablets I bind (*defigere*) [his] business profits and health.

[Side B] Rufa [daughter or slave] of Pu[b]lica: hands, teeth, eyes, arms, belly, nipples, chest, bones, merilas, belly ...., shin, mouth, feet, forehead, nails, fingers, belly, navel, genitals, womb, groin: I bind [these parts] of Rufa [daughter or slave] of Pu[b]lica in these tablets.

Two tablets from Gaul, c. 172 CE, yield a judicial binding spell. These tablets were buried together with a tom-cat whose body had been pierced and the head twisted backward, a vivid example of 'sympathetic magic' on the principle of like unto like.

---

[19] *merilas*: an otherwise unknown word, perhaps marrow.

12.13 GRAF (1997) 124 AND 136-7. I announce to the persons mentioned below, Lentulus and Tasgillus, that they must appear in court before Pluto.[20] As this cat has not harmed anyone, in such a way... that they cannot win this trial. And in the same way that the mother of this cat was unable to defend him, let their lawyers be unable to defend them, let these adversaries... [there follows either garbled Latin or a series of magic words].

Let them be turned away from this trial in the same way that this cat is turned away and cannot get up. Let it be thus for them as well. Let them be pierced through like the cat.

> Agonistic spells were sometimes deposited at turning points of the race track where the danger was greatest, invoking disaster on both horse and charioteer.

12.14 ILS 8753. I call on you, demon, whoever you are, and ask that from this hour, from this day, from this moment, you torture and kill the horses of the Green and White factions,[21] and that you kill and crush completely the drivers Clarus, Felix, Primulus, and Romanus, and that you leave not a breath in their bodies.

12.15 GRAF (1997) 155. I call on you, demon, who lie here [in the grave from which the text comes]: I deliver these horses to you so that you hold them back and that they get tangled up [in their harness] and are unable to move.

Sorcery and witchcraft

> The poet Lucan (39-65 CE), in his epic *Pharsalia*, describes the Thessalian witch Erichtho and her practice of collecting the remains of the dead to use on living victims, usually for ill.

12.16 LUCAN, PHARSALIA 6.515-541. The face of the witch is lean and loathsome with age, her appearance has a hellish pallor that has never seen the light of day, and she is weighed down by her uncombed hair. Whenever black storm clouds take away the stars, then she comes forth from rifled tombs and tries to capture the nocturnal lightning. Her tread blights the seeds of the fertile crop and her breath destroys air that previously was not deadly.

She does not pray to the gods of the heavens, nor does she invoke divine help with a suppliant's chant, nor does she have knowledge of the entrails that propitiate the gods. She rejoices to lay on the altars funeral fires and incense snatched from the blazing pyre. At the first words of her prayer, the gods grant every impiety, in fear of hearing a second spell....

She snatches the smoking ashes and burning bones of the young from the middle of the pyre, and the very torch that their parents were holding.[22] She collects pieces of the bier as they flutter in the black smoke, and the grave-clothes

---

[20] *Pluto*: god of the underworld.

[21] *Green and White factions*: teams racing under different colors.

[22] Cicero, *Against Vatinius* 14, accuses Vatinius of the practice of calling up souls from hell and of appeasing the gods of the underworld with the entrails of children.

as they melt into ashes, and the cinders that smell of the corpse. But when the dead are entombed in stone… then she eagerly savages their limbs, plunging her hands into their eyes, rejoicing as she digs out the stiffened eyeballs, and gnawing the pallid nails from withered hands….

> Pliny was only making a slight exaggeration when he claimed that there was no one who did not fear the power of spells. References in a variety of literary sources indicate that sorcery was not confined to the lower classes. Although several of the following excerpts imply skepticism on the part of the author, allegations of sorcery indicate that the practice was widespread and thus feared.
>
> In discussing orators with weak memories, Cicero recalls one of his opponents, who blamed his inability to speak on sorcery on the part of the defendant. Although Cicero clearly did not believe the excuse, he realized that he had to accept it.

12.17 CICERO, *BRUTUS* 217. One day when, in a very important private case, I had finished my plea for Titania, a client of Cotta, …Curio completely forgot his whole speech, but kept on saying that this had happened because of the spells and incantations of Titania (*veneficiis et cantionibus*).

> The poet Ovid speculates on the reason for his impotence.

12.18 OVID, *LOVE AFFAIRS* 3.7.27-30. Has my body been bewitched by some Thessalian potion (*venenum*)?[23] Is it some spell (*carmen*) or drug (*herba*) that has brought this misery upon me? Has some sorceress written (*defixit*) my name on crimson wax and driven a needle in my liver?[24]

> The historian Tacitus reports that early in Tiberius' reign a young man, who came from the family of Augustus' first wife Scribonia, was put on trial for dabbling in various forms of the occult. The underlying reason for the trial evidently was political.

12.19 TACITUS, *ANNALS* 2.27-32. It was about this time [16 CE] that Marcus Scribonius Libo Drusus was accused of subversive plotting…. Libo was a thoughtless young man with a propensity for silliness. One of this closest friends, a senator, … interested him in the predictions of astrologers,[25] rites of magicians and interpreters of dreams….

Finally, a certain Junius, whom Libo had approached to summon the spirits of the dead by means of spells (*carmina*), reported him to Lucius Fulcinius Trio, a man known for his talent as an informer and his eagerness for notoriety. Trio immediately pounced on Libo, went to the consuls, and demanded a senatorial inquiry….

Papers belonging to Libo were produced that were preposterous. In one, he enquired whether he would become rich enough to pave the Via Appia with

---

23   *Thessalian potion*: Thessaly in northern Greece was the stereotypical location of witchcraft or sorcery.

24   *liver*: the traditional seat of the emotions.

25   On astrology see 12.23-32.

money as far as Brundisium. There was more in the same vein, stupid, vacuous or, if more indulgently regarded, pitiable. But in one paper, the prosecutor argued, sinister or mysterious marks had been added by Libo's hand against the names of imperial personages and some senators.[26] When the defendant denied this, it was decided to question under torture the slaves who had identified his handwriting. [Libo committed suicide before a verdict was announced.]

The senate also ordered the expulsion of astrologers and magicians from Italy. One of their number, Lucius Pituanius, was thrown from the Rock, another, Publius Marcius, was executed by the consuls according to the ancient custom, to the sound of bugle, outside the Esquiline Gate.[27]

> Tacitus reports evidence of sorcery in the death of Germanicus, the designated heir of the emperor Tiberius. When Germanicus became seriously ill, he believed that he had been put under a spell by Piso, the governor of Syria.

12.20 TACITUS ANNALS 2.69. The cruel force of the disease was intensified by Germanicus' belief that Piso had poisoned him. Examination of the floor and walls of his room revealed the remains of human bodies, spells (*carmina*), curses (*devotiones*), the name of Germanicus inscribed on lead tablets, partially burnt ashes smeared with blood,[28] and other devices of black magic that are believed to consecrate the souls to the powers of the underworld. At the same time, men sent by Piso were accused of spying on the ravages of Germanicus' illness.

> Germanicus' widow, Agrippina, remained convinced that her husband had been poisoned, and she was a persistent problem to Tiberius, even though Piso had been put on trial and anticipated the verdict by suicide. Several years after Germanicus' death, Claudia Pulchra, a cousin of Agrippina, was accused of various crimes, including that of commissioning spells and curse tablets against Tiberius; she was convicted.

12.21 TACITUS, ANNALS 4.52. He [Domitius Afer] accused her of unchastity, adultery, and of invoking spells (*veneficia*) and curse tablets (*devotiones*) against the emperor.

> In the reign of Nero, a woman named Servilia was accused of consulting magicians against the emperor.

12.22 TACITUS, ANNALS 16.31. When the accuser asked if she [Servilia] had sold the jewelry from her dowry… in order to get money for performing magical rites… she exclaimed, 'I have resorted to no impious gods, to no curse tablets….'

---

[26] The charge was probably that Libo had prepared curses against a number of enemies, using magic characters or pictorial representations.

[27] *the Rock*: the Tarpeian Rock on the Capitoline hill from which traitors were thrown. The Esquiline gate was a regular place of execution, but this was evidently a ritual execution for a religious crime. The mode of execution 'according to ancient custom' would have been decapitation if the victim was of high rank, as Publius Marcius perhaps was. Otherwise the victim was tied to a stake and beaten to death.

[28] Compare the excerpt from Lucan, see 12.16.

Astrology

Astrology, another method of divination,[29] seems to have become popular in Rome in the early second century BCE, though it was never accepted as part of official Roman religion. The literary sources evince several instances of astrologers being expelled from Rome, usually at times of political unrest. Such expulsions and several negative views of astrology underscore its popular appeal.

During the republic auspices and prodigies had played a large part in the religious life of the city, as the Romans strove to maintain the *pax deorum* in the midst of various crises. With the collapse of the republican system of government, however, religion came under the control of the emperor rather than the Senate, as our brief survey of Augustus' assumption of religious offices has indicated.[30] Livy, writing during the reign of Augustus, expresses his awareness of a disregard that has led to a disbelief in divine warnings. Because of this, he says, portents are no longer officially reported or recorded in the annals (43.13.1).

Livy's observations are borne out by the dearth of references to portents and prodigies in the extant sources for the empire. Writing about the mid-fourth century CE, the historian Ammianus Marcellinus remarks that portents were not expiated by state ritual as they had been in the past, but passed by, unheard and unknown (19.12.19). Rather than turning to the Sibylline books and their interpreters, several emperors including Augustus himself and Tiberius consulted their own astrologers. Barton has observed that 'Astrologers belonged with the sole ruler, as the state diviners belonged with the Republic.'[31]

In the dialogue *On Divination*, Cicero has his brother, who generally argues in favor of divination, be scornful of fortune tellers, men who prophesy for money, and necromancers, as he supports his case with a quotation from a play of Ennius (235-169 BCE) which contains one of the first references to astrologers in Rome.

12.23 CICERO, *ON DIVINATION* 1.132. 'Finally, I say that I set no store by Marsian augurs, village *haruspices*, astrologers who haunt the circus, Isis-seers, or dream interpreters,' for they are not diviners either by knowledge or by skill.

'Rather they are superstitious bards,[32] soothsaying quacks, lazy, or mad, or ruled by want, men who do not know their own path though they show the way to others. They beg money from those to whom they promise wealth.'

Later in the same dialogue, speaking in his own persona, Cicero scornfully questions the credibility of astrology, citing some recent examples of its fallibility.

---

[29] See 1.14.

[30] See 11.3.

[31] Barton (1994) 38.

[32] *bards*: the Latin *vates* literally means prophet or seer.

12.24 CICERO, *ON DIVINATION* **2.99.** Was the birthday of Rome also subject to the influence of the moon and stars? Assume it is important what the arrangement of the stars is when a child draws its first breath. But does it also follow that this has any influence over the bricks and cement of which the city is built?

But why say more? Every day we have cases to refute such a theory. I recall many prophecies that the Chaldaeans made to Crassus, to Pompey and many to Caesar himself, that no one of them would die except in old age, at home and in great glory. And so it would seem miraculous to me that anyone, especially at this time, should trust men whose predictions he sees disproved every day by the actual outcome.

> Cato the Elder, ever the pragmatist, was clearly distrustful of the accuracy of astrology, at least where estate management was concerned.

12.25 CATO, *ON AGRICULTURE* **5.4.** The bailiff must not consult a *haruspex*, augur, prophet or astrologer.

> Astrologers were expelled from Rome in 139 BCE.

12.26 VALERIUS MAXIMUS, *MEMORABLE DEEDS AND WORDS* **1.3.3.** In the consulship of Marcus Popillius Laenas and Lucius Calpurnius, Gnaeus Cornelius Hispalus, the *praetor peregrinus*,[33] by edict ordered the Chaldaeans[34] to depart from the city and from Italy within ten days, because they were profiteering by their lies and creating darkness in the minds of the fickle and stupid by their fallacious interpretation of the stars.... Therefore Cornelius Hispalus expelled the Chaldaeans from the city, ordering them to leave Italy within ten days to prevent them selling their foreign knowledge (*peregrina scientia*). The same Hispalus also banished from the city Jews who were trying to pass their sacred rites on to the Romans....[35]

> But consulation of astrologers was not confined to the 'fickle and stupid.' Before his return to Rome from Greece after the assassination of Julius Caesar, the young Octavian who later became Augustus is reported to have consulted an astrologer.

12.27 SUETONIUS, LIFE OF AUGUSTUS **94.** Augustus with Agrippa as his companion went up to the observatory of the astrologer Theogenes. Agrippa was the first to have a consultation, receiving almost incredible predictions. Augustus, in fear and shame that his should prove to be inferior, persisted in silence, refusing to reveal his time of birth. After much persuasion, he finally gave it with difficulty and great hesitation. Theogenes leaped up and threw himself at Augustus' feet. From that time on, Augustus had such faith in his destiny (*fatum*) that he published his horoscope and issued silver coinage bearing the sign of the constellation Capricorn, under which he was born.

---

[33] *praetor peregrinus*: an official in charge of foreign affairs, as opposed to the *praetor urbanus*, the city praetor.

[34] Astrologers were frequently referred to as *Chaldaeans*, the tradition being that astrology originated in Babylon, the land of the Chaldaeans.

[35] On this expulsion of Jews, see 14.1.

Tacitus recounts the initial meeting between Tiberius and Thrasyllus, who then becomes astrologer to Tiberius and also Augustus.

12.28 TACITUS, *ANNALS* 6.21. Thrasyllus... was interrogated [by Tiberius] and impressed him by intelligent forecasts of his accession and of future events. Tiberius then asked if Thrasyllus had cast his own horoscope: what was the character of that year and of that day? Thrasyllus, after measuring the positions and distances of the stars, hesitated, then showed signs of fear. The more he looked, the more he trembled in astonishment and fright. Finally he cried out that a critical and almost fatal emergency was upon him. Tiberius promptly embraced him, congratulating him that he had perceived his danger and that he would escape it. Thrasyllus' pronouncements were regarded as oracular and he was admitted among Tiberius' closest friends.

Despite his predilection for Thrasyllus, Tiberius expelled astrologers who might be a political threat.[36]

12.29 SUETONIUS, *LIFE OF TIBERIUS* 36. Tiberius also banished all astrologers except those who asked his forgiveness and promised to make no more predictions.[37]

Tacitus, in writing of the year of the four emperors (69 CE), betrays his cynicism about astrology as he relates how astrological predictions encouraged Otho in his bid to become emperor.

12.30 TACITUS, *HISTORIES* 1.22. The astrologers—a breed of men untrustworthy for the powerful, deceitful for the ambitious, a breed that will always be both forbidden and yet retained in our state—also urged Otho on, declaring from their observation of the stars that there were revolutionary moves afoot and that this year would bring him glory.

Many of these astrologers, the worst possible tool for the wife of an emperor, had shared Poppaea's secret plans,[38] and one of them, Ptolemy, who had been with Otho in Spain, had promised him that he would survive Nero. Having established his credibility by the outcome of that prophecy, using guesswork and the gossip of those who compared Galba's old age with Otho's youth, he had persuaded him that he would become emperor. But Otho accepted these prophecies as if they were the genuine predictions of fate disclosed by Ptolemy's skill—such is the desire of human nature to believe too freely in the occult.

After the defeats and deaths of Otho and Vitellius, Vespasian's supporters cite prophecies and astrology as they encourage him to bid for power.

12.31 TACITUS, *HISTORIES* 2.78. They [Vespasian's supporters] gathered about him, encouraging him and recalling the prophecies of seers and the movements of the stars. Nor indeed was he entirely free from such superstition, as soon became clear when he became emperor and openly kept at court an astrologer called Seleucus as his guide and oracle. Old omens came back to his mind....

---

[36] See also the case of Libo, 12.19.

[37] Suetonius earlier reports that Tiberius was purging foreign cults at this time, particularly the rites of the Jews and of Isis, see 14.11.

[38] *Poppaea*: the wife of Nero who had previously been married to Otho.

Firmicus Maternus, a senator writing in the reign of Constantine (312-337 CE), advises astrologers how to avoid questions of a political nature.

12.32 FIRMICUS MATERNUS, *MATHESIS* 2.30.3-4. You will give your answers rationally in public and will warn those who come to consult you that you are going to respond in a clear voice to everything they ask you, so they will not happen to ask questions that it is not lawful to ask or to say.

Be careful to say nothing about the state or the life of the emperor, if anyone should enquire. For it is neither necessary nor lawful. We must not be moved by criminal curiosity to speak of the condition of the country.

An astrologer who replies when he is asked about the fate of the emperor is a criminal and deserves all the punishment he gets....

SKEPTICISM OF TRADITIONAL RELIGION: EPICUREANISM AND STOICISM

From the early third century BCE Greek culture had a profound impact on many aspects of Roman life. Excerpts from the plays of Plautus have shown the questioning of traditional Roman religion in the late third and early second centuries BCE. We have seen the theory of the Greek politician and historian Polybius that the cohesiveness of the Roman state was due to *deisidaimonia*, fear, awe, or respect for the supernatural. Some excerpts from Cicero have indicated his ambivalence and even skepticism about certain aspects of religion. Close reading of several authors, particularly Livy and Tacitus, reveals their skepticism about many of the stories they were recounting. During the political and social upheavals of the late republic two schools of Greek philosophy, the Epicurean and the Stoic, had a particular appeal to educated Romans.

Epicureanism

Lucretius (c. 99-55 BCE), an ardent disciple of the Greek philosopher Epicurus (341-270 BCE), wrote a didactic poem, *De Rerum Natura* (*On the Nature of Things*), in order to free men's minds of *religio*, which is best translated as 'superstition' in an Epicurean context. After extolling Epicurus' achievement, Lucretius inveighs against the power of *religio*.

13.1 LUCRETIUS, *ON THE NATURE OF THINGS* **1.62-79.** When human life lay grovelling for all to see, crushed by the weight of Superstition (*religio*) which showed her head from the regions of the sky and threatened mortals with her horrendous features, a man of Greece[1] was the first to dare to uplift men's eyes against her, the first to make a stand against her. Neither stories of the gods, nor thunderbolts, nor the sky with its threatening roar quelled him. Rather they so provoked the keen excellence of his mind that he longed to be the first to shatter the confining bars of nature's gates.

---

[1] *man of Greece*: Epicurus, the founder of Epicurean philosophy.

The lively power of his mind prevailed, ranging far outside the flaming walls of the world, as he traversed the immeasurable universe in thought and spirit. Returning victorious, he brings for us the knowledge of what can come into being, what cannot, how each thing has a limited power and a deep-set boundary. Thus Superstition is now in her turn crushed and trampled underfoot. But we, because of his victory, are raised to the level of the heavens.

> Among the wicked and impious deeds induced by *religio* is the sacrifice of Iphigenia by her father Agamemnon in order to get favorable winds to sail to Troy.

13.2 LUCRETIUS, *ON THE NATURE OF THINGS* 1.80-101. What I fear in this matter is that you may think you are beginning a godless (*impia*) philosophy and entering on a path of wickedness. On the contrary. Too often that very Superstition has produced wicked and godless deeds. As when at Aulis, the chosen leaders of the Greeks, the foremost heroes, foully stained the altar of Diana with the blood of Iphianassa.[2] As soon as the headband[3] was bound upon her maiden locks hanging down evenly on each cheek, so soon she saw her father standing sorrowfully before the altar, the attendants beside him hiding the knife, and the people shedding tears at the sight of her. Dumb with fear, she sank to the ground on her knees. Nor at this time could it help the poor girl that she had been the first to bestow the name of father on the king. Uplifted by the hands of men, she was brought trembling to the altar, not to be escorted by the loud wedding song amidst solemn and sacred ritual, but so that she, a pure maiden, at the very age of wedlock, would fall a sorrowful victim slaughtered by her father's hand: all this to ensure that a fair and fortunate voyage be granted to the fleet.

Such was the power of Superstition to induce so great an evil deed.

> Superstition and prophecy thrive because men fear punishment after death and think their problems will go on forever. Such fears will be dispelled once the nature of the universe is explained by the doctrines of Epicureanism.

13.3 LUCRETIUS, *ON THE NATURE OF THINGS* 1.102-116, 127-135, 146-148. Someday you yourself, conquered by the terrifying words of prophets,[4] will seek to depart from my teachings. Indeed, how many dreams can they invent for you that have the power to overturn the principles of your life and throw all your fortunes into a confusion of fear! And not without cause. For if men could see that there is a definite end-point for their troubles, they would in some way have the strength to withstand religious superstitions and the threats of prophets. But as it is now, they have no means or power to resist, because eternal punishment is to be feared after death. For they are ignorant of the nature of the soul, whether it is born or finds its way into men at birth, and whether it is destroyed by death and perishes along with us, or whether it travels to the

---

[2]   *Iphianassa*: an alternative form of the name Iphigenia.

[3]   *headband*: a symbol worn by a sacrificial victim.

[4]   *prophets*: the Latin *vates* means prophets or seers.

shadows of Orcus, or finds its way into other animals....[5]

Therefore we must have an explanation (*ratio*) of celestial phenomena, how the movements of the sun and the moon come about, and by what power things happen on earth. Then with acute reasoning (*ratio*) we must investigate in particular the composition of the soul (*anima*) and the nature of the mind (*animus*), and what it is that we encounter when we are awake and that terrifies our intelligence (*mentes*) when we are ill or buried in sleep, so that we seem to see and hear right in front of us those who have died and whose bones the earth embraces ....

This terror and darkness of the mind must be dispelled, not by the rays of the sun nor the bright shafts of the day, but by looking at nature and explaining the way she works.

> Epicurus taught that the universe consisted of infinite space or void and an infinite number of atoms, a word that derives from the Greek *atomos*, 'uncuttable' or 'indivisible.' These atoms were constantly in motion, forming different combinations to make the world that we know. All these combinations were perishable, though the atoms themselves were not. When the combinations were dissolved, the atoms formed new compounds.
>
> The aim of Epicureanism was to secure a happy life. Happiness was defined as pleasure, but not a sensual pleasure—rather, peace of mind or freedom from anxiety (*ataraxia*). The human soul was mortal and perished along with the body at the time of death. Epicurus did not deny the existence of gods, but believed that they had no influence or interest in human affairs. Thus Epicureans denounced religion and fear of the gods because they prevented an individual from achieving *ataraxia*.
>
> The first principle: nothing can be created from nothing. Therefore the creation of the universe is not to be attributed to divine agency.

13.4 LUCRETIUS, *ON THE NATURE OF THINGS* **1.149-158.** We will derive nature's first principle from this: nothing is ever created by divine power out of nothing. The reason that dread constrains all mortals is that they cannot visualise a rational explanation for the causes of many things they see happening in heaven and on earth. And so they think these things happen through some divine power.

But once we have seen that nothing can be created from nothing, then we will more accurately perceive what we are seeking, both the source from which each thing can be made and the manner in which everything happens without the working of gods.

> The second principle is that nature does not destroy completely but merely dissolves all compounds into their constituent atoms.

13.5 LUCRETIUS, *ON THE NATURE OF THINGS* **1.215-216, 225-228, 234-237.** Add to this the principle that nature dissolves all things into their constituent atoms and does not reduce things to nothing....

---

[5] *Orcus*: the underworld. *finds its way into other animals*: an allusion to the Pythagorean doctrine of the transmigration of souls.

Moreover, if time consumes all the material and utterly destroys whatever is immobilized by age, from what matter does Venus bring back the various species of animals into the light of life?[6] ...

But if in a previous era there have been bodies in that space from which the universe is composed and replenished, then assuredly they are endowed with an imperishable nature. Therefore things cannot individually return to nothing.

> The constant motion of atoms results in one compound being diminished, while another is increased. Change results from movement of the atoms.

13.6 LUCRETIUS, *ON THE NATURE OF THINGS* 2.72-79. Whenever bodies [atoms] depart from a thing, they diminish that from which they withdraw and increase that to which they have come, thus forcing the former to fade and the latter to flourish. Nor do they linger there. In this way the universe is always being renewed, and mortal creatures live dependent upon each other. Some peoples increase, whereas others become smaller; in a short space of time the generations of living creatures are changed and, like runners, hand on the torch of life.

13.7 LUCRETIUS, *ON THE NATURE OF THINGS* 2.1002-1006. Death does not destroy by annihilating the bodies of matter, but by breaking up their combination; it then links them in different combinations, causing them all to change their shapes and take on different colors, receiving and giving up sensation in an instant.

> In his second invocation of Epicurus, Lucretius proclaims that Epicureanism has driven away the terrors of the mind with the result that one can see the true nature of the universe in which the gods have their own abodes and enjoy their own *ataraxia*. Nor is there any sign of the underworld.

13.8 LUCRETIUS, *ON THE NATURE OF THINGS* 3.14-30. For as soon as your reasoning (*ratio*) begins to proclaim the nature of things revealed by your god-like mind (*divina mens*), then the terrors of the mind (*animus*) flee away, the walls of the universe open up, and I see action throughout the whole void. The majesty (*numen*) of the gods is revealed and their peaceful abodes, which no winds shake nor clouds sprinkle with rain, which no fall of white snow defiles as it congeals with bitter frost. But air that is ever cloudless covers them, laughing with its wide-spread light. Nature, moreover, supplies them with everything and nothing at any time detracts from their peace of mind.[7]

On the other hand, however, nowhere are the halls of Acheron to be seen.[8] Nor is the earth any obstacle to seeing everything that goes on beneath our feet throughout the void. Therefore, a certain god-like pleasure and a shuddering awe overwhelm me because, by your power, Epicurus, nature is so clearly revealed and unveiled in every part.

---

[6]   *Venus*: by metonomy, the power of procreation. This mention of the goddess of love does not negate Lucretius' basic assertion that the gods are not responsible for the creation of the universe.

[7]   peace of mind (*pax animi*) is the equivalent of the Greek *ataraxia*.

[8]   *Acheron*: the underworld.

Now that he has explained the basic principles of Epicureanism, Lucretius examines mens' fear of death.

13.9 LUCRETIUS, *ON THE NATURE OF THINGS* **3.31-40, 79-86.** I have shown the nature of the beginnings of all things: how they vary in shape as they fly of their own accord, driven in everlasting motion, and how everything can be produced from these. So now it is apparent that I must next explain in my verses the nature of the mind (*animus*) and soul (*anima*). I must drive headlong the fear of Acheron that throws men's lives into utter confusion, suffusing everything with the blackness of death and leaving no pleasure clear and pure....

Often, through fear of death, men are so gripped by a hatred of living and looking on the light that, with anguish in their hearts, they kill themselves, forgetting that this fear is the source of their anxieties. It is this fear that persuades one man to violate honor, another to break the bonds of friendship and, in a word, overturn piety (*pietas*). For often men have betrayed their fatherland and their beloved parents, in seeking to avoid the halls of Acheron.

Traditional stories about punishment in the underworld are untrue: men make their own hell on earth.

13.10 LUCRETIUS, *ON THE NATURE OF THINGS* **3.978-1023.** Indeed everything that is said to exist in the depths of Acheron is here in this life. There is no wretched Tantalus fearing the great rock that hangs in the air above him, as the story goes, paralyzed with vain terror. Rather it is in life that empty fear of the gods presses upon mortals as they fear what blow that chance may bring to each.

Nor are there any birds assailing Tityus as he lies in Acheron; nor indeed for all eternity can they find anything to probe in that mighty breast.[9] Let him cover not only nine acres with his limbs outstretched but even the whole earth, he will not be able to bear the pain forever or always provide food from his own body. But Tityus is here among us, the man who is prostrated by love. Winged cares tear at him or rend him with some other passion, as agonising anguish devours him. Sisyphus also is here in life for us all to see, the man who is absorbed in seeking the emblems of political office from the people, who is always defeated and retires in gloom.[10]....

Cerberus, the Furies, absence of light and Tartarus belching forth horrendous fires from his jaws, these nowhere exist nor indeed can they exist. Fear of punishment for evil deeds is here in life, a fear as enormous as the enormity of the crime. Here too is atonement for crime, prison, the terrifying flinging from the Rock,[11] whipping, executioners, the rack, boiling pitch, red-hot plates, firebrands. Even if these tortures are absent, the mind, conscious of its guilt,

---

[9]   *Tityus*: one of the traditional figures of the underworld who was condemned eternally to have his liver constantly probed by two vultures. He had tried to violate Leto and was killed by her two children, Apollo and Artemis (Diana).

[10]   *Sisyphus*: another of the traditional tortured figures of the underworld. He was condemned to roll a large rock up a steep hill. As soon as he neared the summit, the rock rolled back and Sisyphus had to start all over again.

[11]   *Rock*: traitors were thrown to their death from the Tarpeian rock on the Capitoline hill.

anticipates these fears, applying its goads and tormenting itself with whips. Nor does it see what can be the end to its troubles or a final limit to its punishment, but fears that they may be even heavier after death. In the end, the life of fools becomes a hell on earth.

> The gods' abode is outside of our universe; the idea that the gods created the world for the sake of man is foolish.

13.11 LUCRETIUS, *ON THE NATURE OF THINGS* 5.146-167. Likewise you can't possibly believe that the sacred abodes of the gods exist in any part of our world. For the nature of the gods is thin (*tenuis*) and far removed from our senses, and so is barely discerned even by the mind's intelligence. Since it eludes the touch and impact of our hands, it can have no contact with anything that is tangible to us. That which cannot be touched cannot itself touch. Therefore the gods' dwelling places must be different from ours and be thin in accord with their bodies....

It is foolish to say that the gods deliberately created the glorious nature of the universe for the sake of men, and that therefore it is fittingly praised as the laudable work of the gods, thinking that it will be eternal and immortal.... For what benefit could the immortal and blessed ones obtain from our gratitude that they should attempt to do anything for our sake?

> Men have made themselves miserable by imagining that the gods control the universe and are capable of anger. True piety is not the performance of ritual sacrifice, but rather contemplation with a mind at peace.

13.12 LUCRETIUS, *ON THE NATURE OF THINGS* 5.1183-1203. Men noticed the orderly succession of the celestial phenomena and the various seasons of the year and were unable to understand why this happened. And so they took refuge in attributing everything to the gods and making everything dependent on their nod....

O unhappy human race, to attribute such actions to the gods and to throw in the notion of their bitter anger! What griefs they created for themselves and what wounds for us, what tears for posterity! It is no piety (*pietas*) to appear often with covered head, turning to a stone, approaching every altar, nor to fall prostrate on the ground, with palms outspread before the shrines of the gods, showering the altars with the blood of beasts and piling vow upon vow. Piety is rather the ability to contemplate all things with a mind at peace....

Stoicism

> Seneca the Younger (d. 65 CE), a Stoic himself, defines happiness as the ultimate good (*summum bonum*) of Stoic philosophy.[12]

13.13 SENECA THE YOUNGER, *LETTERS* 124.7, 14. We Stoics define happiness as that which is in accordance with Nature....

---

[12] Compare other excerpts from Seneca, 1.6 where he writes of the religious awe inspired by nature, and 11.23 where he satirizes the deification of the emperor Claudius.

Only that which is perfectly in accordance with nature as a whole is truly perfect. And Nature as a whole is possessed of reason.

13.14 SENECA THE YOUNGER, *LETTERS* **48.7-9.** Do you want to know what philosophy offers to mankind? Philosophy offers advice (*consilium*). Death summons one man, poverty burns another, wealth, either his own or that of a neighbor, tortures a third. That man is afraid of bad luck, this man longs to escape his good fortune. Some are mistreated by men, others by the gods....

Everyone on all sides stretches out their hands to you; lives that are in ruin or in danger of ruin are begging for help. Men's hopes, men's resources depend on you. They beg that you rescue them from this great restlessness, that you reveal to them, scattered and wandering as they are, the clear light of truth. Tell them what nature has made necessary, and what superfluous. Tell them how easy are the laws that nature has laid down, how pleasant is the life, how unimpeded it is for those who follow these laws, how bitter and complicated it is for those who have put more trust in opinion than in nature.

Seneca reflects on the problem of why good men encounter misfortune.

13.15 SENECA THE YOUNGER, *ESSAY ON PROVIDENCE* **2.1-4.** You may ask, 'Why is it that many misfortunes often befall good men?'

Nothing that is truly evil can happen to a good man. Opposites do not mix. Just as the numerous rivers, heavy rains falling from heaven, and the volume of mineral springs do not alter the salty taste of the sea, or even dilute it, so too the onslaught of misfortunes does not affect the mind of the brave man. His mind remains steadfast, and adapts whatever happens to its advantage. For it is more powerful than all external events. I am not saying that the good man is insensible to these events, but he prevails over them and remains serene and calm in the face of every assault. He regards every misfortune as a training exercise....

13.16 SENECA THE YOUNGER, *ESSAY ON PROVIDENCE* **4.11-13.** In dealing with good men, the gods follow the same plan that teachers follow in dealing with their students: they demand more work from those of whom they have greater expectation.... Why are you surprised if God tests noble spirits harshly? The proof of one's *virtus* is never an easy thing. Fortune beats and lashes us, but we should patiently endure. This is not cruelty, but a contest. The more often we engage in it, the stronger we will be. The firmest part of the body is that which gets the most use.... By enduring evils, the mind acquires the ability to despise the endurance of them.

13.17 SENECA THE YOUNGER, *ESSAY ON PROVIDENCE* **5.4-7.** Good men toil, spend and are spent, but this is of their own free will. They are not dragged by Fate; they follow and keep up with it. If they had known how, they would have anticipated her....

I'm not being forced into anything and I'm not putting up with anything against my will. Nor am I a slave to God but his follower,[13] all the more so because I

---

[13]   *God*: the Stoic God was variously identified with Reason, Fate, Nature, Providence, or the Mind of the Universe. Thus God pervades the universe.

know that all things are determined and run a course according to a valid law for all eternity. Fate is our guide, and the first hour of our birth has allotted what length of time remains for us. Cause is linked to cause, and all public and private matters are directed by a long sequence of events. Therefore everything must be endured with fortitude because everything does not, as we suppose, happen but rather it simply comes.

> Seneca reflects on how to behave at the Saturnalia and gives advice on preparing for adversity.

13.18 SENECA THE YOUNGER, *LETTERS* **18.1-6.** It is the month of December and the city is in a particular sweat. Licence is given to the general public for indulgent behavior. Everywhere there is the sound of great preparations, as if the Saturnalia were any different from all the regular business days.[14] Indeed there is no difference, so much so that the man was quite right who said, 'Once December was a month; now it's a year.'[15] If you were here with me, I would gladly discuss what you think we ought to do: whether we should make no change in our daily routine or whether, in order not to seem out of sympathy with the general behavior, we should dine in merry fashion, abandoning our togas for leisure wear. Nowadays we Romans have changed our dress for the sake of pleasure and festivity, whereas earlier it was only the custom when the state was in a serious crisis.[16] If I know you well, I guess that you would have played the arbitrator and wished that we should neither be like the felt-capped throng in all ways nor be dissimilar from them in every way.[17]

But it is perhaps precisely on these days that we should give orders to our soul (*animus*), bidding it be unique in refraining from pleasures when the whole mob is wallowing in them. For this is the surest proof that a man can have of his own strength of mind, if he neither approaches nor is lured into the blandishments that draw one into self-indulgence....

One can observe a festival without extravagance.... Set aside a certain number of days on which you will be content with the scantiest and cheapest food and a rough, coarse garment. Say to yourself, 'Is this what I feared?' It is in this time of freedom from care that the soul should prepare itself for adversity and, while Fortune is kind, strengthen itself to encounter her injustices. In the midst of peace the soldier practices maneuvers and builds ramparts; though no enemy is near, he wearies himself with superfluous exertion so that he can be ready when exertion is needed. If you don't want a man to panic in a crisis, you must train him in advance of the crisis.

---

[14] On the Saturnalia, see 6.17-6.21.

[15] Originally the Saturnalia was a one day festival, but by Seneca's time it extended over several days, despite efforts to curtail it.

[16] See section 6.19 on the celebration of the Saturnalia during the Hannibalic War.

[17] *felt-capped throngs*: the felt cap or bonnet was usually worn by freedmen; here it is an allusion to the reversal of roles by masters and slaves at the Saturnalia (see 6.18), as is also the reference to leisure wear.

The Stoic attitude to suicide, and to the nature of death.

13.19 SENECA THE YOUNGER, *LETTERS* **65.21-22.** I was born for greater things than to be the slave of my body. I consider my body as nothing else but a chain that restricts my freedom. Therefore I set my body as an buffer to Fortune and will not allow any wound to penetrate to the real me. My body is the only part of me that can suffer injury. In this dwelling that is exposed to harm, my soul (*animus*) lives free. And never will this flesh drive me to feel fear, or to assume a pretence that is unworthy of a good man. Never will I lie in order to honor this petty body.

Whenever it seems the right time, I will end my connection with the body.[18] Even now, while we are still bound together, we will not be allies on equal terms. The soul will bring all questions of justice before its own tribunal. Contempt for one's body is absolute freedom.

Seneca's asthma causes him to reflect on the nature of death.

13.20 SENECA THE YOUNGER, *LETTERS* **54.1-7.** Ill-health had given me a long respite, when suddenly it attacked me again.... An attack is of brief duration, like that of a storm at sea, and usually ends within an hour.... I have encountered all the ills and dangers of the flesh, but nothing seems to me more troublesome than this.... Yet in the midst of my difficult breathing I never ceased to find rest in cheerful and brave thoughts.

Why, I say to myself, does death so often put me to the test? Let it do so. I myself have long tested death. When, you ask. Before I was born. Death is non-existence. I already know what that is like. What preceded me will succeed me. If there is any suffering in this condition, there must also have been suffering before we came into the light of day. But we felt no discomfort then. I ask you, wouldn't you say that it is the height of folly to think that a lamp was in worse state when it was extinguished than before it was lighted? We mortals are also extinguished and lighted. In the intervening period we suffer, but on either side there is a deep freedom from anxiety (*securitas*)....

Whatever condition existed before our birth, is death. For what difference does it make whether you do not begin or whether you leave off, since the effect of both of these states is non-existence?

I have not ceased to encourage myself with words of this kind, silently of course, since I was not able to speak. Little by little this shortness of breath, which had now become panting, came on at longer intervals, slowed down, and finally abated. But, although it is has abated, my breathing does not yet flow naturally.[19] I feel a certain hesitation and delay in breathing. Let it do as it wishes, as long as I don't really gasp for breath.

But take my word for it: I will not be afraid when the final moment comes. I am already prepared, and do not plan a full day ahead. But you should praise and imitate the man who enjoys life but is not reluctant to die. For what virtue

---

[18]   Seneca committed suicide in 65 CE rather than live under Nero's regime.

[19]   Compare the precept in 13.13 and 13.14 to live in accordance with nature.

is there in leaving when you are being thrust out anyway? Yet there is some virtue even in this: I am indeed being thrust out, but it is as if I were going away willingly.

For that reason the wise man is never in the position of being thrust out, because that would imply removal from a place that he was unwilling to leave. But the wise man does nothing unwillingly. He escapes necessity because he choses of his own free will to do what necessity is about to force on him.

> The historian Tacitus ponders different theories about what directs human affairs, reflecting on Epicureanism, Stoicism and astrology.

13.21 TACITUS, ANNALS 6.22. When I hear this and similar stories,[20] I feel uncertain whether human affairs are directed by fate and unchangeable necessity or by chance. You will find that the wisest of the ancients and their followers differ. The opinion is engrained in many that neither our birth nor our death is of any concern to the gods — nor, in fact, are human beings.[21] Thus the good often suffer while the wicked flourish. Others disagree, maintaining that fate is indeed in harmony with events, not, however, as a result of the movements of the stars but because of the principles and processes of natural causation.[22] Nevertheless, they leave us free to choose our life; but once that choice is made, the order of the future is fixed. Nor, they maintain, are evil and good what most people think. For many people who seem to be stricken with adversity are happy, provided that they endure their hardships with firmness, whereas greater numbers despite their wealth are most wretched, if they use their prosperity unwisely. Most men, however, are convinced that the future of an individual is determined from birth, but that some things fall out differently from what was predicted because of the dishonesty of men who didn't know what they were talking about.

> Stoic influence is apparent as the satirist Juvenal gives advice on prayer to those who insist on observing traditional rituals.

13.22 JUVENAL, SATIRES 10.346-366. Is there nothing then for which men shall pray? If you ask my advice, you will leave it to the divine powers (*numina*) themselves to provide what is good for us and what serves our interests. For instead of providing what is pleasing, the gods will give us what is best. Man is dearer to them than he is to himself. For we are impelled and driven by a strong and blind desire in our hearts to ask for a wife and offsping. But the gods know the true nature of your future wife and sons. Still, so that you may have something to ask for and be able to offer the entrails and consecrated sausages of a white porker at the shrines, you should pray for a sound mind in a healthy body.[23]

---

[20] *this and similar stories*: Tacitus has just related the story of Tiberius' meeting with Thrasyllus; see 12.28.

[21] An allusion to Epicureanism.

[22] An allusion to Stoicism.

[23] *sound mind in a healthy body*: Latin *mens sana in corpore sano*.

Ask for a brave spirit that has no fear of death, a spirit that considers the length of one's life the least of Nature's gifts, that can endure any kind of toil, that knows neither anger nor desire, that thinks the troubles and harsh labors of Hercules are better than the loves, banquets and feathered cushions of Sardanapalus.[24] What I teach you, you can give to yourself. The one and only path to a tranquil life lies through virtue. If we had but wisdom, you, Fortune, would not be regarded as divine; it is we that make you a goddess and place you in the heavens.

---

[24] *Sardanapalus*: the last king of Assyria whose sensuality and opulence were notorious.

THE JEWS IN THE ROMAN WORLD

There is a paucity of information about Rome's first contacts with the Jews. The first extant reference to the presence of Jews in Rome is problematic, since it is not clear whether the proselytizing Jews that were expelled from the city in 139 BCE were transients or permanent residents. In either case, the numbers involved would have been small.

14.1 VALERIUS MAXIMUS, *MEMORABLE DEEDS AND WORDS* **1.3.3.** The same Hispalus also banished from the city Jews who were trying to pass their sacred rites on to the Romans. He removed their private altars from public places.

By the late republic a substantial permanent Jewish community was resident in Rome. Pompey's conquests in the eastern Mediterranean had put an end to the Seleucid dynasty, bringing many Jews under Roman control in the new province of Syria. Many were also resident in the provinces of Asia and Cilicia. Roman authorities were thus faced with the problem of dealing with a people whose ancestral customs and conventions were totally different from their own. The monotheism of the Jews was incompatible with the polytheism of Roman state religion. Special dispensation had to be granted in order for them to have the right to assemble for worship.[2] The Jewish sabbath and their festivals and dietary laws conflicted with Roman requirements for military service. The annual tax paid by all adult Jewish males to the Temple in Jerusalem also called for special consideration. Such political privileges or exemptions were not always granted by the Roman authorities; when they were, it often caused resentment among their neighbors.

Rome and the Jews in the late republic and early empire

The Jewish historian Flavius Josephus (37-c. 100 CE), who was taken to Rome as a war captive and became a friend of the emperor Vespasian, gives several

---

[1] *Hispalus*: the *praetor peregrinus* who was in charge of cases of justice involving citizens vs. non-citizens. He also expelled astrologers; see 12.26.

[2] On the restriction on the right to assemble, see chapter 9 n.8.

instances of Rome's special treatment of the Jews. In 49 BCE the Roman consul, who was attempting to raise troops for Pompey in the civil war against Julius Caesar, granted the Jews of Ephesus exemption from military service.

14.2 JOSEPHUS, *JEWISH ANTIQUITIES* **14.228.** Lucius Lentulus, the consul, declared: Those Jews who are Roman citizens and observe Jewish rites and practise them in Ephesus, I released from military service on religious grounds ....

> After the defeat and death of Pompey, Julius Caesar granted Roman citizenship and other privileges to Antipater, the father of Herod the Great, thus making him a client of Rome and of himself.[3]

14.3 JOSEPHUS, *JEWISH WAR* **1.194.** Later, when Caesar had settled affairs in Egypt and returned to Syria [c. 47 BCE], he bestowed upon Antipater Roman citizenship and made him an object of envy, by other honors and marks of friendship

> In illustrating Roman favor towards the Jews, Josephus cites an exemption granted by Julius Caesar to the Jews of Rome allowing them to assemble for worship, despite the Roman restrictions on the right of assembly. The governor wished to apply these exemptions in his own province.

14.4 JOSEPHUS, *ANTIQUITIES* **14.213-16.** Julius Gaius,[4] consul of the Romans, to the magistrates and council and people of Parium,[5] greetings: The Jews in Delos and some of the neighboring Jews, in the presence of some of your ambassadors, have appealed to me declaring that by decree you are preventing them from following their ancestral customs and sacred rites.[6] Now it is not pleasing to me that such decrees should be passed against our friends and allies, and that they should be prevented from living in accordance with their customs and from contributing money to common meals and sacred rites, when they are not prevented from doing this even in Rome.

For example, Gaius Caesar,[7] our consul, by edict prohibited religious associations from meeting in the city [of Rome]; but these people alone [i.e., the Jews] were not prohibited from collecting contributions of money and holding common meals.[8] Likewise, I also ban other religious associations, but allow these people alone to assemble and hold meals in accordance with their ancestral customs and conventions. And, if you have passed any decree against

---

[3]   *client*: Rome had developed the practice of appointing client kings as her surrogates either within a province or to serve as a buffer state outside the boundaries of the Roman empire. The practice was an extension of the patron-client relationship among the Romans themselves.

[4]   *Julius Gaius*: perhaps a governor of Asia whose identity is otherwise unknown.

[5]   *Parium*: in northwest Asia Minor, although some would read 'Paros,' an island in the Aegean near Delos.

[6]   *Delos*: an island in the center of the Aegean, originally sacred to Apollo, which at this time was an important center for trade.

[7]   *Gaius Caesar*: Julius Caesar

[8]   Compare the Roman concern with such matters in context of Bacchic worship, 6 and 7.

our friends and allies, you would be well advised to annul it, because of their assistance and goodwill towards us.[9]

The Romans exempt the Jews of Asia Minor from military service, allowing them to observe their native customs.

14.5 JOSEPHUS, *ANTIQUITIES* **14.225-7.** In the presidency of Artemon, on the first day of the month of Lenaeon [24 January 43 BCE], Dolabella, Roman Commander, to the magistrates, council and people of Ephesus, greetings: Alexander, son of Theodorus, ambassador of Hyrcanus, son of Alexander, the High Priest and Ethnarch of the Jews, has pointed out to me that his fellow-Jews cannot undertake military service since they are not able to bear arms or march on the days of the sabbath. Nor can they obtain the traditional foodstuffs to which they are accustomed. I, therefore, like the governors before me, grant them exemption from military service and allow them to observe their native customs, to assemble for their sacred rites in accordance with their law and to make contributions towards their sacrifices.[10] I wish to inform the various cities of these things in writing. It is my wish that you write these instructions to the various cities.

The emperor Augustus publicises a ruling that protects the Jews of Asia Minor by having it inscribed on a prominent part of his temple in Ancyra.

14.6 JOSEPHUS, *ANTIQUITIES* **16.162-5.** Caesar Augustus, *pontifex maximus*, with tribunician power,[11] decrees as follows: since the Jewish nation has been found well-disposed towards the Roman people not only at the present time but also in the past, and especially in the time of my father the Imperator (*autokrator*) Caesar, as has their High Priest Hyrcanus, it has been decreed by me and my council under oath, with the consent of the Roman people, that the Jews should follow their own customs in accordance with their ancestral law, just as they did in the time of Hyrcanus, High Priest of the Most High God. Their sacred monies are to be inviolable, and must be despatched to Jerusalem and handed over to the treasurers in Jerusalem.[12] Nor do they need to give bond [to appear in court] on the Sabbath or on the day of preparation for it after the ninth hour.

And if anyone is caught stealing their sacred books or their sacred monies from a synagogue or community hall,[13] he shall be regarded as sacrilegious and his property made over to the public treasury of the Romans. As for the resolution they have offered to me in honor of the dutifulness (*eusebeia*) that

---

[9] An apparent reference to the help given by two Jewish leaders to Julius Caesar when he was besieged in Alexandria in 48/47 BCE.

[10] *contributions...*: compare the restrictions imposed by the Bacchic decree of 186 BCE.

[11] *tribunician power*: missing from the text at this point is a numeral that would have given the year of Augustus' tribunician power. That he is styled as *pontifex maximus* indicates that the decree dates after 12 BCE.

[12] A reference to the annual tax of two drachmas paid by all adult Jewish males to the Temple in Jerusalem.

[13] *community hall*: a banqueting hall or lounge, found in many synagogues.

I show towards all men and in honor of Gaius Marcius Censorinus,[14] I order that it and this edict be set up on the most conspicuous part of the temple assigned to me by the federation of Asia at Ancyra. If anyone contravenes any of the above ordinances, he shall pay a heavy penalty.

> Philo, a Jew born in Alexandria who went as a delegate to the emperor Caligula (Gaius) in 39/40 CE, recalls Augustus' consideration of the Jews and their ancestral traditions.

14.7 PHILO, *EMBASSY TO GAIUS* 155-8. Augustus knew that a large part of Rome on the far side of the Tiber was occupied and inhabited by Jews. The majority of them were freedmen who were now Roman citizens. They had been brought to Italy as captives and then freed by their owners.[15] They were not forced to violate any of their ancestral traditions. Augustus knew that they have places for prayer meetings and meet together in these places, especially on the holy sabbaths when they come together as a group to learn their ancestral wisdom.

He also knew that they collect money for religious purposes from their first-fruits, sending this money to Jerusalem with people to offer the sacrifices. However, he did not banish them from Rome or deprive them of their Roman citizenship just because they were careful to maintain their identities as Jews. Nor did he take violent action against their houses of prayer; nor did he forbid them to gather to receive instruction in the laws, nor did he oppose their first-fruit collections...

In regard to the monthly grain doles, when everyone receives his share of money or grain,[16] Augustus never deprived the Jews of this charity. But even if the distributions happened to occur on the holy sabbath, when no Jew is allowed to receive or give anything or to do any regular business, particularly mercantile business, he ordered the officials in charge of the distribution to reserve for the Jews until the next day the portion of the welfare that belonged to all.

> Although the situation between the Jews and Alexandrian Greeks was somewhat alleviated by the assassination of Caligula, in 41 CE the new emperor Claudius wrote to the people of Alexandria urging them to adopt a more tolerant attitude to the Jews living in their city. He also issued stern warnings to the Jews.

14.8 CPJ 2.153 LINES 73-103. With regard to the disturbances and rioting, or rather, if the truth must be told, the war against the Jews, and who was responsible, although your ambassadors, and especially Dionysios, son of Theon, argued earnestly and at length in their own defence, I was nevertheless unwilling to conduct a detailed enquiry, but I do feel within myself an implacable anger against those who renewed the conflict. I tell you simply that, unless you stop this destructive and stubborn anger towards each other, I shall be forced to

---

[14] *Censorinus*: consul in 8 BCE and proconsul of Asia in 2/3 CE.

[15] *freed*: they had probably been captured during Pompey's conquest of Syria.

[16] *money or grain*: Philo here is inaccurate; money was rarely distributed.

show you what a benevolent ruler can be like when turned to righteous anger. Therefore, I beg you, Alexandrians, to behave gently and benevolently toward the Jews who have long lived in the same city as you. Do not dishonor any of the traditional practices connected with the worship of their god, but allow them to observe their customs as they did under the deified Augustus, customs that I, having listened to both sides, have confirmed.

But, on the other hand, I order the Jews not to agitate for greater privileges than they had before, nor in future to send out two embassies as if they lived in two cities. For such a thing has never been done before.... Nor are they to bring in or invite Jews to come in by sea and river from Syria or Egypt. For such actions will force me to become more deeply suspicious. If they do, I shall prosecute them in every way as fostering a common plague for the whole world. If, however, both sides give up their quarrels and are willing to live together in gentleness and benevolence toward each other, then I too will show the utmost care for the city that has been closely connected with us for generations.

Repressive measures against Jews in the early empire

Opposition to foreign cults manifests itself as the emperor Tiberius, Augustus' successor, banishes Jews from Rome because four Jews had embezzled contributions from a Roman noblewoman who was a proselyte.

14.9 JOSEPHUS, *ANTIQUITIES* **18.81-84.** There was a certain Jew, an utter scoundrel, who had fled his own country because he was accused of breaking certain laws and feared punishment on this account. He was resident at Rome and presented himself as an interpreter of the Mosaic law and its wisdom. He enlisted three accomplices who were no better in character than himself. When Fulvia, a woman of noble birth who had become a Jewish proselyte, began to meet with them regularly, they urged her to send purple and gold to the Temple in Jerusalem. But they took the gifts and used them for their own personal expenses, which had been their original intention in soliciting these gifts.

Saturninus, Fulvia's husband, at her prompting, duly reported this to the emperor Tiberius, whose friend he was. The emperor ordered the whole Jewish community to leave Rome. The consuls drafted four thousand of these Jews for military service and sent them to the island of Sardinia. But they punished a good many of those who refused to serve because they feared breaking the Jewish laws. Thus, because of the wickedness of four men, the Jews were banished from the city.

Tacitus (c. 56-120 CE) and Suetonius (c. 69-150 CE) connect the incident with the suppression of Isiac religion which involved a Roman woman of noble birth who had become a devotee of Isis.

14.10 TACITUS, *ANNALS* **2.85.** There was a debate [in the Senate] about the banning of Egyptian and Jewish rites. A senatorial decree directed that four thousand descendants of enfranchised slaves who were tainted with that superstition (*superstitio*) and of a suitable age should be sent to Sardinia to suppress brigandage. If they succumbed to the pestilential climate, the loss would be small. The rest were ordered to leave Italy, unless they had renounced their impious rites by a certain date.

14.11 SUETONIUS, *TIBERIUS* 36. Tiberius suppressed foreign cults (*externae caerimoniae*), especially the Egyptian and Jewish rites, forcing those who were in the grip of that superstition (*superstitio*) to burn their religious vestments along with all their cult paraphernalia.[17] Those Jews who were of military age he assigned to provinces of a less healthy climate; the rest of that race and those who held similar beliefs he banished from the city, on pain of slavery for life if they did not obey.

> The historian Dio (c. 160-230 CE) attributes the expulsion to the increased number of Jews in Rome and their proselytizing.

14.12 DIO 57.18.5A. As Jews were flocking to Rome in great numbers and converting many of the [Roman] people to their ways, Tiberius banished the majority of them.

> In 41 CE, the emperor Claudius closes the synagogues in Rome, but does not place a complete ban on their right to worship.

14.13 DIO 60.6.6. The Jewish population of Rome had again increased so much that it would have been difficult to bar them from the city without causing immense disorder because of the numbers involved. Claudius, therefore, did not drive them out. Instead he forbade them to assemble. At the same time he permitted them to observe their traditional way of life.

> C. 49 CE Claudius expels Jews from Rome because of disturbances within the Jewish community. Apparent is a lack of distinction between Jews and Christians.

14.14 SUETONIUS, *CLAUDIUS* 25.4. Because the Jews were constantly causing disturbances at the instigation of one Chrestus, Claudius expelled them from Rome.[18]

> In Corinth the apostle Paul, himself a Jew, encounters two Jews expelled from Rome and lodges with them as he preaches to both Jews and Greeks.

14.15 *ACTS OF THE APOSTLES* 18.1-4. After this, Paul departed from Athens and came to Corinth. There he discovered a Jew called Aquila, a native of Pontus, and his wife Priscilla.[19] He had recently come from Italy because of Claudius' order that all the Jews should depart from Rome. Paul went to see them, and because they were of the same trade he stayed with them and worked. For they were tent-makers by trade.[20] Each sabbath, Paul held discussions in the synagogue [at Corinth] and he tried to win over both Jews and Greeks.

---

[17] On the worship of the Egyptian goddess Isis, see 9.9–9.12.
[18] 'Chrestus' is generally identified with Jesus Christ; see also 15.1.
[19] *Pontus*: the Roman province bordering on the southern shore of the Black Sea.
[20] Tent-making was a skilled and lucrative profession, catering to military needs.

14.16 *ACTS OF THE APOSTLES* **18.5-11.** When Silas and Timothy came from Macedonia, Paul continued with his preaching and testifying to the Jews that Jesus was the Messiah.[21] When they opposed him and verbally abused him, he shook his garments and said to them, 'Your blood be upon your own heads! I am guiltless. From now on I shall go to the Gentiles.' Then he left and went to the house of a man called Titius Iustus, a god-fearing man whose house was next door to the synagogue.[22]

Crispus, the official of the synagogue, became a believer in the Lord, together with all his household. Many of the Corinthians, on hearing Paul, believed and were baptized. One night the Lord spoke in a vision to Paul: 'Do not be afraid, but speak and do not be silent. For I am with you and no one shall lay a hand upon you to harm you. There is a great number of people in this city for me.' Paul therefore settled down for eighteen months, teaching the word of God among them.

The new Roman governor refuses to be involved in Jewish opposition to Paul.

14.17 *ACTS OF THE APOSTLES* **18.12 17.** But when Gallio became proconsul of Achaea [c. 52 CE], the Jews made a united attack on Paul and brought him before the [Roman] tribunal, declaring: 'This man is persuading people to worship God contrary to the law.' Paul was about to open his mouth when Gallio said, 'If some crime or wicked misdeed were at issue here, O Jews, then I would be justified in giving you a hearing. But if it is a question of words, names and your law, see to it yourselves. I do not wish to be a judge of these things.' And he dismissed them from his tribunal.

Then all of them seized Sothenes, the official of the synagogue, and beat him in front of the tribunal. But Gallio paid no attention to these things.

The First Jewish Revolt (66-73 CE)

Trouble erupted between the Greeks and Jews living in the port city of Caesarea in the province of Judaea. The local Roman authorities failed to deal with the situation, protest broke out in Jerusalem, and the whole province revolted. The emperor Nero dispatched one of his leading generals, Vespasian, to put down the rebellion. After Nero's death, in the so-called year of the four emperors, Vespasian was proclaimed emperor by the Roman armies in the east and so he returned to Rome, leaving his son Titus to capture Jerusalem. The Temple was destroyed, the Jewish council of the Sanhedrin and the office of High Priest were abolished, proselytizing forbidden, and the tax previously paid to the Temple was henceforth to be paid to the Roman god, Jupiter Capitolinus.

---

[21] *the Messiah:* the Christ. Silas and Timothy were disciples of Paul.

[22] *god-fearing man*: a non-Jew who regularly attended the synagogue but was not formally converted.

14.18 Dio 65.7.2. Thus was Jerusalem destroyed on the very day of Kronos,[23] a day that even now Jews reverence more than any other. From that time it was ordered that those who continued to observe their ancestral customs should pay an annual tribute of two drachmas to Capitoline Jupiter. Both generals received the title of *imperator*,[24] but neither got the title *Judaicus*, although all the other honors that were appropriate to such a victory were voted to them including triumphal arches.[25]

14.19 Josephus, *Jewish war* 7.218. The emperor Vespasian imposed a tax on all Jews, wherever they lived. He ordered that every Jew should pay two drachmas to the Capitol, just as formerly they had made contributions to the Temple in Jerusalem.

> The biographer Suetonius recalls an instance of the rigor with which the tax on Jews was levied during the reign of Domitian (81-96 CE).

14.20 Suetonius, *Domitian* 12. Besides other taxes, that on the Jews was levied with the utmost rigor. Prosecutions were brought against those who either lived as Jews without acknowledging their faith or who concealed their origin and did not pay the tax imposed upon their race. I recall that as a young man I was present when a ninety-year-old man was physically examined before the procurator and a very crowded court, to see whether he was circumcised.

A Roman view of the Jews

> The historian Tacitus, writing more than a generation after the First Jewish Revolt, gives the following account of the Jews and their religion. He presents a curious mixture of reliable and distorted information, the latter reflecting the stereotypical prejudices that had apparently become prevalent as a result of the revolt.

14.21 Tacitus, *Histories* 5. 4-5. To establish his influence over his people for all time, Moses introduced new rites that were different from those of all other men. In these everything that we regard as sacred is held to be profane. On the other hand they permit things that for us are taboo. In their inmost shrine they dedicated a statue of the animal whose guidance enabled them to put an end to their wandering and thirst, sacrificing a ram in apparent mockery of Ammon.[26] They also offer a bull, since the Egyptians worship the Apis bull. They abstain from pork in memory of a plague because they were once infected by the scabs to which this animal is subject.[27] To this day they bear witness to the

---

[23] *Kronos*: the Greek counterpart of the Roman Saturn, thus Saturday, i.e., the sabbath.

[24] *both generals*: Titus and Vespasian. The title *imperator* is an acknowledgment of their military success, not a political title.

[25] *triumphal arches*: the Arch of Titus commemorating the taking of Jerusalem and Titus' triumph is still standing in the Roman forum today.

[26] *the animal whose guidance*: there was a story that the Temple contained the head of an ass. *Ammon*: an Egyptian deity.

[27] See Deuteronomy 14.8 and Leviticus 11.7.

long hunger by frequent fasts, and Jewish bread is still made without leaven as a reminder of their hurried meal.[28] They say that they decided to rest on the seventh day because it brought an end to their toils; then the charms of inertia led them to give over the seventh year also to inactivity....

These rites, whatever their origin, are maintained by their antiquity. The other customs of the Jews are weird and abominable, and have prevailed because of their depravity. Wretches of the worst kind, scorning their ancestral religions,[29] were always sending tribute and contributions to Jerusalem, thus increasing the wealth of the Jews.[30] They are extremely loyal toward one another and always ready to show compassion, but toward every other people they show hate and enmity. They eat apart and sleep separately. Although as a race they are very prone to lust, they abstain from intercourse with foreign women; yet among themselves nothing is illicit. They adopted circumcision to show that they are different from others.

Those who are converted to their ways follow the same practices, and the first lesson they are taught is to despise the gods, to disown their country and to have little thought for their parents, children and brothers.[31] However, they are concerned to increase their numbers. For they regard it a crime to kill a late-born child, and they consider the souls of those killed in battle or by the executioner to be immortal.[32] Hence their passion for begetting children and their scorn of death. They bury their dead rather than cremate, thus following the custom of the Egyptians. They devote the same care to the dead and hold the same beliefs about the underworld. But their ideas of heavenly things are quite different. The Egyptians worship many animals and composite images. With the mind alone, the Jews conceive of one god only. They regard as impious those who fashion from perishable materials the images of the gods in the likeness of men. The supreme and eternal being is for them inimitable and immortal. Therefore they set up no statues in their cities, let alone in their temples. No flattery is paid to their kings, no honor to the Caesars [emperors]. But since their priests used to chant to the pipe and cymbals and wear garlands of ivy, and because a golden vine was found in their temple, some have thought that they were worshippers of Father Liber, the conqueror of the east.[33] But this is incompatible with their customs. For Liber established rites that are festive and joyous, whereas the practices of the Jews are preposterous and sordid.

---

[28] See Exodus 12.15-20 and 34-39.

[29] *scorning their ancestral religions*: an allusion to proselytes.

[30] *increasing the wealth of the Jews*: as early as 59 BCE Cicero had criticized the flow of money to Jerusalem in the speech *On behalf of Flaccus* 66-9. This attack was politically, not racially, motivated.

[31] *disown their country...*: The concept of leaving one's country and family would have been completely alien to traditional Roman religion and its concept of piety. Cf. Genesis 12.1: Now the Lord said to Abram: 'Go from your country and your kindred and your father's house to the land that I will show you.'

[32] *late-born child*: a child born after the father had made his will.

[33] *Father Liber*: Bacchus or Dionysus.

The Revolt of Bar Kochba (132-135 CE)

After the suppression of a second revolt in Judaea, the emperor Hadrian banned Jewish access to Jerusalem (135 CE). The city was colonized by gentiles and the province renamed Aelia Palestina. Note that the following excerpt was written in the fourth century CE by a Christian bishop.

14.22 EUSEBIUS, *HISTORY OF THE CHURCH* **4.6.3-4.** Hadrian commanded that by a legal decree and ordinances from that time on, the whole nation be completely banned from setting foot on the territory around Jerusalem. This ensured that not even from afar could they see their ancestral land....

Thus, when the Jewish nation was deported from the city and the old inhabitants had all died, it was colonized by foreigners. The Roman city that developed afterwards changed its name and was called Aelia in honor of the reigning emperor Aelius Hadrian. The church there consisted of gentiles ....

CHRISTIANITY

The history of the development of Christianity in the Roman empire is
sparsely and sporadically documented. In the preceding chapter 'The Jews in
the Roman World' we saw the earliest reference in Greco-Roman literature
to the presence in Rome during the reign of Claudius of people for whom
Jesus was the Messiah (the Christ) — people who later would come to be
called Christians.[1]

15.1 SUETONIUS, *CLAUDIUS* 25.4. Because the Jews were constantly causing
disturbances at the instigation of one Chrestus, Claudius expelled them from
Rome.

> A few years later, at the end of the 50s CE, the apostle Paul, a Jew who had
> persecuted the first Christians but then experienced a conversion and became
> an ardent missionary to both Jews and gentiles, was arrested in Jerusalem
> and handed over to the Roman authorities. Since he was a Roman citizen, he
> requested trial before the emperor and so was sent to Rome.[2] On his arrival
> there, Paul introduced himself to the leaders of the Jewish community. This
> passage occurs at the conclusion of *Acts of the Apostles*, a major source for
> Paul's journeys in the eastern Mediterranean.

15.2 *ACTS OF THE APOSTLES* 28.16-31. When we came to Rome, Paul was allowed to
lodge on his own with a soldier to guard him. Three days later he summoned
the leaders of the Jews. When they had assembled, he said to them: 'I have
done nothing against the people or our ancestral laws, brothers, but I was
handed over from Jerusalem as a prisoner into the hands of the Romans. After
investigating the case, they wanted to release me because there was no capital
charge against me. When the Jews objected, I was forced to appeal to Caesar,

---

[1]   See also commentary and footnote at 14.14.

[2]   *citizen*: governors in provinces were forbidden to punish a Roman citizen, although
they had almost supreme power over non-Romans. Thus Paul was sent to Rome to
face trial. See *Acts of the Apostles* 22.25-27.

although I did not have any charge to bring against my own people. This is the reason I have asked to see and speak with you since it is for the hope of Israel that I am in chains.' They said to him, 'We have received no letters about you from Judaea, nor has any of the brothers arrived with news of you or gossip about you. We would like to hear from you what you think, for what we know about this sect is that everywhere people speak against it.'

A day was fixed and large numbers came to his lodging. From dawn to dusk he spoke urgently, testifying to the kingdom of God, trying to persuade them about Jesus with reference to the law of Moses and the prophets. Some were persuaded by his words, others did not believe. They were dispersing without reaching agreement with each other when Paul made one more statement: 'The Holy Spirit was right when he spoke to your fathers through the prophet Isaiah saying: "Go to this people and say: You will hear with your ears but not understand. You will look with your eyes but not see. For this people's heart has become dull of understanding; their ears are hard of hearing and their eyes are closed. Otherwise their eyes might see, their ears hear and their hearts understand, and they might turn again and I would heal them." [3] So let it be known to you that this salvation of God has been sent to the gentiles; they will listen.' [4]

He stayed there for two full years at his own expense and received all who traveled to see him, proclaiming the kingdom of God and teaching about the Lord Jesus Christ quite openly and without hindrance.

> In a letter written during his imprisonment in Rome, Paul exhorts his readers and hearers to emulate Christ's humility and quotes a hymn that would have been well known to his audience. The hymn presents God exhibiting a humility that would have been alien and even offensive to Roman religion.

15.3 *PHILIPPIANS* 2.5-11.

Let the same mind be in you that was in Christ Jesus,
    who though he was in the form of God,
        did not regard equality with God
        as something to be exploited.
But he emptied himself,
    taking the form of a slave,
    being born in the likeness of a man.
And being found in human form,
    he humbled himself
    and became obedient to the point of death – death on a cross.
Therefore God also highly extolled him
    and gave him the name
    that is above every name,

---

[3] Isaiah 6.9-10.

[4] *they will listen*: these words would have reminded Jewish hearers of the book of Jonah in the Hebrew Scriptures, where Jonah is sent to Nineveh to gentiles who listened to him.

so that at the name of Jesus every knee should bend,
in heaven and on earth and under the earth,
and every tongue should confess
that Jesus Christ is Lord, to the glory of God the Father.

Christians as scapegoats

> Although the author of *Acts* states that Paul preached 'quite openly and without hindrance,' Christian views and proseletyzing created tensions even before the First Jewish Revolt and the destruction of the Temple (70 CE). A few years after Paul's arrival in Rome, the emperor Nero made the Christians scapegoats after a great fire (64 CE), an action that indicates their increased presence in the city. It was about this time that Paul and Peter were executed in Rome. Tacitus reports on the reactions of the authorities after the fire.

15.4 TACITUS, *ANNALS* **15.44.** Means were now sought for appeasing the gods. The Sibylline books were consulted. On their recommendation public prayers were offered to Vulcan, Ceres and Proserpina, while Juno was propitiated by the matrons, first on the Capitol, then at the nearest point on the sea-shore where water was drawn for sprinkling the temple and the goddess. Ritual banquets (*sellisternia*) and all-night vigils were celebrated by women who had living husbands.[5]

But neither human resources, nor the emperor's generosity, nor offerings made to the gods dispelled the scandalous report that an order was believed to have been given to start the fire. To suppress the rumor Nero substituted as culprits and punished with cruel refinements those who were hated for their wickedness and popularly known as Christians. The originator of their name, Christus, had been executed in the reign of Tiberius by the procurator Pontius Pilate. The deadly superstition (*superstitio*) was checked for a time only to break out again, not only in Judaea, the source of the evil, but even in the capital itself, where all things hideous and shameful collect from everywhere and and become all the rage.

First self-acknowledged Christians were arrested. Then, on their evidence, a large number were found guilty, not so much on a charge of arson as for their hatred of the human race.[6] Their deaths were made an object of mockery. Covered with the skins of wild beasts, they were torn in pieces by dogs, or they were fastened on crosses[7] and, when daylight failed, they were set alight to serve as torches by night.[8] Nero had offered his gardens for the spectacle and put on an exhibition in his Circus, mixing with the crowd in the dress of a charioteer, or mounted on his chariot. Thus, despite a guilt that had deserved ruthless

---

[5] Widows were thought to be ill-omened.

[6] *hatred of the human race*: either the Christians were considered to hate the human race because of their exclusivity and non-participation in Roman rituals and festivals, or because the human race detested them. The former interpretation is more likely.

[7] *fastened on crosses*: the text is uncertain at this point.

[8] *set alight*: the usual punishment for arson was execution by fire.

punishment, there arose a feeling of pity because of the impression that they were being sacrificed to one man's brutality rather than for the welfare of the state.

A Roman governor asks the emperor Trajan (98-117 CE) for guidance in dealing with Christians

In 112 CE Pliny the Younger, the newly-appointed governor of the province of Bithynia-Pontus (in modern Turkey on the southern coast of the Black Sea), writes to the emperor Trajan, asking his advice on what policy he should adopt towards Christians against whom criminal allegations were being made. It was the responsibility of the local magistrate to decide whether or not a charge was deserving of punishment.

As in the case of the outbreak of new forms of Bacchic worship in 186 BCE, it is likely that the Roman authorities feared political insurrection. From Pliny's account it is apparent that the spread of Christianity was causing pagan temples to be deserted, thus implying a fear that the *pax deorum* would be disrupted. Reference to a lack of demand for sacrificial animals suggests that economic considerations may also have motivated the allegations.

Pliny describes in detail the procedures he has been using in order to test those alleged to be Christians, including a requirement to worship a statue of the emperor.

15.5 PLINY, *LETTERS* 10.96. It is my practice, my lord, to refer to you all matters on which I am doubtful. For who can better guide my uncertainty or inform my ignorance? I have never taken part in the trials of the Christians, and so I do not know what method and limits are customary in either examining or punishing them. I hesitated not a little whether any distinction should be made because of age, or whether the young and their elders should be treated differently. Several other questions arise. Should pardon be granted for repentance, or should it be of no help to an individual who was once a Christian to have recanted? Is the name itself punishable even if there are no criminal offenses? Or should only the criminal offenses associated with the name be punished?[9]

In the meantime, I have employed the following procedure in dealing with those who have been denounced to me as Christians. I asked them directly if they were Christians. If they admitted it, I repeated the question a second and third time, threatening them with capital punishment. If they still persisted, I ordered them to be executed. For I was in no doubt, whatever they confessed to, that their stubborness and inflexible obstinacy certainly ought to be punished. There were other similar fanatics, and these, because they were Roman citizens, I ordered to be sent to Rome.[10]

---

[9]   These last two questions are the crux of Pliny's dilemma, suggesting that there was no law or edict covering the situation.

[10]   *sent to Rome...*: see n. 2.

As a result of the actual procedure, as often happens, the accusations spread, and more kinds of trouble have come to light. An anonymous pamphlet was presented to me, containing many names. Those who denied that they were or ever had been Christians, I thought should be released when they had repeated after me an invocation to the gods and made a supplication of incense and wine to your image which I had ordered to be placed for this purpose with the statues of the gods.[11] They had also cursed Christ. All these are actions that those who are true Christians, so it is said, cannot be forced to do.

Others who had been named by an informer said that they were Christians and then denied it. They had been, but had stopped some three years ago, others several years before, and a few as much as twenty-five years ago. All of these worshipped your statue and the images of the gods. They also cursed Christ. They affirmed, however, that the sum of their guilt, or error, was that they had been accustomed to meet on a fixed day before dawn and sing a hymn in alternate verses to Christ as if to a god, and to bind themselves by an oath, though not for a criminal purpose, vowing not to commit any fraud, theft, or adultery, not to break their word, and not to deny a contract when called upon.[12] After this it had been their custom to separate and then to reassemble to take food — but food of an ordinary and innocent kind.[13] They had abandoned this practice after my edict, by which, in accordance with your orders, I had forbidden political societies.[14] I considered it more essential to seek out the truth, with the help of torture, from two female slaves who were said to be deaconnesses (*ministrae*).[15] But I found nothing except depraved, excessive superstition (*superstitio*).

I therefore adjourned the proceedings and have hastened to consult you. For it seemed to me to be worthy of your consideration, especially in view of the number of those at risk. Many of every age and rank, from both sexes, are and will be involved in the prosecution. The contagion of this superstition (*superstitio*) has spread not only to the cities but also to the villages and countryside, but it can probably be arrested and cured. It is quite clear that

---

[11] *image*: see chapter 11 on imperial cult.

[12] Compare the concern about oath-taking in the Senate's decree on the Bacchanalia, 9.7.

[13] food of an ordinary and innocent kind; for allegations of cannibalism on the part of the Christians, see 15.9.

[14] *had forbidden political societies*: an indication of the authorities' fear that Christianity was politically subversive. In Rome the Senate had long imposed restrictions on the functions of political societies (*collegia*) and the size of the funds they could accumulate. Again compare the Senate's concern about Bacchic worship in 186 BCE.

[15] *deaconesses*: the feminine plural *ministrae* is Pliny's translation of the Greek *diakonissai*. These deaconesses were also slaves (*ancillae*), since they were subject to torture. That women held positions of authority in the early Christian church is attested also in Paul's *Letter to the Romans* 16:1: 'I commend to you our sister Phoebe, a deacon of the church at Cenchreae [near Corinth].' In contrast to Pliny's deaconesses, Phoebe was evidently a woman of some means, since Paul notes her as a benefactor or patron (*prostatis*) of himself and the church.

the temples which had been almost deserted for a long time have begun to be frequented, that the sacred rituals that had long lapsed are being revived, and that there is a general demand for sacrificial animals which, for some time, were finding very few buyers. From this it is easy to infer what a large number of people can be reformed, if an opportunity for repentance is offered.

> The emperor's rescript, a response that had the authority of law, prescribed the death penalty for those who persisted in confessing their faith. Trajan was insistent that Christians were not to be sought out: each case was to be tried on an individual basis. Trajan's rescript was generally followed for almost a century and a half until the reign of the emperor Decius (249-251 CE) who initiated systematic persecutions throughout the empire.

15.6 PLINY, *LETTERS* 10.97. You have followed the necessary procedure, my dear Pliny, in investigating the cases of those denounced to you as Christians. It is not possible to lay down any general rule that could provide a fixed standard. No search should be made for these people. If they are denounced and proved guilty, they must be punished. However, an individual who denies that he is a Christian and gives proof of this by supplicating our gods, even if he has been suspected in the past, will be pardoned as a result of his repentance. But anonymous pamphlets must have no place in a criminal proceeding. For this is a most dangerous precedent and not in keeping with the spirit of our age.

Alleged Christian practices

> Minucius Felix (mid-second to mid-third century CE), himself a Christian, plays devil's advocate as he lists various allegations and wild rumors about Christian practices.

15.7 MINUCIUS FELIX, *OCTAVIUS* 8.4-5. These people gather together the illiterates from the very dregs of society and credulous women who are easily influenced because of their sex. They organize a rabble of wicked conspirators who congregate at night with ritual feasts and inhuman dinners and band together not for a religious ceremony, but for an expiatory sacrifice.[16] They are a secret tribe that shuns the light, silent in public, talkative in hidden corners. They despise temples as if they were tombs, they spit on the gods, and laugh at our sacred rites. Pitiful themselves, if it is right (*fas*) to say so, they pity our priests. They despise political offices and purple regalia, while they themselves go around half-naked.[17]

---

[16] *conspirators... banded together*: compare the prominence of conspiracy in the Bacchanalia episode.
inhuman dinners: an allusion to the charge of cannibalism.

[17] *despise political offices*: since participation in public pagan sacrifices was an essential part of political office-holding, many Christians would have regarded themselves as unable to take part in political life.

15.8 MINUCIUS FELIX, *OCTAVIUS* **9.2.** They recognise each other by secret signs and marks. They are in love with each other almost before they know the individual. Everywhere they mingle in a kind of religion (*religio*) of lust, promiscuously calling each other brother and sister so that any sexual intercourse becomes incest under the cover of a sacred name.

15.9 MINUCIUS FELIX, *OCTAVIUS* **9.5-6.** Stories about their initiation of novices are as deplorable as they are notorious. A baby is wrapped in bread dough to deceive the unwary and is placed beside the person being initiated. The novice is induced to strike the surface of the bread with blows that are apparently harmless. Thus the infant is killed unintentionally by wounds the assailant does not see. And then what a godless act (*nefas*)! They greedily lick up the blood of the infant and eagerly tear apart its limbs.[18] Over this sacrificial victim they swear alliance, pledging themselves to mutual silence by complicity in this crime. These rituals are more foul than any sacrilege. And their feasts are notorious.... On an appointed day, they gather for a banquet with all their children, sisters, and mothers, people of both sexes and all ages. There after much feasting, the party heats up and the passion of incestuous desire inflames them in their drunkenness.

A Christian examines some allegations

> Tertullian (c. 160-230 CE) reiterates and refutes various allegations made against the Christians.

15.10 TERTULLIAN, *APOLOGY* **10.1.** 'You don't worship the gods' you say, 'and you don't offer sacrifices on behalf of the emperors.'

15.11 TERTULLIAN, *APOLOGY* **24.1.** The Christians' response that there is no God except the One whose servants we are is sufficient to repel the allegation that we harm Roman religion.[19]

15.12 TERTULLIAN, *APOLOGY* **30.1.** On behalf of the well-being (*salus*) of the emperors, we invoke the eternal God, the true God, the living God ...

15.13 TERTULLIAN, *APOLOGY* **30.4.** We Christians are continually offering prayers for the emperors, as we look upward, with our hands out-stretched, because innocent, with our heads bare,[20] because we do not blush, and without a prompter, because we pray from the heart.[21] We pray that they may have a long life, secure rule, a safe home, strong armies, a faithful Senate, honest

---

[18] *tear apart its limbs*: this and earlier references to bread and wine are evidently a distorted version of the Eucharist combined with an allusion to the Bacchic *sparagmos*, the tearing apart of a sacrificial animal.

[19] *harm Roman religion*: such a charge would imply a breach of the *pax deorum* and could thus be treasonous.

[20] *with our heads bare*: traditional Roman religion required the head to be covered when praying.

[21] *without a prompter*: in traditional Roman religion set prayers were read aloud by one individual to ensure that there was no mistake (*vitium*); see 4.4.

subjects, and a peaceful world – everything for which a man and a Caesar can pray.

15.14 TERTULLIAN, *APOLOGY* **31.3.** Clearly and explicity it is said, 'Pray for kings and princes and worldly powers so that your lives may be tranquil.'[22] For when the Empire is shaken and the rest of its members are shaken, we too find ourselves in some part of the disaster, although we are not counted as belonging to the masses.

15.15 TERTULLIAN, *APOLOGY* **35.1.** The Christians are considered public enemies because they will not give the emperors vain, false and rash honors, and because they celebrate the emperors' festivals as men of true religion, in their hearts rather than in licentious behavior.[23]

15.16 TERTULLIAN, *APOLOGY* **39.1-3.** I will now show that the proceedings of a Christian association are honorable (I have already proved that they are not evil). We are a society (*corpus*) with a common religious feeling, a common body of teachings, and a common bond of hope. We gather to meet and congregate so that we approach God in prayer .... We nurture our faith with the sacred words, we lift up our hope, we strengthen our confidence, but we also strengthen our teachings by the inculcation of divine precepts....

15.17 TERTULLIAN, *APOLOGY* **39.5-6.** Even if there is a kind of treasury, it is not made up of money paid as an entrance fee, as if religion could be bought.[24] Each individual once a month, or whenever he wishes, gives a small donation, but only if he wishes and only if he can. For no one is compelled; the offering is voluntary. These are, as it were, the trust funds of piety. For they are not spent on banquets or drinking parties, nor on thankless eating-places, but to feed and bury the poor, for boys and girls who lack property and parents, for elderly slaves and ship-wrecked mariners,[25] any who may be in the mines, islands or prisons, provided that the expenditure is for the sake of God's school, who thus become the nurtured (*alumni*) of their confession.

Local persecutions[26]

In his history of the Christian church, Eusebius (c. 264-340 CE), himself a bishop, describes the martyrdom of Polycarp at Smyrna in Asia Minor, c.157 CE.[27] A less prominent Christian had been thrown to the beasts, but the

---

[22] *pray for ... may be tranquil*: quotation from a letter of Paul (1 Timothy 2.2).

[23] Christians disapproved of the wild, drunken behavior that often accompanied the traditional Roman festivals.

[24] *treasury*: the establishing of a common fund was one of the things that were forbidden in the Senate's decree concerning Bacchic worship in 186 BCE; see 9.5 and 9.6.

[25] *elderly slaves*: the Latin could also mean the elderly who were confined to their homes.

[26] *persecution*: the English word derives from the Latin *persequi*, to follow, pursue, go after, bring a case against an individual.

[27] *martyr*: originally a Greek word which literally means 'witness.' Thus a martyr is one who bears witness to his faith by undergoing capital punishment.

crowd was not satisfied and demanded that Polycarp be hunted down. When eventually discovered, Polycarp refused pleas to worship the emperor and curse Christ.

15.18 EUSEBIUS, *HISTORY OF THE CHURCH* **4.15.26-29.** The governor sent his herald to announce three times in the middle of the stadium: 'Polycarp has confessed to being a Christian.' And when the herald had said this, the whole mob of pagans and of Jews who lived at Smyrna cried at the top of their voices with uncontrollable anger, 'This is the teacher of Asia, the father of the Christians, destroyer of our gods, one who teaches many not to sacrifice or prostrate themselves.'[28] With these words, they shouted a demand for Philip the Asiarch to let a lion loose on Polycarp.[29] But he said that he could not since he had officially ended the games. Then, unanimously, they decided to shout for Polycarp to be burnt alive .... The crowds immediately gathered wood and sticks from workshops and baths, and the Jews were particularly eager to help with this, as they usually are.[30]

Eusebius later describes the persecution of Christians in Gaul in 177 CE.

15.19 EUSEBIUS, *HISTORY OF THE CHURCH* **5.1.7-9, 14-15.** First the Christians nobly endured all that was heaped upon them by the mob: verbal abuse, beatings, draggings, being plundered, stoned and imprisoned and all those things that an enraged group of people usually does to supposed foes and enemies. They were dragged into the marketplace by the tribune and the city officials; they were indicted and confessed [to being Christians]. They were then imprisoned until the arrival of the governor. When he arrived, they were led before him, and he brought all his cruelty to bear upon them....

Some foreign slaves who belonged to our church were also arrested because the governor had publicly ordered that we were all to be questioned. These slaves were caught in the snare of Satan and were terrified of the tortures that they saw the saints suffering. At the urging of the soldiers, they falsely accused us of Thyestean banquets and Oedipodean incest, and things that it is not right for us either to say or think or even believe that such things could ever happen among men.[31] When these accusations spread, everyone turned like wild beasts against us, with the result that even people who had formerly been moderate towards us because of personal friendship now became intensely angry and furious.

---

[28] *destroyer of our gods... not to sacrifice or prostrate themselves*: these words imply a fear of endangering the *pax deorum*.

[29] *Asiarch*: governor or chief magistrate in Asia Minor.

[30] Note Eusebius' antipathy and prejudice towards Jews.

[31] *Thyestean banquets and Oedipodean incest*: mythical allusions implying cannibalism and sexual relations with close family members. Thyestes' brother Atreus fed him the flesh of his own children at a feast. Oedipus married his own mother who bore children to her own son.

Persecution as imperial policy

In the middle of the third century, a period of chaos and disorder throughout the empire, the emperor Decius (249-251 CE) initiated systematic persecutions of the Christians when he ordered that all inhabitants of the Roman empire, except the Jews, should sacrifice to the gods. Decius' decree thus accentuated the otherness, or social alienation, of the Christians, making them vulnerable to widespread persecution. His principal aim was to restore the traditional religion and places of worship and so ensure the *pax deorum* in a time of political, military and economic instability. Roman religion was one of the few remaining bonds that could serve to unify the highly disparate inhabitants of the empire.

The test of suspected Christians was similar to that employed by Pliny, but now they were also required to participate in the sacrificial system as a whole: the offering of incense, pouring of libations and tasting of the sacrificial victim. They were, moreover, required to attest that they had *always* performed such sacrifice, thus involving many in the necessity to lie. Commissioners were appointed to enforce the decree and, in doubtful cases, certificates were issued, signed by two officials who had witnessed the sacrifice.[32]

Persecution was renewed by the emperor Valerian in 257 CE, but stopped three years later by Gallienus. Again the crucial test was the performance of pagan sacrifice. Those who did not follow Roman religion *(religio)* were required to observe Roman religious ceremonies. Prominent individuals, both in the church and in politics, who refused to sacrifice were subjected to confiscation of property, exile and even death. As the governor of Africa who was trying the case of bishop Cyprian is reported to have said, 'You have long persisted in your sacrilegious views, and you have joined to yourself many other vicious men in a conspiracy. You have set yourself up as an enemy of the Roman gods and their religious rites.' [33]

In an attempt to restore central authority, the emperor Diocletian (284-303 CE) sought to ensure the favor of the gods by a return to traditional Roman values.

15.20 EDICT OF DIOCLETIAN, *IN COMPARISON OF MOSAIC AND ROMAN LAWS* 6.4.1 (*FIRA* **2. 559**). For in this way there is no doubt that the immortal gods themselves will look with favor, as they always have, on the Roman Name and be placated, if we see that everyone who is under our rule cultivates a pious, religiously scrupulous, peaceful and chaste life in all respects.

Diocletian's ruling against the Manichees (297 CE), devotees of a new religion that spread westward from Persia in the mid-third century, defined rejection of traditional Roman religion as a crime.

15.21 EDICT OF DIOCLETIAN, *IN COMPARISON OF MOSAIC AND ROMAN LAWS* 15.3.2-3 (*FIRA* **2. 580**). But the immortal gods in their providence have seen fit to ordain

---

[32] See Lane Fox (1986) 455-7.

[33] *Acts of Cyprian* 1.1.

and dispose what is good and true in such a way that it should be approved and established by the judgment of many good and outstanding men of the greatest wisdom and remain unimpaired. It is not right to obstruct or resist this, nor should old religion be criticized by a new one.

It is the greatest crime to revoke things which, once established and determined by the ancients, hold and maintain their position and course. For this reason it is our great desire to punish the obstinacy of the perverted minds of utterly evil men. These men, who set up new-fangled and unheard-of sects in opposition to the older religious practices, are using their perverted judgment to shut out what heaven once bestowed upon us.

The evolution of imperial policy during the fourth century CE

Diocletian's efforts culminated in the so-called Great Persecution. In 302 CE, soldiers and members of the imperial court were ordered to sacrifice to the traditional Roman gods. In the following year, Christian worship was declared illegal. Christian clergy were imprisoned and only released after they had performed pagan sacrifice. In 304 CE all the inhabitants of the empire were ordered to sacrifice, holy books were confiscated, and churches destroyed. The overall extent of the persecutions is impossible to discern from the extant sources which focus on a few atrocities. Similarly difficult to discern are the motives of Diocletian and Galerius, his co-ruler. Implicit, however, in the accounts of the persecution is the increased organization of the church, with a hierarchy of bishops and other officials, a factor that had doubtless caused the emperors considerable disquiet. Ultimately the persecution failed and, on his deathbed in 311 CE, Galerius repented and issued the edict of Religious Toleration.

15.22 EDICT OF GALERIUS IN LACTANTIUS, *DEATHS OF THE PERSECUTORS* 34. We had previously wished to correct everything in accordance with the ancient laws and public discipline of the Romans and see to it that the Christians also, who had abandoned their ancestors' way of life, should return to good sense....

But as very many persisted in their determination and we saw that these same people neither exhibited the worship and respect owed to the gods, nor did they worship the god of the Christians, we have decided, in view of our lenience and clemency and because of our long-lasting practice of customarily granting pardon to all, that the readiest indulgence should be extended to these people too, so that once again they may be Christians and hold their meetings, provided they do not act contrary to the public discipline....

In 312 CE Constantine defeated Maxentius, his rival for the throne, at the battle of the Milvian Bridge, and entered Rome in triumph. Of Constantine's so-called conversion, Beard, North and Price comment: 'The conversion of Constantine was one of the most unexpected events in Roman history, and remains highly controversial. Even supposing that what happened at and before the battle was central to Constantine's support of Christianity (which is, of course, far from certain), almost every aspect of that support has been debated ever since. Was he sincere in his adherence to Christianity? How far did he conflate Christianity with elements of traditional cults? From what date is Constantine's firm support of Christianity to be dated – from AD 312 or later?... The questions are unanswerable.'[34]

In 313 CE the so-called Edict of Milan expanded religious toleration.

15.23 LACTANTIUS, *DEATHS OF THE PERSECUTORS* **48.** Among the other things that we saw would be of benefit to the majority, or thought should be dealt with first, was the issue of reverence (*reverentia*) for divinity, so that we might grant Christians and everyone the freedom to follow the religious observance that each person wished, so that whatever divinity there is in the seat of heaven may be placated and propitious to us and to all who are under our rule.

> But such toleration was not achieved. In 341 CE Constantius, one of Constantine's three sons and successors, passed a law enjoining that 'superstition must cease and the madness of sacrifice be abolished,' a law that applied to traditional Roman religion in its entirety. However, in the following year, some concessions were granted to those pagan rituals that provided entertainment for the populace.

15.24 *LAW CODE OF THEODOSIUS* **16.10.3.** Although all superstitions must be abolished, we nevertheless desire that the temples situated outside the walls should remain untouched and undamaged. Because certain plays and spectacles of the circus or contests originated in some of these temples, such structures must not be torn down, since they provide the regular performance of long-established amusements for the Roman people.

> Constantius again attempted to ban pagan sacrifice (346 or 354 CE).

15.25 *LAW CODE OF THEODOSIUS* **16.10.4.** It is our pleasure that in all places and every city the temples be immediately closed and access to them forbidden so that the immoral be deprived of the possibility of misbehavior. Moreover we wish that all should refrain from sacrifice. But if anyone should perpetrate any such a criminal act, he shall be killed by the avenging sword.

We also decree that the property of the executed shall be claimed by the Treasury and that the governors of the provinces shall be similarly punished if they fail to take measures against such crimes.

> In 356 CE Constantius reaffirmed the ban on pagan sacrifices and the closing of pagan temples, decreeing that 'capital punishment be the penalty for those proved to have engaged in sacrifices or worshipped statues (*Law Code of Theodosius* 16.10.6). Three years later Julian the Apostate (361-363 CE) rescinded the laws hostile to the traditional Roman religion. Subsequent emperors, however, legislated against pagan practices.

> But paganism did not disappear overnight. The influential old Roman aristocracy maintained its adherence to the traditional cults, and the populace continued to enjoy the pagan festivals and the games. Valentinian I banned nocturnal prayers and sacrifices (*Law Code of Theodosius* 9.16.7), and Theodosius banned

---

[34] BNP 1.366.

sacrifices in daylight if they were for divination.

15.26 *Law code of Theodosius* **16.10.7.** If any madman or sacrilegious person, so to speak, should involve himself in forbidden sacrifices for divination, by day or by night, and if he should suppose that he should employ, or think that he should approach a shrine or temple for the commission of such a crime, he shall know that he will be subject to proscription, since we give warning that God must be worshipped by chaste prayers and not be profaned by dire incantations.

> The story of the 'triumph of Christianity' is material for another book. Our selection of sources for Roman religion is perhaps best concluded with an excerpt from the petition of Symmachus, the pagan prefect of Rome, who wrote to the emperor Valentinian II asking him to restore the altar of Victory which had earlier been removed from the Senate house by the emperor Gratian, who had also refused the title of *pontifex maximus*.[35] This letter articulates a plea for toleration, while also reflecting the distinctive features of traditional Roman religion that have been described throughout our survey.
>
> It should be noted that many of the sources cited in this chapter, notably Eusebius, were writing from the perspective of the eastern Mediterranean Greek-speaking world. Moreover, Constantine and most subsequent emperors were principally resident in the New Rome, Constantinople, where growing disputes in and about Christianity were not necessarily viewed in the same way as they were in the west, in old Rome.

15.27 Symmachus, *Dispatches to the Emperor* **3.8-10.** Every man has his own way of life (*mos*) and his own religious practices (*ritus*). Similarly, the divine mind has given to different cities different religious rites (*cultus*) which protect them. As souls are apportioned to men at birth, so, too, does each nation receive a Genius which guides its destiny. In addition there is also the bestowal of favors (*utilitas*) which, more than anything else, proves to man the existence of the gods. For, since all human reasoning is obscure on this matter, from where else does knowledge of the gods more correctly come than from the recollection and evidence of success? If the long passage of time gives authority to religious rites, we must keep faith with so many centuries and we must follow our fathers, who followed their fathers and so prospered.

Let us imagine that Rome herself is standing here now and addressing these words to you: 'Best of emperors, father of the fatherland, respect the number of years that the dutiful performance of religious rites (*pius ritus*) has brought to me. Let me enjoy the ancient ceremonies, for I do not regret them. Let me live according to my own custom (*mos*), for I am free. This is the worship (*cultus*) which made the whole world obedient to my laws. These are the rituals (*sacra*) which drove back Hannibal from my walls and the Senones from my Capitol.[36]

---

[35] The altar of Victory had been set up by Augustus in the Senate house after his return from Egypt after defeating Antony and Cleopatra.

[36] *Senones*: a Gallic tribe, an allusion to the Sack of Rome by the Gauls in 390 BCE.

Have I been preserved only to be criticized in my old age? I will consider the changes which people think must be instituted, but correction (*emendatio*) in old age is insulting and too late.'

And so we are asking for amnesty (*pax*) for the gods of our fathers, our native gods. It is reasonable to assume that whatever each of us worships is one and the same. We look up at the same stars, the same sky is common to us all, the same universe encompasses us. What difference does it make which system each of us uses to seek the truth? It is not by just one route that man can arrive at so great a mystery.

GODS

Aesculapius: god of healing, the Greek Asclepius, whose cult was imported to Rome in the early third century BCE.

Apollo: originally a Greek god, son of Zeus and Leto (Roman Latona) whose cult as healer was imported to Rome in 432 BCE during a time of plague. His cult was later promoted by Augustus, who built a temple to him on the Palatine and had the Sibylline books placed there rather than in the temple of Jupiter Capitolinus.

Bacchus/Dionysus: a Greek god, son of Zeus and Semele, who was worshipped in Rome as Liber Pater in the early fifth century. A revival of this cult was suppressed by the Senate in 186 BCE because of its orgiastic aspects which were thought to be politically subversive.

Ceres: ancient Italo-Roman goddess of growth, usually identified with the Greek Demeter. Her temple on the Aventine dates to the early fifth century BCE.

Cybele or **Cybebe**: the great Anatolian mother goddess who was imported to Rome during the Hannibalic War and worshipped on the Palatine hill as Magna Mater, the Great Mother. Her eunuch priests were called Galli. She was worshipped along with her consort Attis.

Diana: an Italian goddess often identified with Artemis, the sister of Apollo and daughter of Zeus and Leto. She was worshipped at Aricia in Latium and in a temple on the Aventine. Her original Italic cult seems to have been that of a goddess of the wilderness and of margins.

Janus: god of doors and gates, openings and beginnings. He was usually represented as facing two ways, like a door.

Jupiter: one of the pre-eminent Roman deities, often identified with Zeus. He was worshipped on the Capitoline hill as Jupiter Optimus Maximus, in a tripartite Etruscan-style temple shared with Juno and Minerva that was built at the end of the sixth century BCE. He was also worshipped in Rome as Jupiter Tonans (Thunderer) and Jupiter Stator (Stayer-in-battle).

Juno: an ancient and important Italic deity, later identified with the Greek goddess Hera. She was worshipped with Jupiter in the temple of Jupiter Optimus Maximus, but also had her own temple on the citadel nearby where she was worshipped as Juno Moneta, an epithet usually interpreted as the 'Warner' because her sacred geese warned the Romans of the approach of the Gauls in 390 BCE. The cult of Juno Regina was brought to Rome by the ritual of *evocatio* from Veii on the capture of that city in 396 BCE. At Lanuvium, near Rome, she was worshipped as Juno Sospita (Protector).

Isis: an Egyptian goddess whose cult infiltrated Rome in the early first century BCE. Several attempts were made to suppress her worship, but she was finally accepted and given a temple during the reign of Claudius.

Magna Mater: the 'Great Mother', see above, Cybele.

Mars: apparently originally an Italic god of vegetation who soon became associated with war, and so was assimilated with the Greek war-god Ares. Augustus built a temple to Mars Ultor (the Avenger) in recognition of his victory over Caesar's assassins.

Mercury: patron god of circulation, especially trade and commerce. Probably of Italic origin, though he is later identified with the Greek god Hermes. Mediator between gods and mortals, patron of businessmen, shopkeepers, traders, travelers and brigands. His temple on the Aventine is traditionally dated to the early fifth century BCE.

Minerva: an Italic goddess of handicrafts and thus identified with Athena, daughter of Zeus. She first appears in Rome as part of the Capitoline triad, and thus may have come through contact with the Etruscans.

Mithras: an ancient Indo-Iranian god whose worship was widespread in the Roman empire, especially among the lower ranks of the military. The cult involved initiation. A relatively large number of shrines have been discovered in Rome and in Ostia.

Neptune: an Italic god of water, later identified with the Greek god Poseidon.

Quirinus: a god, probably of Sabine origin, who is associated with the deified Romulus. Little is known of this deity, except that his functions resemble those of Mars. He is often associated with Mars and Jupiter, since all three deities had their own *flamen*.

Saturn: a deity thought by some to be an Italic god of sowing or seed-corn. Others consider him to be of Etruscan origin. His cult is celebrated according to the Greek rite, which raises a further question about his origin. He was celebrated at the Saturnalia, a period of rest and merry-making.

Venus: the goddess of sexual desire who was assimilated with the Greek Aphrodite. The cult of Venus Genetrix was especially promoted by Julius Caesar, whose family claimed descent from Venus via her son and grandson, Aeneas and Iulus (Ascanius).

Vesta: Roman goddess of the fire of the hearth, worshipped as the living flame in a circular shrine in the Roman forum. This fire and her cult were tended by the Vestal virgins, who were required to maintain strict sexual purity during a minimum thirty-year service.

Vulcan: ancient Roman god of destructive and volcanic fire who was identified with the Greek Hephaestus.

Glossary

Arval Brethren: an ancient college of priests that had ceased to function in late republican times but was revived by Augustus.

augurs: official Roman diviners who were both experts and priests. They held office for life and were members of the augural college.

augury: auspices or signs that pertain to both substance and time that could only be conducted by augurs, as opposed to auspices which only pertained for one day.

auspices (*auspicia*, singular *auspicium*): literally the observation of birds, but more widely applied to a variety of signs that were considered to have been sent by the gods as an indication of their favor or disfavor toward an action that was already in progress or under consideration. These signs were interpreted by divination. Auspices were valid for one day only, that is, they pertained only to time, not to substance; cf. augury. All public, i.e., state, actions were undertaken after auspices had been sought.

Aventine: one of the seven hills of Rome that originally lay outside the *pomerium* or sacred boundary of Rome. The area is associated with the lower classes or plebeians.

client: a free man who entrusted himself to another (his patron), and in return received protection such as food and legal assistance when needed. The client would support his patron both in political and private life, demonstrating his loyalty by going to his house each morning to offer a formal greeting (*salutatio*).

Comitium: the chief place of political assembly during the republic. An inaugurated space, consecrated as a *templum*, north of the Roman Forum, at the foot of the Capitoline hill.

consuls: the two chief magistrates of Rome who during the republic were elected annually and held both civic and military power.

decemviri: see quindecimviri

devotio: the vow of a military commander to give his own life to the gods in return for victory.

divination: the interpretation of messages or signs believed to have been sent by the gods. These signs—auspices, portents, prodigies, dreams and prophecies—could be solicited or unsolicited, could refer to the present, past or future and could indicate prediction, warning, displeasure, prohibition, or approval. Three groups of experts interpreted these signs: augurs, harsupices and quindecimvirs.

duumviri: see *quindecimviri*

Etruscans: non-Indo-European speaking peoples, living to the north of Rome in Etruria. Their power expanded to control Rome and areas of Campania in the sixth and early fifth centuries BCE.

expiation: (*piaculum*) an action aimed at making amends or atonement for an offense to the gods.

fas: an action that is lawful in the eyes of the gods, as opposed to *nefas* (an impiety).

fetials (*fetiales*): priests whose duties were the making of treaties and declaration of war

flamen (plural, *flamines*): Roman priests within the college of the pontifices. There were three major and twelve minor *flamines*, each assigned to a specific deity, although this did not preclude them from participating in the worship of other deities. Of the three major *flamines*, one served Jupiter (*flamen Dialis*), another Mars, and a third Quirinus.

flamen Dialis: a priest of Jupiter on whom many taboos were imposed, making it virtually impossible for him to pursue a political or military career.

Genius: A divine 'double', as it were, of an individual, usually a male. The Genius of the *pater familias* was thus a part of family religion, and the whole household had its Genius. This Genius protected family and client relationships. Augustus developed the cult of his own Genius.

haruspices (singular, *haruspex*): diviners who originally came from Etruria. They dealt with signs that were thought to indicate future happenings in the entrails of sacrificial victims, lightning and prodigies. The term *haruspex* is also used more generally of soothsayers and diviners. They, unlike the *pontifices* and augurs, were not official priests of the state until the time of Claudius (42-54 CE).

intercalation: the insertion of an additional month in the Roman year of 355 days in order to keep the Roman calendar in synchronisation with the solar year of 364 days. Intercalation was one of the duties of the pontifices, but was not always regularly performed. During the civil wars of the late republic, it was neglected for a number of years, resulting in Julius Caesar's reform of the calendar.

lar (plural *lares*): the spirit or deity which guarded and protected the household and its members. In each home there was a shrine to this deity where sacrifices were made regularly by the head of the household (*pater familias*).

Laws of the Twelve Tables: a collection of statutes into twelve 'tables', traditionally dated c. 450 BCE. This collection is the foundation of Roman law.

lectisternium: literally a draping of couches (*pulvinaria*), a banquet in honor of the gods at which the statues of the gods were placed on draped couches outside the temples.

libation: a liquid offering to the gods, usually of wine.

manes: spirits of the dead.

nefas: an action that is unlawful in the eyes of the gods, an impiety.

oracle: a divine utterance, or prophecy, made by a god through a priest or priestess. The word can also apply to the priest or priestess making the utterance, e.g., the Delphic oracle.

pax deorum: the favor or benevolence (literally the peace, as opposed to anger, *ira*) of the gods. This cannot be ensured, but may be obtained by prayer and sacrifice.

Palatine: one of the seven hills of Rome, reputedly the oldest settlement. It came to be the most desirable residential area, and thus was inhabited by the emperors. English 'palace' derives from *palatium*.

penates: household gods that protected the pantry or store-cupboard.

pomerium: the sacred boundary of the city of Rome, said to have been established by Romulus.

pontifex (plural, *pontifices*): official priests of the state who held office for life and who belonged to the pontifical college. They were experts and interpreters of ritual matters, including flaws in performance (*vitia*).

pontifex maximus: chief pontifex.

portent: an unusual or unnatural occurrence, either solicited or unsolicited, that was thought to have been sent by the gods as an indication of a future event. A portent could become a prodigy only if so decreed by the state authorities.

praetor: an elected official or magistrate.

praetor peregrinus: the magistrate concerned with the business of foreigners in the city of Rome, as opposed to the city praetor (*praetor urbanus*).

prodigy: an unusual or unnatural occurrence that was considered to have been sent by the gods as an indication of a future event. A prodigy could be solicited or unsolicited, though the latter is more common. The term prodigy (*prodigium*) should strictly refer to a sign that has been accepted by the state authorities as indicating that the *pax deorum* has been broken or is about to be ruptured, although both ancient and modern writers often refer to the more unfavorable or sinister portents as prodigies (*prodigia*).

pulvinaria: couches or platforms on which the statues of the gods were placed at a *lectisternium*.

quindecimvirs: A board of priests who were in charge of the performance of sacred rites (*sacris faciundis*). Their principle function was the guardianship of the Sibylline books. Their number increased from two (*duumviri*) to ten (*decemviri*) then fifteen (*quindecimviri*) and finally sixteen, although the title *quindecimviri* remained unchanged.

Quirites: an ancient title of the Romans, perhaps to be connected with the god Quirinus.

rex sacrificulus or *rex sacrorum*: literally 'king of sacrifices.' This official is said to have taken over the religious functions of the king, when the monarchy was abolished.

Rostra: the speakers' platform in the Roman Forum.

Senate: an advisory body consisting of ex-magistrates, whose chief function was to advise the magistrates on matters of domestic and foreign policy, finance and religion.

Sibylline books: a collection of oracles that was kept in the temple of Jupiter on the Capitoline Hill, said to have been bought from the Sibyl of Cumae by Tarquin the Elder. The books were later transferred by Augustus to the temple of Apollo on the Palatine.

supplicatio: a ritual of collective prayer that was performed on behalf of the citizen body in order to elicit the favor of the gods, expiate a prodigy or give thanks for the fulfilment of an earlier petitionary prayer. This ritual, in which the people themselves often participated by visiting all the *pulvinaria*, seems to have been of Greek origin and to have been adopted during the fifth century. Expiatory supplications were frequently performed on the advice of the decemvirs, after consultation of the Sibylline books.

vitium: a flaw or error in the performance of ritual. The flaw could be in the performance of the prayer, in the accompanying sacrifice, or in the entrails of a victim after sacrifice.

CHRONOLOGY

Some of the earlier dates are traditional or approximate.

c. 753 BCE	traditional date of the founding of Rome
c. 509	expulsion of the kings and dedication of temple of Jupiter Capitolinus
c. 450	Laws of the Twelve Tables
433	temple vowed to Apollo
399	first *lectisternium*
396	*evocatio* of Juno of Veii
340	*devotio* of Decius Mus
c. 300	plebeians admitted to major priesthoods
291	temple of Aesculapius on Tiber island
264-241	First Punic War
249	Publius Claudius and the sacred chickens
218-201	Second Punic or Hannibalic War
217	battle of Trasimene and death of Flaminius
216	battle of Cannae followed by sacrifice of two Gauls and two Greeks
205	summoning of Magna Mater to Rome
186	attempt to suppress Bacchic cult
146	Rome sacks Carthage and Corinth
139	expulsion of Jews and astrologers from Rome
46	Caesar's reform of the calendar
44	assassination of Julius Caesar
31	battle of Actium and defeat of Antony and Cleopatra
29	dedication of temple of Divus Julius
28	dedication of temple of Apollo on the Palatine
27	Octavian takes the title Augustus
14 CE	Tiberius becomes emperor
19	suppression of cult of Isis and expulsion of Jews from Rome
c.36	Conversion of Paul on road to Damascus

41	Claudius becomes emperor
43	temple of Isis dedicated in Campus Martius
c.49	Claudius' expulsion of Jews/Christians from Rome
46-58	Paul's mission to the gentiles in Asia Minor and Greece
54	Nero becomes emperor
58	Paul accused of blasphemy, arrested by Roman authorities in Jerusalem and sent to Rome
64	Christians as scapegoats after fire of Rome
64, 65, or 66	execution of Paul and Peter in Rome
66-73	First Jewish Revolt
70	Titus sacks Jerusalem
79	eruption of Vesuvius
111	Pliny's letter from Bithynia re Christians, and Trajan's rescript
133	revolt of Bar Cocheba
135	defeat of revolt, dispersal of Jews, reorganization of Syria Palestina
c. 157	martyrdom of Polycarp at Smyrna
177	persecution of Christians in Gaul under Marcus Aurelius
202	Septimius Severus bans conversion to Christianity and Judaism
249-251	persecutions under Decius who orders all inhabitants of the Empire except Jews to sacrifice to unspecified (pagan) gods
257	Valerian starts new persecution of Christians; confiscations of Church property
260	Gallienus ends Christian persecution
303-311	persecution of Christians under Diocletian and Galerius
311	Galerius' deathbed repentance; Edict of Religious Toleration
312	battle of Milvian Bridge and so-called conversion of Constantine
313	Edict of Milan expands religious toleration
325	Council of Nicaea. Arianism condemned as heresy
330	Constantinople becomes imperial residence
337	death of Constantine
346 (or 354)	Constantius' edict attempting to ban pagan sacrifice
360-363	Julian the Apostate rescinds laws hostile to paganism
382	Gratian renounces the title of Pontifex Maximus, removes altar of Victory from Senate House and confiscates endowments of Vestal Virgins and ancient priestly colleges
384	Petition of Symmachus to Valentinian II to restore altar of Victory
391	edicts against paganism; destruction of Serapeum in Rome
392	Theodosius' ban on sacrifices

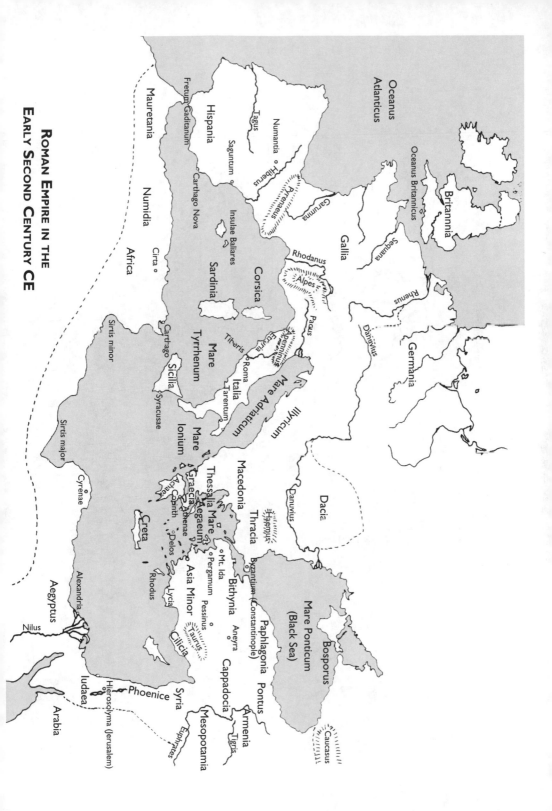

ROMAN EMPIRE IN THE
EARLY SECOND CENTURY CE

Oceanus
Atlanticus

Mauretania

Hispania

Numantia

Tagus

Saguntum

Hiberus

Pyrenaeus

Fretum Gaditanum

Numidia

Africa

Cirta

Carthago Nova

Insulae Baliares

Sardinia

Corsica

Garumna

Gallia

Rhodanus

Alpes

Padus

Oceanus Britannicus

Britannia

Sequana

Rhenus

Germania

Danuvius

Sirtis minor

Carthago

Sicilia

Syracusae

Mare
Tyrrhenum

Tiberis

Etruria

Roma

Italia

Tarentum

Apenninus

Mare Adriaticum

Illyricum

Sirtis major

Cyrenae

Creta

Mare
Ionium

Graecia

Corinth.

Athenae

Delos

Rhodus

Achaea

Thessalia

Aegaeum

Mare

Macedonia

Thracia

Haemus

Danuvius

Dacia

Byzantium (Constantinople)

Bithynia

Pergamum

Mt. Ida

Asia Minor

Lycia

Pessinus

Taurus

Cilicia

Aneyra

Cappadocia

Paphlagonia

Pontus

Mare Ponticum
(Black Sea)

Bosporus

Armenia

Tigris

Caucasus

Alexandria

Aegyptus

Nilus

Iudaea

Hierosolyma (Jerusalem)

Phoenice

Syria

Euphrates

Mesopotamia

Arabia

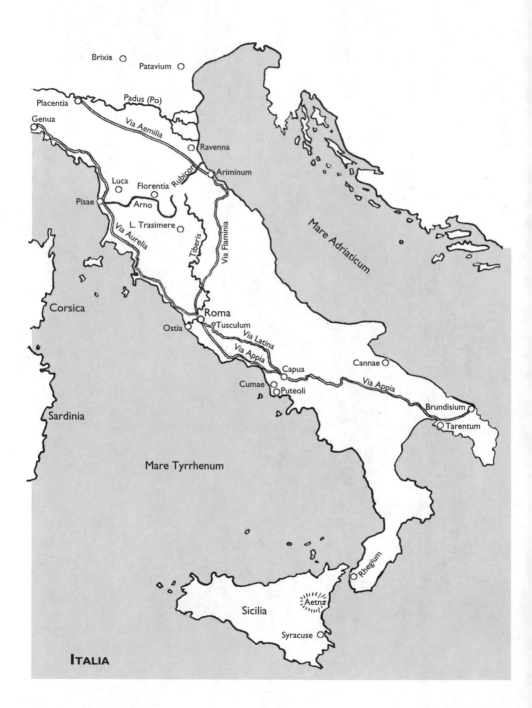

Brixia ○

Patavium ○

Placentia ○

Genua ○

Padus (Po)

Via Aemilia

Ravenna ○

Luca ○

Florentia ○

Ariminum ○

Rubicon

Pisae ○

Arno

Via Aurelia

L. Trasimere ○

Tiberis

Via Flaminia

Corsica

Roma ○

Tusculum ○

Ostia ○

Via Latina

Via Appia

Mare Adriaticum

Capua ○

Cumae ○

Puteoli ○

Cannae ○

Via Appia

Sardinia

Brundisium ○

Tarentum ○

Mare Tyrrhenum

Rhegium ○

Aetna

Sicilia

Syracuse ○

ITALIA

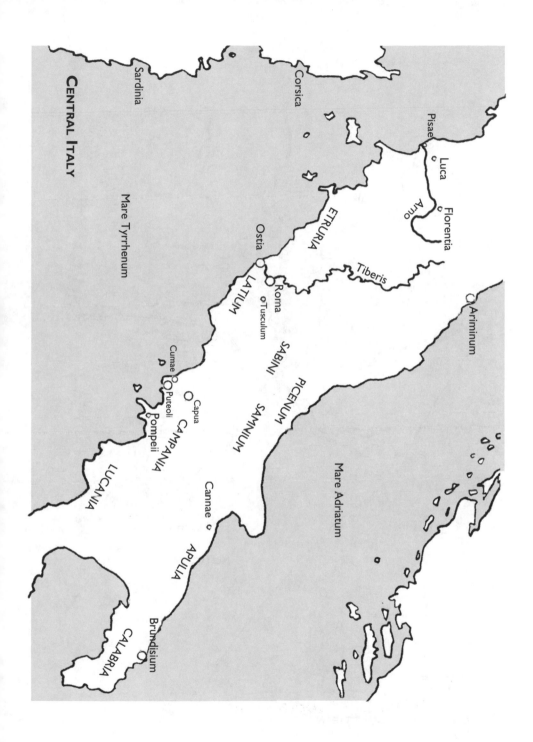

CENTRAL ITALY

Sardinia

Corsica

Pisae

Luca

Arno

Florentia

ETRURIA

Ostia

Tiberis

Ariminum

Mare Tyrrhenum

LATIUM

Roma

Tusculum

SABINI

PICENUM

Cumae

SAMNIUM

Puteoli

Capua

Pompeii

CAMPANIA

Mare Adriatum

LUCANIA

Cannae

APULIA

Brundisium

CALABRIA

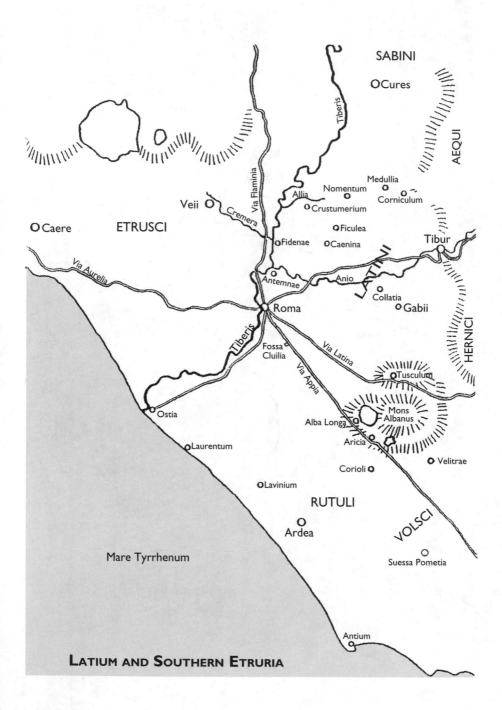

SABINI

O Cures

AEQUI

Tiberis

Medullia
Nomentum   O
                Corniculum
Allia
Veii O   O Crustumerium
      Cremera
                    O Ficulea
O Caere   ETRUSCI
                O Fidenae   O Caenina   Tibur
Via Aurelia
                                              LATINI
              O Antemnae   Anio
                                    O Collatia
              Roma   O Gabii
                                                HERNICI
Tiberis   Fossa
           Cluilia   Via Latina
                  Via Appia
                                    Tusculum
O Ostia   O
                                    Mons
                        Alba Longa Albanus
   O Laurentum   O
                        Aricia O
                                    O Velitrae
                   Corioli O

              O Lavinium

                   RUTULI

              O
              Ardea   VOLSCI

Mare Tyrrhenum
                        O
                        Suessa Pometia

                              Antium
                              O

LATIUM AND SOUTHERN ETRURIA

Ager Vaticanus

Tiberis

Campus Martius

Quirinalis

Viminalis

niculum

Capitolium

Forum
Romanum

Esquiliae

Roma
quadrata

Palatium

Caelius

Vallis Murcia

Tiberis

Aventinus

Porta Capena

Moenia antiqua

ROMA ANTIQUA

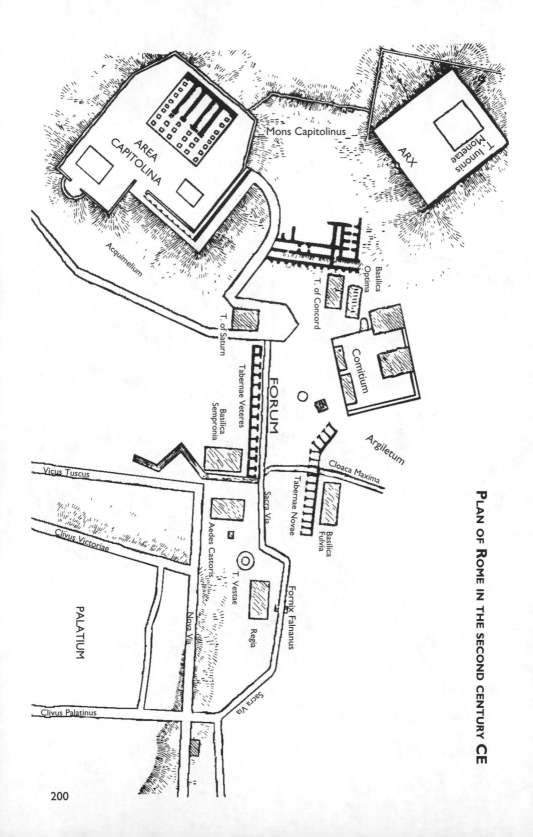

PLAN OF ROME IN THE SECOND CENTURY CE

Mons Capitolinus

AREA CAPITOLINA

ARX

T. Iunonis Monetae

Acquimelium

Basilica Optima

T. of Concord

T. of Saturn

Comitium

Tabernae Veteres

FORUM

Basilica Sempronia

Argiletum

Cloaca Maxima

Tabernae Novae

Basilica Fulvia

Vicus Tuscus

Clivus Victoriae

Sacra Via

Aedes Castoris

Clivus Palatinus

PALATIUM

Nova Via

T. Vestae

Regia

Fornix Fabianus

Sacra Via

200

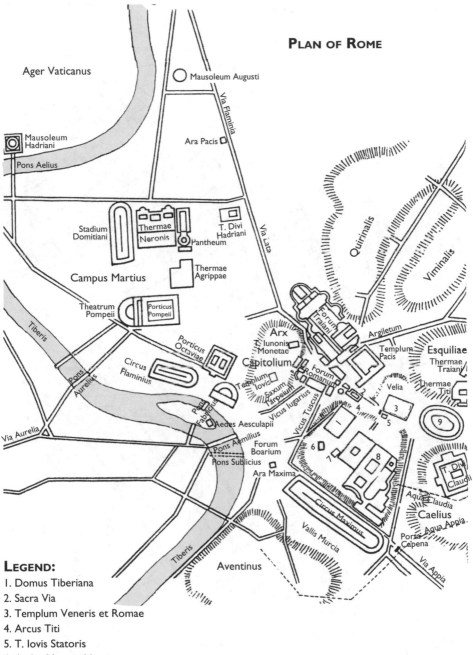

PLAN OF ROME

Ager Vaticanus

Mausoleum Augusti

Via Flaminia

Mausoleum Hadriani

Pons Aelius

Ara Pacis

Stadium Domitiani

Thermae Neronis

T. Divi Hadriani

Pantheum

Via Lata

Quirinalis

Viminalis

Campus Martius

Thermae Agrippae

Theatrum Pompeii

Porticus Pompeii

Tiberis

Pons Aurelius

Porticus Octaviae

Circus Flaminius

Arx

Capitolium

T. Iunonis Monetae

Templum Iovis

Saxum Tarpeium

Forum Traiani

Argiletum

Templum Pacis

Esquiliae

Thermae Traiani

Forum Romanum

Velia

Thermae Titi

Via Aurelia

Pons Fabricius

Aedes Aesculapii

Pons Aemilius

Pons Sublicius

Forum Boarium

Ara Maxima

Vicus Iugarius

Vicus Tuscus

4

3

5

1

6

7

8

9

T. Divi Claudii

Aqua Claudia

Caelius

Aqua Appia

Circus Maximus

Porta Capena

Via Appia

Tiberis

Vallis Murcia

Aventinus

LEGEND:
1. Domus Tiberiana
2. Sacra Via
3. Templum Veneris et Romae
4. Arcus Titi
5. T. Iovis Statoris
6. Aedes Magnae Matris
7. Aedes Apollinis
8. Domus Augustana
9. Amphitheatrum Flavium (Colosseum)

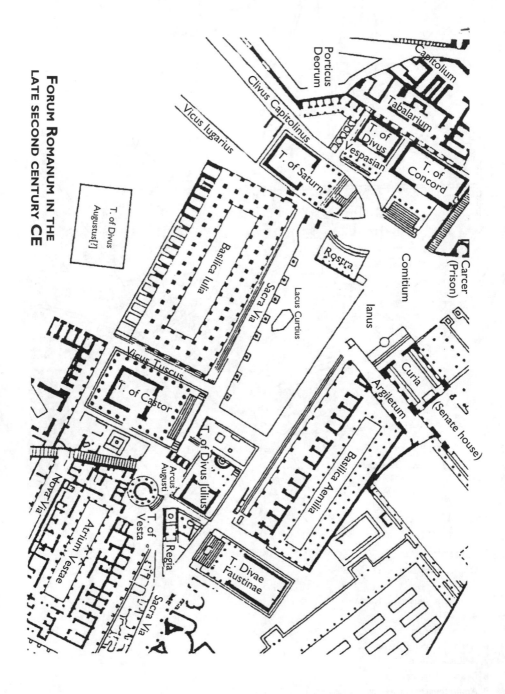

Forum Romanum in the Late Second Century CE

T. of Divus Augustus[?]

Porticus Deorum

Capitolium

Clivus Capitolinus

Tabalarium

Vicus Iugarius

T. of Divus Vespasian

T. of Concord

T. of Saturn

Carcer (Prison)

Basilica Iulia

Rostra

Comitium

Lacus Curtius

Ianus

Sacra Via

Curia (Senate house)

Argiletum

Vicus Tuscus

T. of Castor

Basilica Aemilia

Arcus Augusti

T. of Divus Iulius

Nova Via

T. of Vesta

Atrium Vestae

Regia

Sacra Via

T. Divae Faustinae

ANCIENT SOURCES

Most of the sources translated in this volume are available in the Loeb Classical Library and the Penguin translation series. My translations use either the Loeb texts or the Oxford Classical Texts.

Acts of the Apostles, the fifth book of the New Testament, a major source for the journeys of the apostle Paul.

Aulus Gellius, see below under Gellius.

Apuleius (c. 125-c.170 CE), wrote a novel *Metamorphoses*, also known as *The Golden Ass*, in which the hero Lucius is transformed into an ass, then restored to human form by Isis and finally initiated into her cult .

Augustine (354-430 CE), a major figure in the history of Christianity. Two of his many works are *Confessions* and *City of God*.

Pseudo-Augustine, a Christian writer about the same time as Augustine, author of *Questions on Old and New Testaments*.

Augustus (63 BCE-14 CE) was first known as Octavius, then Octavian after his adoption by Julius Caesar, and finally in 27 BCE Augustus. Towards the end of his life, Augustus had an account of his achievements (*Res Gestae*) set up in stone in various locations throughout the empire.

Cato the Elder (234-149 BCE), a politician and writer who was a strict advocate of the old Roman way of life (*mos maiorum*) and author of *On Agriculture*.

Catullus (c. 84-54 BCE), a Roman poet who wrote in a variety of poetic genres, including much love poetry. He belonged to a 'fast set' in Rome and was in love with a woman he calls Lesbia.

Cicero (106-43 BCE), orator, politician and writer of letters and philosophy which touch on religion and theology, most notably *On divination* and *On the nature of the gods*.

Comparison of Mosaic and Roman Laws, a treatise which seems to date between 390 and 438 CE, but was apparently begun c. 320 CE.

Cyprian (c. 200-258 CE), Bishop of Carthage, martyred in 258 CE, who wrote on the persecutions of Decius.

Dio (c. 160-c. 235 CE), Cassius Dio, a Greek who wrote a history of Rome through to his own times.

Dionysius of Halicarnassus, a Greek resident in Rome 30-8 BCE, who wrote *Roman Antiquities*, a highly detailed account of Rome's early history and customs.

Eusebius (c. 265-340 CE), appointed Bishop of Caesarea c. 311CE. He wrote *History of the Church*, an account in Greek of the early development of Christianity.

Festus (late second century CE), abridged an early first century CE work, *On the Significance of Words*, and was subsequently himself abridged in the 8th century by Paulus.

Gaius (2nd century CE), his *Institutes* constitute the first legal textbook.

Gellius (c. 123-165 CE), Aulus Gellius wrote *Attic Nights*, a twenty-volume collection of essays on a variety of topics which preserve quotations from earlier authors whose works are otherwise lost.

Horace (65-8 BCE),a lyric poet and satirist who was introduced by Vergil to Maecenas, a patron of the arts, who introduced him to Augustus.

Josephus (b. 37 CE, died c. 100 CE), a Jewish historian who had been an officer in the Jewish forces and who was captured by the Romans in 67 CE. After the capture of Jerusalem he was taken to Rome, where he became a friend of the emperor Vespasian and his two sons, Titus and Domitian. He was granted Roman citizenship and died in Rome.

Juvenal lived in the late first and early second centuries CE. He wrote satires denouncing the follies and vices of contemporary Roman society.

Lactantius (c. 240-c. 320 CE), a Christian apologist who became tutor to Constantine's eldest son. His work *Deaths of Persecutors* may have exaggerated the role of Galerius in the persecutions of the early 300s.

Laws of the Twelve Tables, a collection of statutes, traditionally codified c. 450 CE. This collection is the foundation of Roman law. Our knowledge of these statutes derives from quotations in later authors. See *ROL* 3 for Latin excerpts with translation.

Livy (c. 59 BCE-17 CE) wrote a history of Rome in 142 books from its foundation to his own times. Only books 1-10 and 21-45 survive in their entirety. They are a valuable source for Roman religion.

Lucan (39-65 CE), writer of an epic on the civil war between Caesar and Pompey that is generally known as *Pharsalia*, but more correctly as *On the civil war*. Implicated in a conspiracy against Nero, he was forced to commit suicide.

Lucretius (died c. 55 BCE) wrote an epic didactic poem, *On the Nature of Things*, on Epicureanism in order to rid the Romans of supersitious fear (*religio*).

Macrobius, grammarian who lived c. 400 CE and who wrote a seven-volume work, *Saturnalia Conversations*.

Martial (c. 40-104 CE), a poet who wrote fourteen books of epigrams on a wide variety of topics, many of which are satiric.

Minucius Felix, a Christian writer who lived from the mid-second to the mid-third century CE. He wrote *Octavius*, an apology or defense of Christianity.

Ovid (43 BCE-17 CE), a sophisticated and witty poet who wrote love poetry, a mythological epic (*Metamorphoses*), and the *Fasti* which deals with the festivals of the first six months of the year and is a mine of information for Roman religion and folklore. In 8 CE he was exiled from Rome by Augustus for some indiscretion that may have involved the emperor's family.

Paul (died in the early 60s CE), a Jew who converted to Christianity and preached first to Jews and then to Gentiles. His letters, which now form part of the New Testament, were instrumental in defining the doctrines of Christianity. His journeys are described in *Acts of the Apostles*.

Paulus, jurist and teacher who lived at the end of the second and beginning of the third century CE. He published extensively on laws, constitutions and jurisprudence. Extracts from Paulus' writings are incorporated in the *Digest*, commissioned by the emperor Justinian (527-565 CE).

Philo (c. 30 BCE-45 CE), philosopher, political writer and leading exponent of Alexandrian-Jewish culture. As an old man in 39/40 he led a Jewish deputation to the emperor Caligula in an attempt to have the Jews exempted from the imperial cult.

Plautus (c. 254-184 BCE), a Latin playwright who adapted Greek new comedy for Roman audiences. His works closely reflect the language and mind-set of the ordinary man in the street.

Pliny the Elder (23/4-79 CE), author of thirty-seven volumes entitled *Natural History*, an encyclopaedia of contemporary knowledge. He died in the eruption of Vesuvius in 79 CE.

Pliny the Younger (61/2-c. 112 CE) was raised by his uncle the Elder Pliny, pursued a political career and held a series of imperial administrative appointments.. He published much of his correspondence, including letters to the emperor Trajan concerning provincial government. One letter is the earliest extant account of Christian worship and Pliny's method of dealing with this new cult. Also preserved is Trajan's reply.

Plutarch (c. 46-died after 120 CE), Greek philosopher who wrote parallel lives of prominent Greeks and Romans.

Polybius (c. 200-c.118 BCE), a Greek politician who spent the latter half of his life as a hostage in Rome. He moved in Roman political circles and wrote a history explaining to the Greeks Rome's rise to world power in the late third century and the first half of the second century BCE.

Seneca the Younger (c. 4 BCE-65 CE) was appointed as tutor to Nero who became emperor in 54 CE, whereupon Seneca became Nero's chief advisor, but gradually fell out of favor because of his disapproval of the emperor's behavior. In 62 he tried to retire from the court and in 65 was accused of complicity in a plot against the emperor. He anticipated public execution by committing suicide. He was a devoted Stoic, writing extensively on moral and philosophical themes. He may also have written *The Pumpkinification of Claudius*, a satrirical skit on Claudius' deification.

Statius (c. 45-96 CE), a poet whose extant works are *Thebais*, an epic, and *Silvae*, a collection of miscellaneous poems.

Suetonius (c. 69-c. 130 CE), a biographer who wrote the lives of Julius Caesar and the first eleven emperors. These biographies contain much gossip and scandal, but little historical analysis.

Symmachus (c. 340-402 CE), an orator and ardent supporter of the old pagan state religion at a time when Christianity was taking over.

Tacitus (c. 55-118 CE), a historian who had a political career under Vespasian and Domitian. His two best-known works are the *Annals*, covering the period from the death of Augustus in 14 CE to the death of Nero (books 7-10 and the last part of 16 are lost), and the *Histories* which cover the period from the death of Nero to probably the death of Domitian in 96 CE, although only the first four and half books survive. He is a master of innuendo and was highly ciritical of the principate, failing to fulfil his professed aim to write without anger or partisanship (*sine ira et studio*).

Terence, a Latin playwright who flourished in the early second century and died c. 159 BCE. Like Plautus, his plays were modelled on those of Greek new comedy, but were closer to the original, having few Roman intrusions into the Greek setting.

Tertullian (c. 160-c. 230 CE) converted to Christianity and wrote many works about the history and character of the church. In the *Apology* he refutes many of the charges made against Christians.

Theodosian Code (438 CE), a collection of decrees issued by emperors from Constantine onward, commissioned by the emperor Theodosius.

Valerius Maximus, a writer active during the reign of Tiberius (14-37 CE). His work *Memorable Words and Deeds* is a collection of anecdotes, illustrating various aspects of human character.

Varro (116-27 BCE), a learned antiquarian whose work on religion in *Human and Divine Antiquities* survives only in excerpts quoted by other authors. Only two of his many works survive in their entirety: *On the Latin Language* and *On Agriculture* (*de re rustica*).

Virgil (70-19 BCE), a poet whose major work, the *Aeneid*, is an epic poem about the journey of Aeneas from Troy to Italy where he was destined to establish a new home for his people and his gods.

Zonaras, a historian who lived in Constantinople in the late eleventh and early twelfth centuries CE and wrote a history of the world down to 1118 CE. His work preserves an account of a Roman triumph.

BIBLIOGRAPHY

General reference works

Adkins, Lesley, and Roy Adkins, *Dictionary of Roman Religion*. New York: 2000.

Boatwright, Mary T., Daniel Gargola and Richard Talbert, *The Romans and their History: From Village to Empire*. Oxford University Press, NY: forthcoming 2003.

Boardman, John, Jasper Griffin, Oswyn Murray, eds. *The Oxford History of the Classical World: The Roman World*. Oxford: 2001.

BNP = Beard, Mary, John North and Simon Price, *Religions of Rome*, 2 vols. Cambridge: 1998.

CIL = *Corpus Inscriptionum Latinarum*. Berlin: 1863.

CPJ = V. J. Tcherikover, and A. Fuks, *Corpus Papyrorum Judaicarum*, Cambridge, MA: vol. 2, 1960.

FIRA = *Fontes Iuris Antejustiniani*. Florence: vol. 1 1941, vol. 2 1964.

ILS = H. Dessau, *Inscriptiones Selectae*. Berlin: 1962.

OCD 3 = Hornblower, Simon, Antony Spawforth, eds. *Oxford Classical Dictionary*, third edition, Oxford: 1996.

ROL = *Remains of Old Latin*, ed. E. H. Warmington. London and Cambridge MA: 1938.

Further reading

Barton, Tamsyn, *Ancient Astrology*. London and New York: 1994.

Burkert, W., *Greek Religion*. Cambridge, MA: 1985.

Dowden, Ken, *Religion and the Romans*. Bristol: 1992.

Dumezil, G., *Archaic Roman Religion*. 2 vols., Chicago: 1970.

Fantham, E., ed., *Ovid, Fasti Book IV*. Cambridge:1998.

Feeney, Denis, *Literature and Religion at Rome: Cultures, Contexts, and Beliefs*. Cambridge: 1998.

Flower, H., *Ancestor Masks and Aristocratic Power in Roman Culture*. Oxford: 1996.

Gager, John G., *Curse Tablets and Binding Spells from the Ancient World.* Oxford: 1992.

Graf, F., *Magic in the Ancient World.* Cambridge, MA 1997.

Herbert-Brown, G., *Ovid and the Fasti: an historical study.* Oxford: 1994.

Hickson, F., *Roman Prayer Language: Livy and the Aeneid of Vergil.* Stuttgart: 1993.

Hunt, A.S., C.C. Edgar, ed., *Select Papyri,* vol. 1 Loeb Classical Library: 1932.

Huskinson, Janet, ed, *Experiencing Rome: Culture, Identity and Power in the Roman Empire.* Routledge: 2000.

Lane-Fox, R., *Pagans and Christians.* Harmondsworth and New York: 1986.

Liebeschuetz, J. H. W. G., *Continuity and Change in Roman Religion.* Oxford: 1979.

Linderski, J., 'Roman Religion in Livy,' *Roman Questions.* Stuttgart: 1995, pp. 608-625.

————, 'The Augural Law,' *Aufsteig und Niedergang der römischen Welt,* edd. H. Temporini and W. Haase. Berlin: 1986, II 16.3: 2146-2312.

MacMullen, Ramsay, *Paganism in the Roman Empire.* New Haven and London: 1981.

————, *Christianizing the Roman Empire A.D. 100-400.* New Haven and London: 1984.

Michels, A. K., 'The topography and interpretation of the Lupercal,' *Transactions of the American Philological Association* 84 (1953) 35-59.

————, *The Calendar of the Roman Republic.* Princeton: 1967.

Ogilvie, R. M., *The Romans and their Gods.* London 1969.

Orlin, E. M., *Temples, Religion and Politics in the Roman Republic .* Leiden: 1997.

Potter, David S., 'Roman Religion: Ideas and Actions,' *in Life, Death and Entertainment in the Roman Empire,* edd. D. S. Potter and D. J. Mattingly. Ann Arbor: 1999.

Price, S. R. F., *Rituals and Power: The Roman Imperial Cult in Asia Minor.* Cambridge: 1984.

Ramsay, J. T. and A. L. Licht, *The Comet of 44 BC and Caesar's Funeral Games.* Atlanta, GA: 1997.

Rives, J., 'Religion in the Roman Empire,' in Huskinson, *Experiencing Rome: Culture, Identity and Power in the Roman Empire.* London and Routledge: 2000, pp. 245-275.

Roller, Lynn, *In Search of God the Mother.* California: 1999.

Ryberg, I. S., 'Rites of the State Religion in Roman Art,' in *Memoirs of the American Academy in Rome* 22 (1955).

Scheid, John, 'The Religious Roles of Women,' in *A History of Women, I: From Ancient Goddesses to Christian Saints,* ed. Pauline Schmitt Pantel. Cambridge, MA: 1992, 377-408.

Scullard, H. H., *Festivals and Ceremonies of the Roman Republic.* London and Ithaca: 1981.

Shelton, Jo Ann, *As the Roman Did.* 2nd ed. Oxford: 1998.

Takács, Sarolta, *Isis and Serapis in the Roman World.* Leiden: 1995.

Toynbee, J.M.C., *Death and Burial in the Roman World.* London:1971.

Treggiari, Susan M., *Roman Marriage*. Oxford: 1991.

————, *Roman Social History*. Routledge: 2002.

Turcan, Robert, *The Cults of the Roman Empire*. Blackwell: 1996.

————, *The Gods of Ancient Rome*. Routledge: 2000.

Vermaseren M. J. and van Essen, C. C., *The Excavations in the Mithraeum of the Church of Santa Prisca in Rome*. Leiden: 1965.

Versnel, H., 'An Essay on Anatomical Curses,' in *Ansichten griechischer Rituale*, ed. Fritz Graf. Stuttgart and Leipzig: 1998.

Wardman, A., *Religion and Statecraft among the Romans*. London: 1982.

Watson, A., *The State, Law and Religion: Pagan Rome*. Athens, GA :1992.

Warrior, V. M., 'The Roman Bid to Control Bacchic Worship,' in *Euripides' Bacchae*, by Stephen J. Esposito. Focus: 1998.

Williams, Margaret, *The Jews among the Greeks and Romans: a Diasporan Sourcebook*. Johns Hopkins: 1998.

————, *Jews and Jewish communities in the Roman empire,*' in *Huskinson, Experiencing Rome: Culture, Identity and Power in the Roman Empire*, pp. 305-333

Wiseman, T. P., 'Cybele, Vergil and Augustus,' in *Poetry and Politics in the Age of Augustus*, edd. T. Woodman and D. West. Cambridge: 1984.

Zanker, Paul, *The Power of Images in the Age of Augustus*. Michigan: 1988.

INDEX OF TEXTS CITED

1. Literary Texts

2. Inscriptions, Graffiti and Papyri

GENERAL INDEX

Aemilius Paullus, (consul 216 BCE) 7.13, 7.14; (consul 168 BCE), 7.19; (consul 50 BCE), 9.8

Aeneas, 3.23, 6.9, 8.17, 11.15, 11.17

Aesculapius, 8.3, 8.9, 8.10

Agrippa, 11.12, 12.27

Alba Longa, 2.6, 6.2

Alexander the Great, 11.1, 11.4

Ancus Marcius, 7.2

anger of the gods (*ira deorum*), 1.38, 7.11, 10.4

Anubis, 9.10, 9.12

Apollo, 8.4-8.6, 8.13, 8.14

Arval Brethren, 4.3, 11.13

astrologers, 1.14, 12.9, 12.23, 12.25, 12.27-12.32, 13.21

astrology, 12.23-12.32

Attus Navius, 5.6

augurs, 1.11, 1.13, 1.14, 2.4, 5.4-5.6, 11.13, 12.23, 12.25

augury, 2.1, 2.1; augury vs. haruspicy 1.26

Augustus (emperor, 27 BCE-14 CE), 2.2, 7.5, 10.12, 11.7-11.19, 12.27, 14.6, 14.7

auspices, 1.11- 1.13, 2.8, 5.4-5.6; auspices before battle, 1.16; auspices disregarded, 1.24, 7.7, 7.11, 7.14

Aventine hill, 2.1, 2.2, 2.6

Bacchic cult, 9.2-9.7

Bacchus, 4.11;

Bellona, 4:13, 4.18

books, Sibylline: see Sibylline oracles

Caesar (Gaius Julius Caesar, consul 59 BCE, dictator after 49 BCE), 5.15, 6.14, 10.7, 10.10, 10.11, 11.7-11.10, 11.19, 12.24,14.3, 14.5

calendar, 2.5, see chapter 6 *passim*, especially 6.1-6.3

Cannae, 7.13-7.15, 10.14.

Capitoline hill, 2.8

Cato the Elder, 5.15, see Index of texts cited

Ceres, 4.9, 4.11, 5.10, 8.3, 15.14

Cerialia, p. 116

Chaldaeans, 2.26, see also astrologers

Christ, 14.14, 15.1-15.5

Christianity, chapter 15 *passim*; as *superstitio* 15.4, 15.5

Christians, chapter 15 *passim*

Cicero (Marcus Tullius, consul 63 BCE), see Index of texts cited

Claudia Quinta, 8.17, 8.18

Claudius (Pubius Clodius Pulcher, consul 249 BCE) and the sacred chickens, 1.24

Claudius (emperor, 41-54 CE), 11.21-11.23, 14.8, 14.14, 14.15, 15.1

Colosseum (Flavian Amphitheater), 10.16

cultus (worship), pp.3-4

curses, 12.10-12.15, 12.20-12.22

Cybele, see Magna Mater

death and afterlife, honoring the dead, 3.22, 3.23; Epicurean view, 13.7, 13.9, 13.10; Stoic view, 13.19.13.20

decemviri sacris faciundis, see *quindecimviri sacris faciundis*

deification, see chapter 11 *passim*, see also imperial cult

deities, polytheism, anthropomorphism, non-anthropomorphised spirits, assimilation, see Introduction *passim*; accepting new gods, chapter 8 *passim*; control of non-Roman cults, chapter 9 *passim*, Epicurean view of gods, 13.11; for deities of ambivalent gender, see Pales and Robigo, and 8.8; for notes on individual deities, see pp. 187-188

Delphi, 7.15, 8.15

deisidaimonia, 1.35, p. 18 n.12

devotio, 4.18

Diana, 1.20, 8.3, 8.5, 13.2

Diocletian (emperor, 284-305 CE), 15.20,